BICYCLE

service manual · 2nd edition

TECHNICAL PUBLICATIONS

Published By

⬤INTERTEC
PUBLISHING CORPORATION

P.O. Box 12901, Overland Park, Kansas 66212

Cover photo credit: Panasonic, Division of Matsushita Electric Corporation of America, One Panasonic Way, Secaucus, NJ 07094. Al Kruper, photographer.

Contents

INTRODUCTION
Tools...3
Threaded Fasteners 4
Identification................................4
Adjustment....................................5
Inspection....................................5
Maintenance 5

IDENTIFICATION
Frame 7
Front Fork and Steering 8
Front Wheel 10
Pedals, Crank and Chainwheels................12
Chain and Rear Sprockets 14
Derailleur...................................16
Rear Wheel 19
Brakes 20
Serial Numbers 21

GENERAL ADJUSTMENTS
Selection 23
Frame 23
Seat 24
Handlebar and Stem 25
Taping Handlebars 26
Brakes 27
Bearings 30
Chain 31
Multi-Speed Hub 32
Derailleurs 32
Tires and Pressure 32

INSPECTION
Tires 35
Bearings 35
Frame 36

PERIODIC MAINTENANCE
Cleaning.....................................37
Lubrication 37
Bearing Adjustments 39
Brakes 40

SERVICE
Front Wheel and Hub
Remove and Reinstall the Assembly 41
Clean, Inspect and Lubricate Axle Bearings 42
Renew Hub, Spokes or Rim 43
Tighten Spokes and Align Wheels 44
Front Fork, Stem and Handlebars
Remove and Reinstall Handlebars and Stem 46
Remove and Reinstall Fork and Headset Bearings ...46
Pedals, Crank and Chainwheels
Pedal Repair and Lubrication 47
Crank and Crank Bearing Lubrication and Repair ...48
Crank Transmissions 51
Chainwheel Removal and Installation 51
Chain
Chain Tightening 52
Chain Repair 53
Chain Remove and Reinstall 53
Rear Wheel Assembly
Remove and Reinstall the Assembly 54
Clean, Inspect and Lubricate Axle Bearings 54
Renew Hub, Spokes or Rim 55
Tightening Spokes and Aligning Wheels 57

Coaster Brake Rear Hubs
Bendix 58
Centrix K 61
Durex 61
Elgin 61
Excel.......................................61
Hawthorne 61
J.C. Higgins 61
Mattatuck 62
Morrow 62
Musselman 62
Nankai NK75 63
New Departure 63
Perry B-100 64
Perry B-500 64
Pixie 65
Renak 65
Resilion 65
Sachs (Jet, Komet, Komet Super & Torpedo Boy) ...65
Schwinn Approved 66
Shimano 66
Sturmey Archer 67
Styre 67
Swift (100 & 2 Star) 67

Two Speed Rear Hubs
Bendix 2-Speed Yellow Band 68
Bendix 2-Speed Blue Band 71
Bendix 2-Speed Red Band 75
Sachs Torpedo Duomatic 77

Three Speed Rear Hubs
Brampton 79
Hercules 79
Sachs Torpedo 415 79
Sachs Torpedo 515 83
Schwinn Approved Styre 88
Shimano 3.3.3. Without Back Pedaling Brake 88
3.3.3. Tri-Matic With Back Pedaling Brake 91
Schimano 3 CC 92
Sturmey Archer "AW" 93
Other Sturmey Archer 3-Speed Hubs 96
Styre 97

Four and Five Speed Rear Hubs
Sturmey Archer FW and S5 97

DERAILLEUR SYSTEMS
General Adjustments 101
Belri 103
Campagnolo Valentino 103
Campagnolo Nuovo Record 104
Campagnolo Sport Extra 105
Cyclo Benelux 105
Huret Allvit and Super Allvit 107
Huret Avant "700" 108
Huret Jubilee 108
Huret Luxe 109
Huret Svelto 109
Schwinn 109
Shimano Crane, Dura Ace, Eagle, Thunder Bird,
   Titlist, Tourney 110
Schimano Positron 112
Simplex 113
Sun Tour 114
Triplex 116

Introduction

Servicing bicycles requires interest, ability and knowledge. You must already be interested in servicing bicycles or you would not be reading this book. Regardless of your present state, your ability will increase as you gain experience. Your selection of tools may also limit your ability to perform certain services, but these tools can be acquired as your mechanical ability increases. This book explains specific procedures and will help you develop the knowledge of how to service. The purpose of this book is to help you maintain and repair bicycles and is not intended as a "Buyer's Guide". You will develop many personal preferences and will be more sure of what you consider important plus-features of a bicycle after you have serviced and repaired several different types.

Bicycles have been manufactured for a long time and new components are constantly being designed. The editors have included all components for which we were able to find sufficient information.

BMX, Cross Country, Cruisers, Free Style, Mountain, Track Racers, Triathlon and other special purpose bicycles can be serviced using the information in this book.

TOOLS

Some tools are required to begin servicing bicycles. The specific tools required will depend upon the equipment installed on the bicycle and to what extent you want to service it. Professional mechanics that work on several different makes of racing bicycles will, of course, require more tools and will generally prefer better quality, more expensive tools than an occasional user will need. Standard hand tools are required and necessary wrench sizes will usually be smaller than 11/16-inch and 17 MM. Often both metric and inch sizes are required and the use of pipe wrenches, adjustable open end wrenches and locking plier wrenches should be discouraged. The number and quality of tools can be gradually increased as the need becomes apparent. A special chain servicing tool, for instance, is necessary for removing and

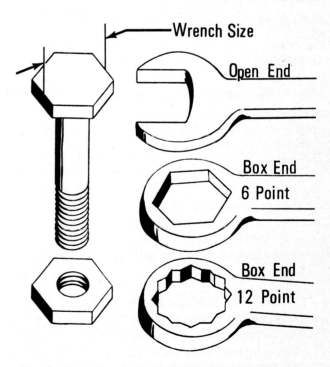

Fig. 2—The size of the screw head or nut determines size of wrench necessary. An open end wrench grips a fastener by two sides, a 6-point box end wrench or socket grips the fastener on all six sides and a 12-point grips the fastener at each of the six corners.

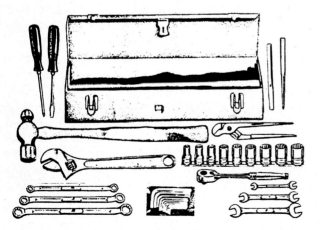

Fig. 1—Only a small number of tools are necessary to begin servicing bicycles. The number of tools can be increased slowly as needs arise.

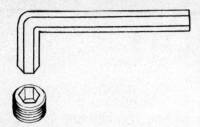

Fig. 3—Allen wrenches and screws are available in both metric and inch sizes. Wrench size is distance across flats and Allen screw size is determined by thread diameter, pitch and length.

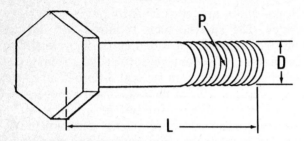

Fig. 4—Screw sizes are not determined by size of head. Shape and pitch of threads (P), length of fastener (L) and diameter (D) determines fastener size.

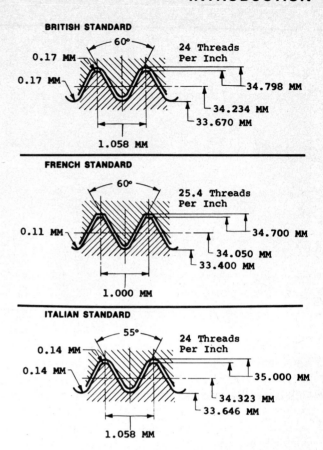

Fig. 5—Distance between threads or pitch and shape of threads may vary between two parts. Be sure that both are manufacturered to the same standard. Do not force.

installing the one piece chain used with derailleurs. The chain used on some bicycles (without deraileur) is equipped with a master link which doesn't require special tools. If only bicycles with master links are serviced, the purchase of a special chain breaker is not necessary. Be careful however, because otherwise serviceable parts can be easily ruined by trying to use a tool that doesn't fit.

Wrench sizes are determined by measuring **across the flats of the hex** as shown in Figure 2. Allen screws and wrenches (Fig. 3) are also available in metric and inch sizes. Some inch and metric sizes are very close such as: 10 MM and 7/16-inch, 13 MM and ½-inch, 14 MM and 9/16-inch. Be careful when measuring and be sure the correct wrench is used. The size of the head determines the size of the wrench used and is related to the size of the screw, but is not the screw size. The size of standard screw fasteners is given as thread diameter (D-Fig. 4), thread pitch (P) and length (L).

THREADED FASTENERS

Be sure the correct threaded fasteners are used. Components used on bicycles may be manufactured in just about any country in the world. Most companies use manufacturing standards commonly used in that country and they may be considerably different than a similar standard used in another country. Obvious differences

occur between metric and inch measuring systems, but more subtle differences occur. The standard thread shape and number of threads in a given distance (pitch) may be different between metric sized parts manufactured in neighboring countries. Check all questionable threaded parts carefully by hand. Threaded parts should be easily joined by hand without looseness. Looseness or tight fitting threaded parts usually indicate incorrectly matched or damaged threads. Occasionally threaded parts are tight fitting (self-locking) to prevent accidentally loosening. These self-locking threaded parts may be threaded completely together smoothly using proper wrenches. Self-locking threaded parts are not often used on bicycles. The most common methods to prevent loosening are through the use of lock washers and lock nuts. The service section for the various components will call attention to these locking devices.

IDENTIFICATION

An important part of service is to know the names of the parts. Each part is given a descriptive name by the manufacturer. **Different manu-**

facturers may call the same (or similar) part by different names. An example of this is a retaining ring, retaining clip, circlip or snap ring. The ring (or clip) may be made of round wire or may be flat, may enter a groove inside a hole or may enter a groove around the outside of a shaft.

The IDENTIFICATION section, which begins on page 7, will be helpful for finding the correct names of components and many parts. This section also includes some explanation of why certain parts are shaped the way they are. Directions such as: Front, Rear, Left, Right, Top, Bottom are given in reference to a rider in normal position. **These directions apply, even when the part is separated from the rest of the bicycle.** The right side of the rear hub is the side that has the sprocket, even when the wheel is removed from the bicycle.

Screws and nuts are normally loosened by turning counter-clockwise and tightened by turning clockwise. Some threaded parts are different from normal

to prevent loosening while in use and are referred to as "Left hand thread". A part with left hand thread is loosened by turning clockwise and tightened by turning counter-clockwise.

ADJUSTMENT

Some adjustment is necessary just to fit the bicycle to the rider. Also, the shape of the rider may change. The bicycle must fit the rider, not only for comfort to the rider, but also in the interest of safety. Safety should be a prime concern of all bicyclists.

Refer to the GENERAL ADJUSTMENTS section, which begins on page 23, for a brief description of many common adjustments.

INSPECTION

Inspection is an important part of bicycle service, but is often included with another function. Simply riding will permit a serviceman to inspect the operation of many different systems. Washing can provide a close examination of many critical parts. Repair includes disassembly and reassembly, but the internal parts of most complex assemblies can only be inspected while the unit is apart. The act of disassembling and assembling will not correct a problem caused by a damaged part. The part must be inspected; then, if damaged, the fault must be corrected before the unit will operate correctly.

The INSPECTION section, which begins on page 35, includes special notes for checking tires, bearings and frame for problems which should be corrected.

MAINTENANCE

Periodic preventive maintenance, accompanied by careful inspection will often be safer, less expensive and easier than permitting a part to fail completely. Lubrication and cleaning are the most obvious forms of regular maintenance and these are naturally accompanied by inspecting the affected parts. The need for additional adjustments or repair should be noted as you perform the routine maintenance.

The most satisfactory interval of time between regular service will depend upon the type of riding as well as the type of bicycle and component. Moisture from any cause will wash lubricant from parts, which need oil or grease, and cause parts to rust or corrode, which should be clean or polished. Wear caused by dirt or dust can also be reduced by prompt maintenance.

Refer to the appropriate paragraphs in the PERIODIC MAINTENANCE section for recommended general procedures. Components which require more detailed specific instructions are included in the SERVICE section. The PERIODIC MAINTENANCE section begins on page 37 and the SERVICE section begins on page 41.

Fig. 6—Directions such as left and right are often used to identify location of parts even when removed from bicycle.

A dictionary definition of a bicycle goes something like this.

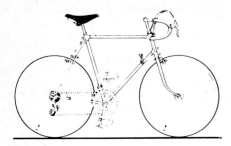

bi cy cle (bi'sikel) noun [French bi-+-cycle] 1. a vehicle with two wheels tandem, usually propelled by pedals and having handlebars for steering and a saddle type seat.

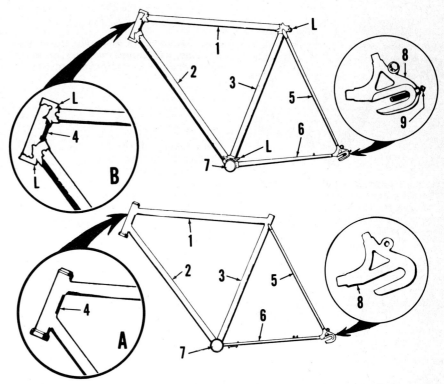

Fig. 1-2—Most bicycle frames are made of steel tubing. Various tubes are joined by butting together as shown in inset "A" or by using lugs (L) as shown in inset "B".

1. Top tube	4. Head tube	7. Bottom bracket
2. Down tube	5. Seat stays	8. Drop outs (fork
3. Seat tube	6. Chain stays	ends)

This definition can keep someone from confusing a bicycle with bananas or automobiles but more information and better identification are needed when servicing. A bicycle consists of the frame (1-Fig. 1-1), front wheel assembly (2), front fork and steering assembly (3), crank and pedals assembly (4), rear wheel assembly (5) and seat (6). There are, of course, other items but these are the largest components or sub-assemblies.

Fig. 1-1—View of right side of a DBS Golden Beam "Girls" three speed bicycle. Right and left sides are determined by position of rider.

1. Frame
2. Front wheel assembly
3. Front fork and steering
4. Pedals and crank assembly
5. Rear wheel assembly
6. Seat

FRAME

The frame is the single most important part of the bicycle. It forms the foundation upon which the remaining parts are attached. The bicycle or frame manufacturer selects the material to use, decides upon the method of attaching the pieces together and designs the shape (geometry) that the frame should have.

Wood, aluminum, plastic, fiberglass, titanium, steel and some other materials have been used to make frames. Steel tubing is currently the most popular material. Common names for the parts used to make a tubular steel frame are listed in Fig. 1-2. Steel frame tubing may be joined by welding or brazing the tubes dir-

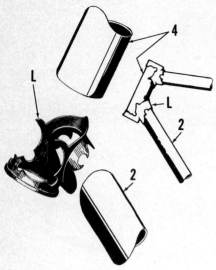

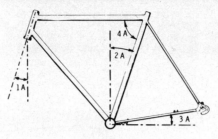

Fig. 1-5—Angles of frame tubes will combine with other features to determine handling characteristics of bicycle.

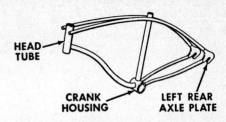

Fig. 1-8—Frame serial number will usually be stamped at one of the three locations indicated.

Fig. 1-6—Lengths of various frame tubes will determine overall size of bicycle. Usually frame size is listed as length of seat tube and other frame tubes are proportionate.

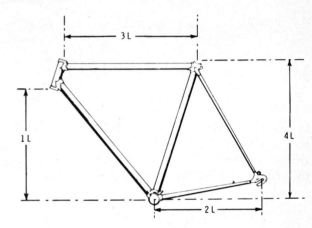

Fig. 1-3—Lugs (L) are often used to join different pieces of tubing when building a bicycle frame. Example shown (L) is lower lug which joins head tube (4) to down tube (2).

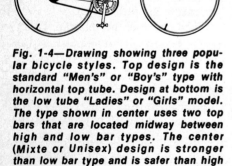

Fig. 1-4—Drawing showing three popular bicycle styles. Top design is the standard "Men's" or "Boy's" type with horizontal top tube. Design at bottom is the low tube "Ladies" or "Girls" model. The type shown in center uses two top bars that are located midway between high and low bar types. The center (Mixte or Unisex) design is stronger than low bar type and is safer than high bar type.

Fig. 1-7—The manufacturer's name will be located on head tube of most bicycles.

ectly together (A-Fig. 1-2) or the pieces of tubing may be brazed or silver soldered in lugs (L-Fig. 1-3). The shape of the frame may permit a step-through mounting procedure or may not (Fig. 1-4). These designs are only a matter of preference. The angle of the head tube, etc. (Fig. 1-5) will determine the riding characteristics (geometry) of the bicycle. The distance between various parts (Fig. 1-6) will change the physical size of the bicycle. The standard method of listing frame size is the measurement from the center of the crank axle to the top of the seat tube. This dimension is usually the only measurement given.

Bicycle manufacturer's name is usually located on the front of the head tube (Fig. 1-7). Model names may be painted on various frame tubes, but should not be confused with the bicycle manufacturer's name. The bicycle serial number is a specific number for each particular frame. The serial number will be stamped at one of three locations (Fig. 1-8): On the frame head tube; on crank housing; on left rear axle (drop out) plate. Removal of the manufacturer's name and/or illegible serial number usually indicates a stolen bicycle.

FRONT FORK

The front fork passes through the frame head tube. Head sets (bearings) are located between these two parts and permit the fork to turn easily in the head tube. A handlebar stem (2-Fig. 1-9) is expanded inside the fork

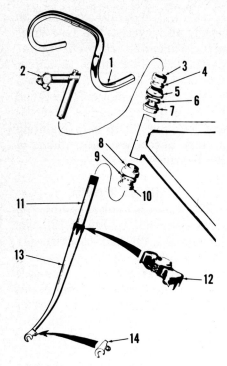

Fig. 1-9—Exploded view of typical front fork and steering. Refer to Fig. 1-10 for different methods of assembling fork.

1. Handlebar
2. Steering (handlebar) stem
3. Lock nut
4. Lock washer
5. Adjustable bearing race
6. Bearing balls and retainer
7. Fixed top race
8. Fixed lower race
9. Bearing balls and retainer
10. Fixed cone
11. Fork tube
12. Fork crown
13. Fork blade
14. Fork ends (drop outs)

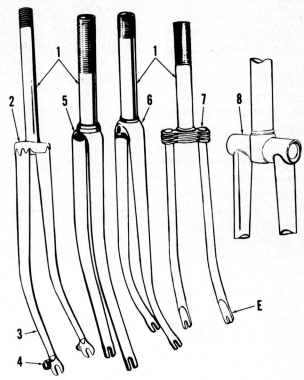

Fig. 1-10—Front forks may be manufactured in a variety of ways.

1. Fork tube
2. Fork crown
3. Fork blades
4. Fork ends (drop outs)
5. Forged fork
6. Stamped fork
7. Fork crown plates
8. Tube fork crown

tube (11) and the handlebars are attached to the stem. Turning the handlebars, turns the steering stem, which turns the front fork that holds the front wheel. The front forks can be manufactured in several different ways as shown in Fig. 1-10. In all cases, the fork is made by attaching at least two pieces together and alignment is very important to the frame geometry. The fork stem (1) may be attached to the forged (5) or stamped (6) fork assembly or to a fork crown (2, 7 & 8). The fork blades (3) are attached to the fork crown and drop outs (4) may be attached to the fork blades. Brazing or welding are the two most common methods of attaching the various parts together. The ends (E) of tubular, forged and stamped forks may be shaped as shown. Some models with a tubular fork use

special drop outs (4) which are attached to the fork blade tubes.

The angle (A & B-Fig. 1-11) of the frame head tube and the amount of trail (T1, T2 & T3) are important to the handling of the bicycle. The angle (A) is determined by the building of the frame. The amount of trail (T) is determined by the amount of axle offset built into the fork and the angle of the head tube. A small amount of fork offset (02) will result in a large amount of trail (T3). More fork offset (04) will decrease the amount of trail (T1). The head tube angle will also affect the amount of trail. Angle (B) is less than angle (A) and the trail (T2) is more than trail (T1) when the offset (04) remains the same. Generally a bicycle with more trail (T3) will be more stable at high speed. Less or zero trail (T1) will be easier to turn and control at very slow speed but may be dangerously unstable at higher speeds. The bicycle manufacturers choose the type of

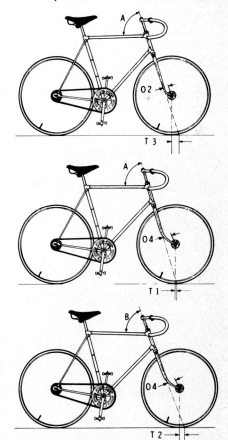

Fig. 1-11—Angle (A or B) of head tube and amount of fork offset (02 or 04) will combine to determine amount of trail (T1, T2 or T3).

handling they desire for a specific model and build the bicycle with those handling features. Usually the steering head angle (A & B) will be between 68 and 75 degrees and the trail will be from 1 inch to 2½ inches. The original angle, offset and trail specifications are often used only for manufacturing purposes. These specifications may be used to select a bicycle that fits a buyers requirements if they are known. The actual head tube angle, fork offset and consequently the trail can also be changed by accidents such as riding the bicycle into a storm drain. Changes in the frame and front fork geometry either by installing different parts or by accident will change the riding characteristics of the bicycle.

The steering stem (2-Fig. 1-9) is usually made of steel or aluminum (on lighter bicycles), but regardless of type, its purpose is to connect the handlebar to the front fork. The handlebar (1) is clamped into the steering stem at the top and the lower end of the steering stem is wedged into the fork tube. At increased speed, the

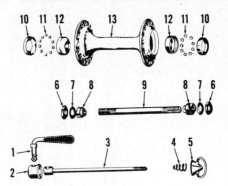

Fig. 1-13—Exploded view of typical front wheel hub with quick release skewer (1 thru 5).

1. Release lever
2. Housing
3. Quick release skewer
4. Spring
5. Adjuster
6. Lock nuts
7. Lock washers
8. Inner races (cones)
9. Axle
10. Dust seals
11. Bearing balls
12. Outer races (cups)
13. Hub

bicycle direction can be controlled by leaning and the front wheel may not need to be turned. However, at low speed it is necessary to turn the front wheel to control and direct the bicycle. Head set bearings (6 & 9) are located between the frame head tube and the fork stem (11) to reduce the effort required to turn the front wheel. Bearings may be either caged bearings as shown or may be loose balls. Renewable bearing

races (5, 7, 8 & 10) are used on nearly all bicycles. Top race (5) is often threaded onto the upper part of the fork stem to adjust the head set bearings. A tongued washer (4) is sometimes installed between the threaded race (5) and lock nut (3) to help maintain a more permanent adjustment of the bearings.

FRONT WHEEL

The front wheel assembly includes the hub (1-Fig. 1-12), rim (2), spokes (3) and the tire (4). The weight of the front part of the bicycle is carried by the axle and the hub rotates around this axle and is held by the spokes attached to the rim. The hub actually hangs from only a few of the spokes at the top. This means that the weight of the front of the bicycle is suspended by only these few spokes. As the wheel turns, the weight is transmitted to the different spokes as they come closer to the top of the rim.

The front hub, axle and axle bearings are usually available either as an assembly or as individual parts. The axle (and thus the front wheel assembly) is retained in the front fork with either nuts or with a clamp (skewer). The nuts may either be standard or self-wrenching type. The clamped type is known as quick release and the front wheel assembly including the hub and axle is removable after releasing the clamp. The hub will almost always rotate on ball type axle bearings. The outer race may be either part of the hub (13-Fig. 1-13) or the outer races (12) may be separately renewable pieces. The inner races (8) are also called cones or bearing cones. The cones are usually threaded onto the axle (9) in order to adjust the axle bearings. The distance between the outer races (12) is not adjustable so the inner races (8) must be positioned so that axle bearings (8, 11 & 12) operate freely without unnecessary loose-

Fig. 1-12—Front wheel assembly consists of hub (1), rim (2), spokes (3) and tire (4).

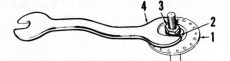

Fig. 1-14—Special thin wrenches called "cone wrenches" (4) are used to hold bearing cones (2) while tightening lock nut (3). Hub is shown at (1).

ness. This bearing adjustment is critical to the safety of the rider and lock washers (7) and/or lock nuts (6) are often used to secure the position of the bearing cones. Special thin wrenches called cone wrenches are often necessary to hold these bearing cones while tightening the lock nuts. Refer to Fig. 1-14.

The spokes may be straight or swaged (1 & 2-Fig. 1-15). Spokes usually break near the ends and therefore may be made larger at the ends to reduce breakage. The complete spoke could be made larger (2) for increased strength, but this would add unnecessary weight. Spoke threading machines such as shown at (4) can be used to roll threads onto the

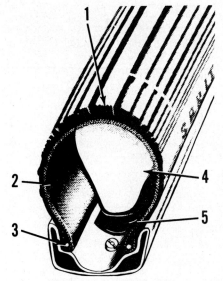

Fig. 1-16—Cross sectional view of clincher (wire-on) tire and typical rim.

1. Tread
2. Cord body
3. Bead wires
4. Tube
5. Nipple protector (liner)

ends of the spokes. Nipples (3) are threaded onto the end of each spoke so that the tension of the spoke can be adjusted. The spoke nipples should be adjusted so that the hub is centered in the rim

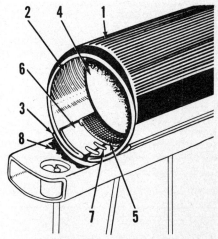

Fig. 1-17—Cross section of tubular (sew-up) tire and typical rim.

1. Tread
2. Cord body (casing)
3. Base tape
4. Tube
5. Chafing tape
6. Hem
7. Stitching
8. Rim cement

and so that the rim is correctly positioned and straight. The rim can be physically bent but most out-of-round and out-of-alignment problems are caused by improper spoke tightening. Broken spokes often result from some spokes being too loose. The weight of the bicycle is held up by only a few spokes at a time and as the wheel turn, the weight is transferred to different spokes. If one or more of the spokes is not tight, the others must hold up the weight that the loose one should and they may break under excessive load.

The front wheel provides the round surface upon which to roll. The tire provides a wear surface and cushions the imperfections in the road surface. The tire can be either of two general types and the rim must be the same type. The clincher (wire-on) type tire is shown in Fig. 1-16 and the tubular (sew-up) type tire is shown in Fig. 1-17. Some rims require special clincher type tires and of course the tire must be the correct size for the rim. The size and type of tire will generally be included in the overall design of the bicycle. Several tread patterns are available from each tire manufacturer for each type and size of tire. Fig. 1-18 shows only a

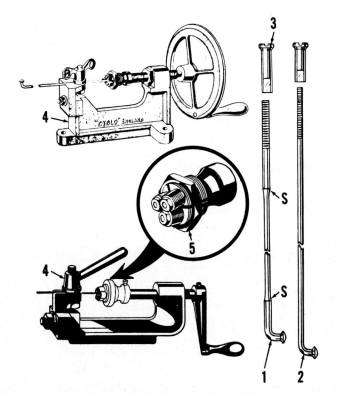

Fig. 1-15—Spoke (1) is swaged and spoke (2) is straight. Nipple is shown at (3) and two different types of threading tools at (4). Head (5) uses rollers to roll threads onto ends of spokes.

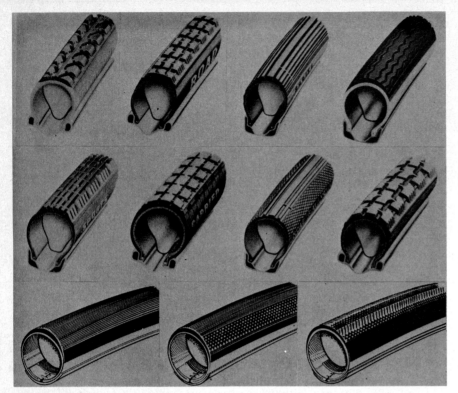

Fig. 1-18—Many tread patterns are available to suit a variety of riding conditions. Some patterns are for front tire only, others for rear only and some are available for strictly styling purposes.

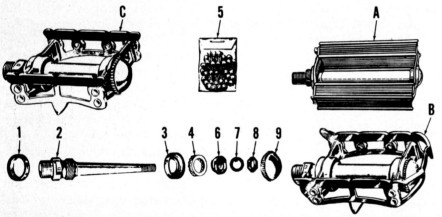

Fig. 1-19—Block type pedal (A) is usually not repairable. Road racing pedal (B) and track pedals (C) usually can be repaired. Loose balls (5) or balls in retainer (4) may be used.

1. Dust seal
2. Pedal Shaft
3. Bearing race (cup)
4. Ball bearing and retainer
5. Bearing balls
6. Bearing inner race (cone)
7. Lock washer
8. Lock nut
9. Dust cap

few of the many patterns available. Selection of thread pattern will depend upon type of riding. Ribbed styles usually contribute to stability at high speed. Pyramid, block and other similar thread patterns provide the better traction needed when accelerating or braking. "Drag Slicks" or "Knobbies" are sometimes selected for styling purposes only.

PEDALS, CRANK AND CHAINWHEELS

Pedals are pushed in order to turn the crank. The chainwheel (or wheels) is attached to the crank and is turned with the crank. The pedals, crank and chainwheel (or wheels) make up the front part of the power train, which changes the linear motion of pushing the pedals to rotary movement of the chainwheel.

Pedal axles are usually threaded into the crank arms. The pedal and crank arm used on left hand side are usually equipped with left hand threads. The most common pedals are either block type (A-Fig. 1-19), road racing (B) and track type (C). Pedals with a steel platform are sometimes called "rat trap" pedals. Toe clips (1-Fig. 1-20) and straps (2) are sometimes attached to rat trap pedals so the pedal can be pulled up as well as pushed down. Special cycling shoes (1-Fig 1-21) are also available that have a built in steel shank. The steel shank distributes the pressure of the steel pedal over a large part of the foot. Cleats (2, 3, 4, 5 & 6) are usually fitted to cycling shoes.

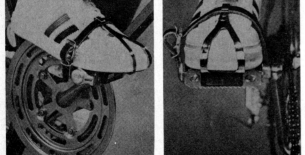

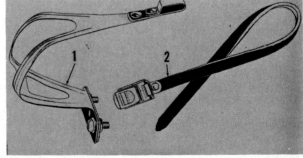

Fig. 1-20—View showing toe clip (1) and strap (2) which are sometimes used to permit pulling pedal up as well as pressing down.

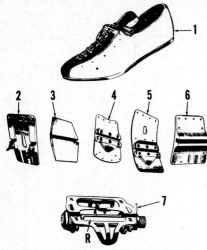

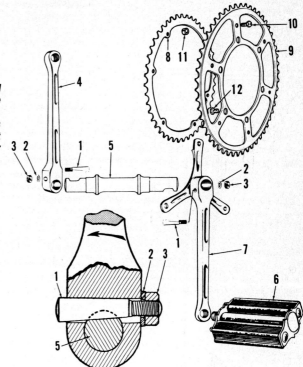

Fig. 1-23—Exploded view of cottered three piece crank assembly. Also shown is cross section showing correct installation of cotter pins.

1. Cotton pins
2. Washers
3. Nuts
4. Left crank arm
5. Crank spindle
6. Pedal
7. Right crank arm
8. Low speed sprocket
9. Fast (large) sprocket
10. Screws
11. Spacers
12. Screws

Fig. 1-21—Special cycling shoes (1) with appropriate cleats (2, 3, 4, 5 or 6) are used by serious cyclists. Groove or notch in cleat locates foot on ridge (R) of pedal (7).

The cleat locates the foot on a ridge (R) of pedal and it is important that the cleat is installed on the shoe in the correct place. Wear the shoes (without the cleats) while riding and ridges (R) will mark the soles so that it will be obvious where to align groove in the cleat.

Crank sets, including spindle and right and left hand crank arms, can be made in one piece or in three pieces. The one piece crank (2-Fig. 1-22) is common on American made bicycles and is

usually manufactured of forged steel. Three piece crank sets are divided into cottered (Fig. 1-23) and cotterless (Fig. 1-24) types. The wedge bolts (1-Fig. 1-23) are called "cotter pins". Cotter pins clamp the crank arms (4 & 7) to the spindle (5). Cotterless crank arms (4 & 13-Fig. 1-24) are provided with a tapered square hole which fits onto the tapered square ends of spindle (10). A bolt (2) tightens the crank arms onto spindle. Most cotterless crank arms are made from an aluminum alloy and can be easily damaged by improper installation or removal procedures. Special

pullers are available for removing most cotterless crank arms.

The crank spindle is turned by pedaling and the spindle must be provided with some type of bearing. Most models use a ball type bearing for the crank. Some are loose bearing balls, while others use bearing balls that are contained in a retainer (7 & 11-Fig. 1-24). The purpose of using a ball type bearing is to reduce friction and this purpose can be defeated if bearing is damaged of improperly adjusted.

The front (drive) sprockets attached to the crank arm or spindle is commonly called a "chain-

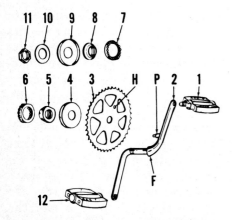

Fig. 1-22—Exploded view of a typical one piece [Ashtabula] crank assembly.

1. Right pedal	7. Bearing balls retainer
2. Crank	8. Adjustable bearing cone
3. Chain wheel	9. Dust seal
4. Dust seal	10. Lock washer
5. Bearing cone	11. Lock nut
6. Bearing balls and retainer	12. Left pedal

Fig. 1-24—Exploded view of typical cotterless crank set. Bearings (7 & 11) may be either loose balls or balls contained in retainers as shown. Bearing inner races (cones) are made as part of spindle (10).

1. Dust cap
2. Retaining screw
3. Washer
4. Left crank arm
5. Lock nut
6. Adjustable race (cup)
7. Bearing

8. Cone	11. Bearing	14. Nut
9. Protecting sleeve	12. Fixed bearing cup	15. Chainwheel
10. Crank spindle	13. Right crank arm	16. Screw

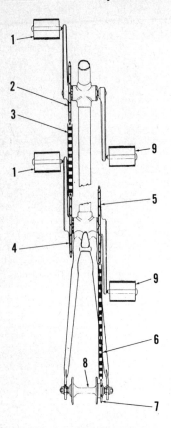

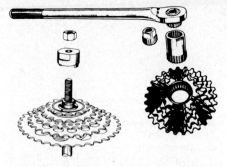

Fig. 1-27—The freewheeling hub is screwed onto rear hub. Special tools are necessary for gripping the hub for removal.

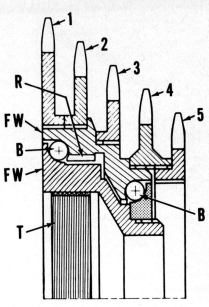

Fig. 1-28—Cross sectional drawing of a typical freewheeling hub with five sprockets. Ratchet (R) locks so that sprockets will drive the wheel, but release so that wheel can coast when sprockets stop. Bearings (B) are used only when freewheeling.

1. Low (1st) speed sprocket
2. Second speed sprocket
3. Third speed sprocket
4. Fourth speed sprocket
5. High (5th) speed sprocket
B. Bearings
FW. Freewheeling hub
R. Ratchet
T. Threads

Fig. 1-25—Power train typical of tandem bicycles. Front chain (3) connects sprockets (2 & 4) so that both cranks turn together. Rear chain (6) connects chainwheel (5) with rear wheel sprocket (7). Connecting chain (3) and sprockets (2 & 4) may be on either side.

1. Left pedals
2. Connecting sprocket
3. Connecting chain
4. Connecting sprocket
5. Chainwheel
6. Chain
7. Sprocket
8. Rear hub
9. Right pedals

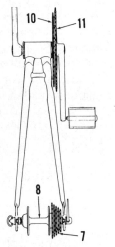

Fig. 1-26—Drawing showing location of chainwheels (10 & 11) and sprockets (7) used on ten speed derailleur bicycles.

7. Rear sprockets
8. Rear hub
10. Small (slow) chainwheel
11. Large (fast) chainwheel

wheel". On one piece forged cranks (2-Fig. 1-22), chainwheel (3) is usually tightened against a flange (F) on the crank by tightening bearing cone (5). A pin (P) on right side crank arm should engage a hole (H) in chainwheel. Right crank arm (7-Fig. 1-23 or 13-Fig. 1-24) on cotter and cotterless crank sets is usually provided with some method of attaching the chainwheel. One chainwheel (3-Fig. 1-22 or 15-Fig. 1-24) is usually installed on single speed bicycles, five speed derailleur models and bicycles with multispeed rear hubs. Two chainwheels (8 & 9-Fig. 1 23) are used on ten speed derailleur bicycles and three chainwheels are used on fifteen speed bicycles.

CHAIN AND REAR SPROCKETS

The sprocket or sprockets at the center of the rear wheel is the rear of the power train. A chain is used to connect the front part of the power train to the rear sprocket. Some track bicycles use a fixed rear sprocket. "Fixed" means that the single rear sprocket is attached directly to the rear hub and turns all the time that the rear wheel turns. Most bicycles provide some method of coasting, or stopping the rear sprocket, while allowing the wheel to run. Single speed bicycles are often equipped with a coaster brake rear hub which includes a coasting (freewheel) mechanism and a back pedaling

brake. Multi-speed hubs (2, 3, 4, 5, etc.) usually contain a freewheeling ratchet and many are also equipped with a back pedaling brake. Popular derailleur bicycles (5, 10 & 15 speeds) are equipped with a freewheeling assembly between the sprockets and the rear wheel hub. The methods of constructing the units are different for the various manufacturers. Some freewheeling units can be disassembled and cleaned but service usually consists of removing the old unit and installing a new one. Special tools are available (Fig. 1-27) for removing most freewheeling hubs. Several different threads are used between the hub and the freewheeling unit. Be certain of the type and do not force an incorrect unit onto the hub. The hub will probably be damaged. Many freewheeling units are available with three or more different thread types.

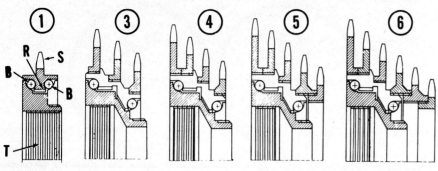

Fig. 1-29—Five sprockets are most common; however, freewheeling hubs are available for use with different numbers of sprockets.

A drive chain is used to connect sprockets together. Inner links (D-Fig. 1-32) are connected together by outer links (E). Offset sections (A) or offset links (B) can be used to provide a chain with an odd (uneven) number of rollers. Chain used on bicycles without derailleurs can be equipped with spring clip connecting link (C) or a cottered connecting link (B). Connecting links are often called "Master Links". The pin with a cotter (1) or the pins with the spring clip (6) project out of side plates and should not be used with derailleurs. Special tools such as the rivet extractor (chain breaker) and riveting or assembling tools (Fig. 1-33) are available for building a chain that is the correct length.

Tandem bicycles use a drive chain (3-Fig. 1-25) to connect the two crank sets together. A chain

FREEWHEELS THREADS

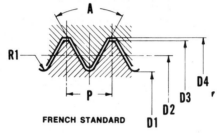

FRENCH STANDARD

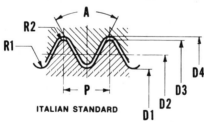

ITALIAN STANDARD

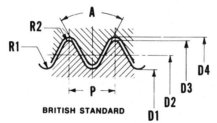

BRITISH STANDARD

Fig. 1-31—The freewheeling hub threads are available in different, but similar designs.

Fig. 1-33—Chain that slides between derailleurs should be riveted together without master links (B or C-Fig. 1-32). Special tools are available for pressing rivets out of chain side plates and reinserting them.

A. Angle
D1. Thread root diameter in wheel hub
D2. Thread mean diameter
D3. Outside diameter of wheel hub thread
D4. Thread root diameter in freewheel
P. Pitch
R1. Fillet radius
R2. Thread top fillet radius

British Standard
A. 60 degrees
D1. 33.670 MM
D2. 34.234 MM
D3 & D4. 34.798 MM
P. 1.058 MM
R1. 0.17 MM
R2. 0.17 MM

French Standard
A. 60 degrees
D1. 33.400 MM
D2. 34.050 MM
D3. 34.700 MM
D4. 34.700 MM
P. 1.000 MM
R1. 0.11 MM

Italian Standard
A. 55 degrees
D1. 33.646 MM
D2. 34.323 MM
D3 & D4. 35.000 MM
P. 1.058 MM
R1. 0.14 MM
R2. 0.14 MM

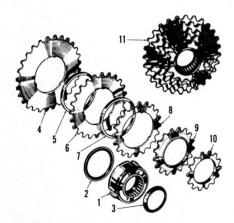

Fig. 1-30—Exploded view of typical five sprockets and freewheeling hub.

1. Freewheeling hub
2. Rear seal
3. Outside seal
4. Low (1st) speed sprocket
5. Spacer
6. Second speed sprocket
7. Spacer
8. Third speed sprocket
9. Fourth speed sprocket
10. High (5th) speed sprocket
11. Assembled sprocket and freewheeling unit

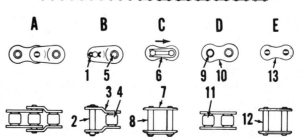

1. Cotter key
2. Pin
3. Offset side plate
4. Roller
5. Bushing
6. Spring clip
7. Side plate
8. Pins
9. Bushing
10. Side plate
11. Roller
12. Rivet
13. Side plates

Fig. 1-32—Drawing of chain showing various parts of typical bicycle chain: Offset section (A); Offset link (B); Spring clip connecting or master link (C); Inner link (D) and Outer link (E).

Derailleur

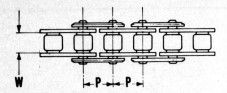

Fig. 1-34—Pitch (P) is the distance between centers of rollers. Width (W) is distance between side plates of inner links.

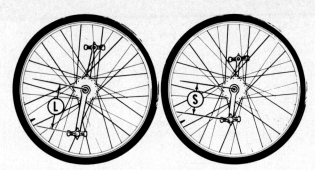

Fig. 1-36—Long crank arms (L) will be easier to move, but distance traveled by pedals will be farther than for short crank arms (S).

(6) is used on nearly all bicycles to transmit movement of the chainwheel (5) to the sprocket (7). Many different types and sizes of drive chain are available for use on many types of equipment. Several different types and sizes of chain have been used on bicycles, but most are equipped with one of three popular sizes. The size is generally listed as length of pitch (P-Fig. 1-34) and width (W). Chain with 25.4 MM (1 inch) pitch and 4.9 MM (3/16-inch) width is used on some bicycles, especially older models. Later one speed bicycles, models with multi-speed rear hubs and three speed rear derailleur are most often equipped with chain that has 12.7 MM (½-inch) pitch and 3.3 MM (1/8-inch) width. Nearly all bicycles with derailleur use chain with 12.7 MM (½-inch) pitch and narrow 2.38 MM (3/32-inch) width. It is very important to use the correct length of chain, as well as the correct type and size.

DERAILLEUR

The length of the crank arm, size of the sprockets and diameter of the wheel combine to determine how easily a bicycle can be pedaled.

Starting with two wheels of the same diameter, pedals can be installed near the center of one and near the outside (rim) of the other (Fig. 1-36). The wheel with pedals near the outside will be easier to pedal because the levers or crank arms (L) are longer than crank arms (S). Regardless of the length of the crank arms, the two wheels will cover the same dis-

tance in one revolution if the diameter of the two wheels are the same. Increasing the diameter (and circumference) of the wheel will result in the larger wheel traveling farther in one revolution than the smaller wheel (Fig. 1-37). The maximum diameter of wheel was determined by the length of a person's legs and by strength. A great amount of force was required to turn a large wheel. The crank can be located away from the wheel using a

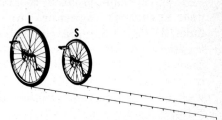

Fig. 1-37—The wheel with larger diameter (L) will travel farther than small wheel (S) for each revolution. The circumference is greater for larger wheel.

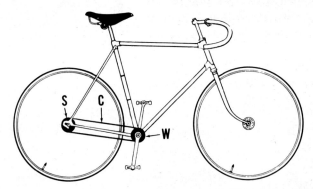

Fig. 1-38—Pedals can be relocated by using chain (C), chain wheel (W) and sprocket (S).

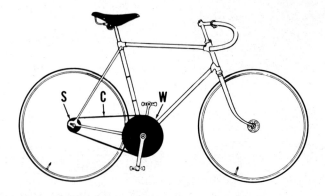

Fig. 1-39—Installation of different sized chain wheel (W) and sprocket (S) will affect the distance traveled for each revolution of pedals.

GEAR TABLE
For 26 and 27in. Wheels. To find any gear not given in this table, multiply the diameter in inches of the rear wheel by the number of teeth on the Chain Wheel, and divide by the number of teeth on the hub sprocket

Chain Wheels	36		38		40		42		44		46		47		48		49		50		51		52	
Wheel Sizes	26″	27″	26″	27″	26″	27″	26″	27″	26″	27″	26″	27″	26″	27″	26″	27″	26″	27″	26″	27″	26″	27″	26″	27″
Sprocket Sizes 12	78.0	81.0	82.3	85.5	86.6	90.0	91.0	94.5	95.3	99.0	99.7	103.0	101.8	105.7	104.0	108.0	106.2	110.2	108.3	112.5	110.8	114.9	113.0	117.0
13	72.0	74.8	76.0	78.9	80.0	83.1	84.0	87.2	88.0	91.4	92.0	95.5	94.0	97.6	96.0	99.7	98.0	101.7	100.0	103.8	102.0	105.1	104.0	108.0
14	66.9	69.4	70.5	73.3	74.3	77.1	78.0	81.0	81.7	84.9	85.4	88.7	87.3	90.6	89.1	92.6	91.0	94.5	92.9	96.4	94.1	98.5	96.6	100.0
15	62.4	64.8	65.9	68.4	69.3	72.0	72.8	75.6	76.3	79.2	79.7	82.8	81.5	84.6	83.2	86.4	84.9	88.2	86.6	90.0	88.6	91.2	90.1	93.6
16	58.1	60.7	61.7	64.1	65.0	67.5	68.3	70.9	71.5	74.3	74.7	77.6	76.4	79.3	78.0	81.0	79.6	82.7	81.3	84.4	82.1	86.1	84.5	87.7
17	55.1	57.2	58.1	60.3	61.2	63.5	64.2	66.7	67.3	69.9	70.3	73.1	71.9	74.6	73.4	76.2	74.9	77.8	76.5	79.4	78.0	81.0	79.5	82.6
18	52.0	54.2	54.9	57.0	57.7	60.0	60.7	63.0	63.5	66.0	66.4	69.0	67.9	70.5	69.3	72.0	70.8	73.5	72.2	75.0	73.1	76.9	75.1	78.0
19	49.3	51.2	52.0	54.0	54.7	56.8	57.5	59.7	60.2	62.5	62.9	65.4	64.3	66.8	65.7	68.2	67.1	69.6	68.4	71.1	69.1	72.9	71.1	73.9
20	46.8	48.6	49.4	51.3	52.0	54.0	54.6	56.7	57.2	59.4	59.8	62.1	61.1	63.5	62.4	64.8	63.7	66.2	65.0	67.5	66.6	68.2	67.6	70.2
21	44.6	46.3	47.0	48.8	49.5	51.4	52.0	54.0	54.5	56.6	57.0	59.1	58.2	60.4	59.4	61.7	60.7	63.0	61.9	64.3	63.3	65.2	64.4	66.8
22	42.6	44.2	44.9	46.6	47.5	49.1	49.6	51.5	52.0	54.0	54.4	56.4	55.5	57.7	56.7	58.9	57.9	60.1	59.1	61.4	60.6	62.1	61.4	63.8
23	40.7	42.3	43.0	44.6	45.2	46.9	47.5	49.3	49.7	51.6	52.0	54.0	53.1	55.2	54.3	56.3	55.4	57.5	56.5	58.7	57.1	59.2	58.8	61.0
24	39.0	40.5	41.1	42.7	43.3	45.0	45.5	47.3	47.7	49.5	49.8	51.7	50.9	52.9	52.0	54.0	53.1	55.1	54.2	56.3	55.6	57.9	56.3	58.5
25	37.4	38.9	39.5	41.0	41.6	43.2	43.7	45.3	45.8	47.5	47.8	49.7	48.9	50.8	49.9	51.8	51.0	52.9	52.1	54.0	53.1	55.2	54.1	56.2
26	36.0	37.4	38.0	39.1	40.0	41.6	42.0	43.5	44.0	45.7	46.0	47.8	47.0	48.8	48.0	49.8	49.0	50.9	50.0	51.9	51.0	52.2	52.0	54.1
28	33.4	34.8	35.3	36.6	37.1	38.6	39.0	40.5	40.9	42.4	42.7	44.4	43.6	45.3	44.6	46.3	45.5	47.2	46.4	48.2	47.3	49.1	43.3	50.1

Fig. 1-40—The combination of sprocket size (number of teeth), chain wheel size (number of teeth) and rear wheel size (diameter) will affect the distance traveled.

Fig. 1-41—Photograph shows bicycle with pedals attached directly to wheels. The ratio of one revolution of the pedals to the distance traveled can be easily seen by these two different units.

sprocket (S-Fig. 1-38) and a chainwheel (W) and a chain (C). The crank is just relocated if the sprocket (S) and the chainwheel (W) are identical in size (diameter).

One revolution of the crank will turn the wheel one revolution. It is possible to change the distance traveled during one revolution of the crank by installing different size sprockets (S-Fig. 1-39) and chainwheel (W).

During one revolution of the chainwheel (W), the sprocket (S) and wheel in the illustration will rotate approximately three complete turns. The distance the bicycle travels will be approximately three times as far as it would if the crank were mounted directly on the wheel. It will also be harder to pedal than if the crank were mounted directly on the wheel. The maximum diameter of wheel was determined by the length of his legs and his strength. The sprockets and

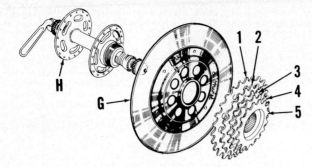

Fig. 1-42—*View of rear wheel hub (H) and sprockets. Guard (G) is used to protect wheel spokes in case chain comes off sprockets. Largest sprocket (1) provides the most power but slowest speed. Smallest sprocket (5) provides fastest speed, but is harder to pedal at slow speed.*

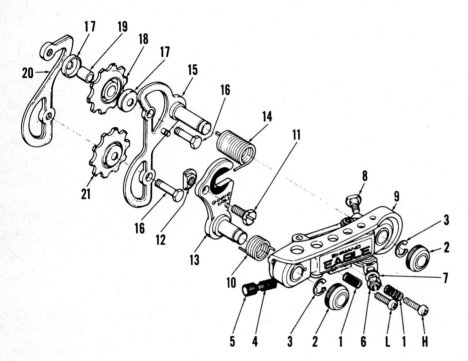

Fig. 1-44—*View of rear wheel sprockets (1, 2, 3, 4 & 5) and derailleur assembly. Chain is guided to different sprockets by derailleur assembly.*

Fig. 1-43—*Exploded view of typical rear derailleur and chain tensioner assembly. Refer to service section for specific repair and adjustment data.*

1. Lock springs
2. Caps
3. Snap rings
4. Lock spring
5. Cable adjuster
6. Cable attachment nut
7. Washer
8. Cable attachment bolt
9. Derailleur mechanism
10. Tension spring
11. Attaching screw
12. Attaching nut
13. Mounting plate and shaft
14. Tension spring
15. Inner cage plate
16. Pulley bolts
17. Pulley caps
18. Pulley
19. Pulley bushing
20. Outer cage plate
21. Pulley
H. High gear adjusting stop
L. Low gear adjusting stop

For instance, a bicycle with a 49 tooth chainwheel and a 21 tooth sprocket on the 26 inch wheel would be equivalent to a crank mounted directly on a wheel 60.6 inches in diameter. A bicycle with 24 tooth chainwheel and a 28 tooth sprocket on a 26 inch wheel would be equivalent to a crank mounted directly to a 22.3 inch diameter wheel. The size of the wheels in Fig. 1-41 are not known but the two extremes of wheel size (reduction) can be duplicated on a modern bicycle without changing the size of the wheel. The effective reduction is changed by using different sprocket and chainwheels.

The derailleur system is simply a method of changing the sizes of the chainwheels and sprockets while moving. On a typical 5 speed bicycle, five sprockets are mounted on the rear wheel but only one chainwheel is used. The pedals turn the chainwheel which pulls the chain which turns one of the rear sprockets. The derailleur guides the chain to one of the rear sprockets. The largest of the rear sprockets (1-Fig. 1-42) is the slowest speed and the smallest

chainwheels are available with many different diameters (number of teeth) to provide for many different riding conditions. The overall riding conditions, of course, must take into consideration the tire size as well as the physical sprocket ratio. Tables

(Fig. 1-40) are available which translate the size of the sprocket, chainwheel and tire into another common number. The common number is the original base of what diameter of tire would be necessary if the crank were mounted directly on the wheel.

sprocket (5) is the fastest speed. The derailleur should guide the chain and hold its position so the chain doesn't accidentally slip onto an unwanted sprocket. The rear derailleur also includes some method of automatically tightening the chain. Refer to Fig. 1-43 for exploded view of typical rear derailleur.

The front derailleur (F-Fig. 1-45) accomplishes the same purpose as the rear, but doesn't include a chain tensioner. The front and rear derailleur assemblies are often designed to operate as a set. The front derailleur guides the chain over two or three sprockets while the rear derailleur may guide the chain over as many as six different sprockets. When the chain is over the smallest front chainwheel and the smallest rear sprocket, the tensioner must keep the chain tight enough that it won't come off. The chain must be long enough to go over the largest rear sprocket and the largest front chainwheel.

Controls for the derailleurs may be located at the unit, but most are remote controlled by cable. The remote control lever may be located any of several places; on the frame, on the han-

Fig. 1-46—Derailleur controls are usually located in one of the positions shown.

dlebar stem or on the handlebars (Fig. 1-46).

REAR WHEEL

The rear wheel assembly consists of the hub, spokes, wheel (rim) and tire. The hub may contain the brake assembly, a multi-speed transmission or may be threaded with a freewheel unit and derailleur sprockets installed. Regardless of the specific design, the rear sprocket turns the hub which in turn rotates the wheel

via the spokes. The rear wheel spokes are used to pull the wheel, turning it and propelling the bicycle. The rear wheel spokes, therefore, should be assembled so that

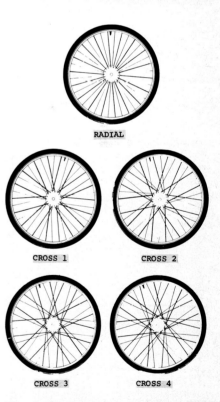

Fig. 1-47—Drawings of assembled 36 spoke wheels showing five of the more popular spoke patterns. Radial and cross 1 lacing are not recommended for any rear wheels. Cross 3 is most common for both front and rear wheels. Cross 4 is sometimes used for tandem bicycles.

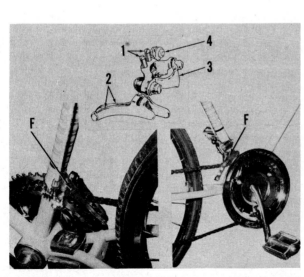

Fig. 1-45—Front derailleur (F) operates like rear unit to guide chain over one of the chain wheels. The chain slides between plates (2). Derailleur bracket (3) is usually clamped to seat tube and cable is attached to arm (4). Adjustment (stop) screws for the Huret unit shown are located at (1).

Fig. 1-48—Early methods of slowing bicycles were very simple; drag something.

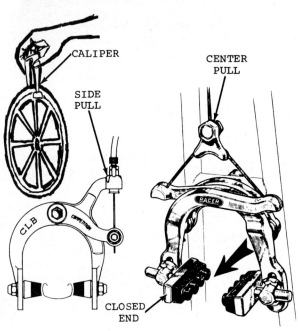

Fig. 1-49—Caliper brakes are available that grip sides of wheel rims. Be especially careful when assembling, to install brake shoes with closed end of holder toward front. The brake shoes will slide out of holder if assembled incorrectly.

CALIPER

SIDE PULL

CENTER PULL

CLB

CLOSED END

the spokes pull on a nearly straight line. Refer to the SERVICE section for specific details, but Fig. 1-47 shows common patterns for spoking wheels. Usually the spokes are laced in a cross three pattern for both front and rear wheels. A radial pattern may be used for some front wheels that only idle. Radially spoked wheels are used on the front wheel of some racers because they weigh less. Cross one pattern is similar and slightly better than radially spoked. Spokes are slightly longer than radial spokes and therefore the assembled wheel will weigh more. At the other extreme, is the cross four pattern. A cross four pattern with a large diameter hub is the strongest for the rear driving wheel, but it will also weigh more than other combinations. This much strength is generally not required except for some tandem bicycles. The most common pattern is the cross three. The rims and tires used for the rear are similar (or identical) to those previously described for the front wheel.

BRAKES

Brakes are necessary in order to slow or stop the bicycle. Early in the history of bicycling, it was necessary to drag a tree branch and the rider's feet in order to slow the bicycle (Fig. 1-48). Later, brakes were developed which are much better and more dependable.

A coaster brake is contained in the rear wheel hub and is actuated by pushing the pedals backward. This type of hub also incorporates a ratcheting mechanism which permits coasting. Back pedaling brakes are available in single speed hubs, two and three speed hubs. The back pedaling brake is actuated by the feet; other types of (hand operated brakes) are also used on bicycles.

Caliper type brakes that grip the wheel rim are commonly used

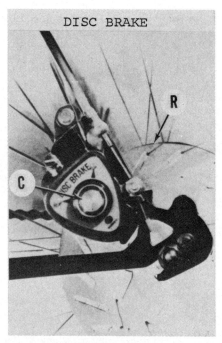

EXTERNAL CONTRACTING

DISC BRAKE

INTERNAL EXPANDING

Fig. 1-50—Disc brakes, external contracting and internal expanding shoe brakes are used on some bicycles. Brakes drum (D) and shoes (S) are used on shoe type brakes. Rotor (R) or disc and caliper (C) is used on disc brake.

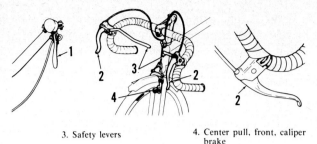

Fig. 1-51—View of different types of handlebar mounted brake control levers. Be sure that control for front wheel brake is operated by left hand.

1. Brake lever for upright handlebars
2. Brake lever for down turned handlebars

3. Safety levers

4. Center pull, front, caliper brake

SERIAL NUMBERS

It is important to identify specific bicycles for certain types of service, but more often serial numbers are required to prove ownership to others such as law enforcement personnel. Photographs can be another aid to help with identification and for insurance claims.

Almost all manufacturers stamp the model number and a unique serial number into the bicycle frame (Fig. 1-52) in one of three locations:

1. Under the crank hanger (A)
2. Outside the left side rear wheel lug (B)
3. On the steering head tube (C)

If the serial number has been disfigured or ground away it is an almost sure signal that the bicycle has been stolen. If you are not able to locate the serial number, contact a bicycle dealer for help. Sometimes the stamped numbers are filled so completely with paint that they are not easily read. Sometimes parts other than the frame are marked

(Fig. 1-49). The control cable may pull from the center or from the side. This type of brake can be operated by hand controls and can be used to stop either front or rear wheels. Be sure that closed side of brake pad holder keeps the pads from sliding out and that pads contact the rim evenly and squarely.

Disc brakes operate the same as caliper brakes except a special disc is used instead of using the wheel rim. Usually the disc is small and is attached to the hub.

Several of the coaster (back pedaling) brake systems are shoe brakes that expand in the drum. A standard expanding shoe brake is also incorporated into some front hubs and is operated by handlebar mounted controls. External contracting brakes have also been used, but are not very common.

Regardless of the type of brake, handlebar mounted remote controls should be installed with control for front wheel brake on left side. Handlebar control for rear wheel should be operated by the right hand.

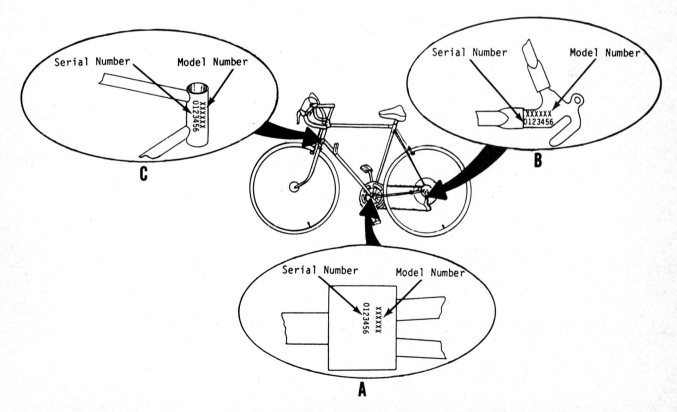

Fig. 1-52—Bicycle serial numbers are usually stamped into the frame at one of the locations shown. Position "A" is the underside of the crank hanger; position "B" is outside of left side rear wheel lug; position "C" is on the steering head tube.

with serial numbers, but usually any other numbers are only to identify the type of part.

Immediately after purchasing a bicycle, all of the serial numbers and other pertinent data should be recorded and stored away from the bicycle. The following space is provided for a convenient place to record this information.

Owner	Brand	Color	Model Number	Serial Number

Fig. 2-1 — Choose a bicycle that is designed for the type of riding you intend to do.

SELECTION

Choose a model that is designed for the type of riding you intend to do. The frame design and each component will contribute in some way to the operation of the bicycle. Some exceptional features for certain types of riding may be completely unsuited for a different type of riding or for a different rider.

Attempts to alter the design of a bicycle by adding or changing components are very often unsatisfactory and costly. Some competent, very experienced riders are able to successfully direct changes or select components, but most will be better satisfied following the direction of a qualified dealer or dealer representative.

Fig. 2-3 — The frame size is given as the seat tube height (H) and rim diameter (R).

FRAME

The frame should fit your physical size. Control may be difficult or impossible if the bicycle is too small or too large, especially during critical maneuvers. Breaking or bending bicycle parts is of course not desired, but riding will be less dangerous and more fun if the bicycle is the correct size for your size and weight.

The frame size is given as the distance from the center of the bottom bracket to the top of the seat tube (H – Fig. 2-3) and the wheel rim diameter (R). Two examples are 21/26 inch frame and 15/20 inch frame. The 21 inch and 15 inch dimensions are the length of the seat tube (H) and the 26 inch and 20 inch are the size (diameter) of the rims (R).

Fig. 2-2 — The frame should fit your physical size.

The rider can change the distribution of his weight between the handlebars, the seat and the pedals as long as he does not exceed his ability (or attempt to defy gravity). Mechanical components of the bicycle determine the geometric transfer of the rider's weight to the ground. As a rule, a forward riding position is more desirable for high speed riding, while more casual riding is more comfortable with the rider's weight toward the rear.

Frame geometry, as well as component selection, will determine the distribution of the rider's weight. Direction control is also governed by the frame angles which determine wheel caster and steering head angle. Only highly qualified personnel should attempt to straighten a bent frame, repair a broken frame or change the frame geometry. A damaged frame should usually be discarded before it causes injury.

Fig. 2-4 — The riding position affects rider comfort and bicycle handling.

SEAT

The selection of seat type, covering material and manufacturing company should be an important consideration for each rider. Improper seat selection or adjustment can quickly change a ride from a good experience into a nightmare. Ideally, you should not be aware of the seat while riding, but it should accomplish several very important jobs unnoticed.

1. **Support the riders upper body** — Legs should be suspended so that muscles can be used for propelling bicycle.
2. **Provide steering control** — Locate rider laterally above the pedals for control around corners.
3. **Provide fore and aft location** — Distribution of rider's weight can be shifted as required for better stability, control and power output.
4. **Assist to absorb impact shock** — Should work in conjunction with legs to prevent injury.

All of the support provided by the seat should be done without restricting leg motion. The most desirable seat must therefore consider the type of riding and the physical shape of the rider. Bone structure differences between men and women have caused special seats to be developed for each sex. Heavy thighs, hip bone width, excess fat or other physical differences should also be carefully considered when choosing a seat.

ADJUSTMENT. Vertical height of the seat should be adjusted so that the rider's knee is bent slightly when rider is against the seat and ball of rider's foot is on pedal that is at lowest position. A study conducted at Loughboro University in England found that best efficiency is possible with seat height set as follows: Measure from the floor to the lowest bony part of the rider's pelvis, while rider is standing without shoes. Multiply this measurement by 1.09 which should be the distance from the center of the pedal spindle to

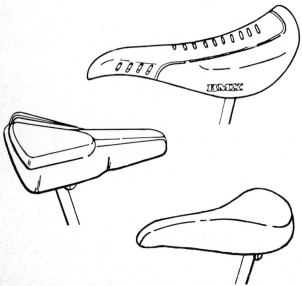

Fig. 2-5 — Seat selection should be determined only after carefully considering the type of riding and the attributes of the rider.

Fig. 2-6 — The seat should be positioned so that the rider's knee is bent slightly when pedal is at the lowest position.

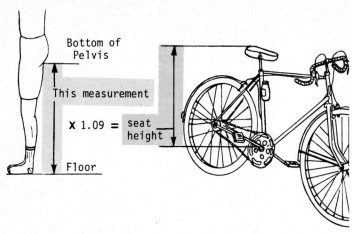

Fig. 2-7—Measure from the floor to the bony part of rider's pelvis, then multiply this measurement times 1.09. The result should be the correct distance from center of pedal spindle to top of seat.

the top of the seat. Small changes may be necessary to suit rider preference. Loosen clamp nut (C – Fig. 2-8) to raise or lower the seat post in the frame's seat tube.

The rider will rock from side to side causing discomfort, if the seat is too high. Pedal crank arms that are too long can also cause rocking and discomfort. If the seat is too low, pedaling force will have less than optimum effect, which can result in leg discomfort. Vertical changes of as little as 1/8 inch can affect comfort and pedaling efficiency.

The seat should be nearly horizontal and should be aligned with the frame tube. Loosen clamp nut (1 – Fig. 2-8) to change the position of seat on top of the seat post. The slant of the seat top and fore/aft position of the seat can be primarily governed by personal preference; however, will effect handling and pedaling efficiency. Slanting the top of seat down at the front or moving seat forward slightly will cause the rider to put more weight on the handlebars. This forward positioning will dramatically affect the rider's comfort and control, but the changes will not always be an improvement.

Major changes should seldom be necessary after initial adjustments, but minor changes can be effectively used to reduce or eliminate discomfort. It may also be necessary to readjust the slant and fore/aft position of the seat after adjusting the handlebar position because the seat and handlebar positions are so interrelated.

HANDLEBAR AND STEM

Styles and shapes for handlebars are nearly endless. Selection should suit the rider's preference, but should be designed for the type of riding planned. Special shapes are available for off road cross country type riding that would be completely unsuitable for standard road touring. High bars which position grips above the rider's shoulders, bars or accessories with unprotected ends or protrusions, improper (upside down, reversed or wrong size) installation and other obvious unsafe practices should always be discouraged.

Stems are available with many different vertical lengths and with different amounts of forward offset. Select stem carefully because the offset cannot be adjusted and vertical adjustment is possible only within a very limited range. Special high strength stems are available for BMX or other types of riding which stress the stem excessively.

Grips, padding or wrapping for handlebars should be installed after handlebars are adjusted and all handlebar mounted accessories are installed.

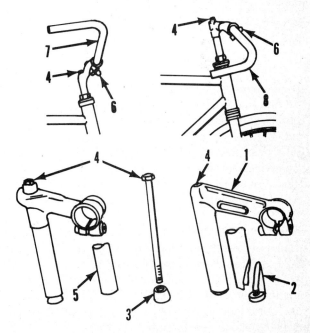

Fig. 2-9—Steering stems and handlebars are available in a variety of shapes. The diameter of the steering stem is larger for early bicycle forks, because later fork tube has the same outside diameter but thicker tubing thickness for increased strength.

	3. Expansion lug	
1. Aluminum stem	4. Wedge bolt	6. Handlebar clamp
2. Split lug	5. Steel stem	bolt

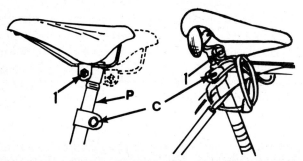

Fig. 2-8—Location of the seat is important to the comfort of the rider and will also affect handling. Height is changed by raising or lowering post (P) after loosening clamp (C).

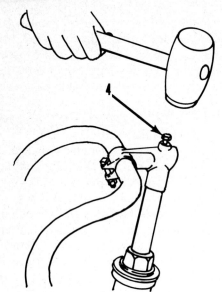

Fig. 2-10 — Loosen steering stem wedge bolt (4), then bump the bolt down to dislodge the wedge.

ADJUSTMENT. The stem can be moved vertically or can be rotated in the fork tube after loosening the wedge between stem and tube. To loosen wedge, first loosen bolt (4 – Fig. 2-10) approximately four turns, then use a soft faced hammer to bump the bolt (and wedge) down. The stem should be able to turn and move vertically with little effort. Use caution to make sure stem is not pulled too far up in the fork tube. Some stems are marked to indicate the maximum upward position in relation to the top of fork tube. Align front wheel and handlebar while tightening the bolt for the stem wedge. Tighten wedge bolt sufficiently to hold stem in fork tube securely after positioning correctly.

Handlebars can be rotated to a comfortable position after loosening clamp bolt or screw (6 – Fig. 2-9). Tighten clamp sufficiently to eliminate possibility of handlebar movement after adjustment is complete.

It is desirable to recheck adjustment of seat and handlebar positions after changing the position of either. Changing the position of the rider's body at either end may alter the desired setting at the other end.

Handlebar mounted controls should be located within easy reach and accessories should be located where they are convenient to use. Brake lever on left should operate the front wheel brake and lever on right should operate rear brake. Similarly, control for front derailleur should be on left; control for rear derailleur should be mounted on right of frame or handlebar.

Brake lever for upturned handlebars should be at comfortable position angled slightly out as shown in Fig. 2-12. On low style handlebars, brake control levers should be straight in front of handlebar as shown.

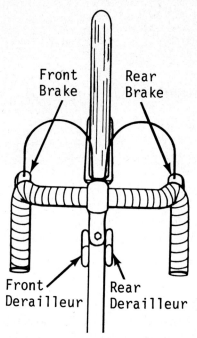

Fig. 2-11 — Brake lever on left side should stop front wheel and derailleur control on left side should operate the front derailleur.

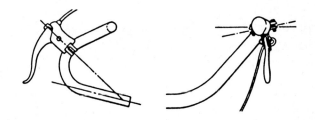

Fig. 2-12 — Handlebar mounted controls should be comfortably located in approximately the positions shown.

TAPING HANDLEBARS. Be sure handlebar mounted controls and accessories are correctly positioned and securely mounted before installing tape. If tape is supplied in one roll, unroll tape and divide into two equal lengths. Each length should be approximately 7½ feet for one side of most handlebars. Tape width may change the length of tape required.

There are many different ways to wrap the handlebars; however, the following notes may be helpful.

Regardless of style, **wrap both sides of handlebars the same.** A common method is stand in front facing handlebars. Wrap across top, around the back of bar and pull tape toward you (forward) from under the handlebar.

Adhesive backed tape should be installed without wrinkles, but relaxed. Too much tension may force adhesive through the cloth and be sticky to the rider's hands.

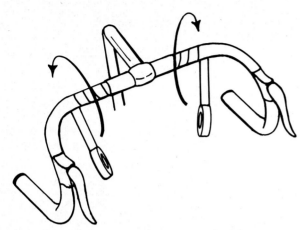

Fig. 2-13 — If wrapped, the tape on handlebars should be installed the same way. The method shown is one method of wrapping from the center outward. Don't become confused while wrapping around brake levers, just continue the pattern already started.

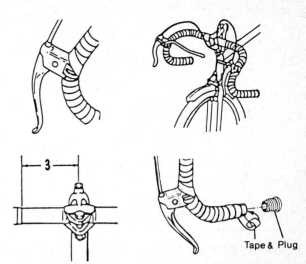

Fig. 2-15 — Views showing some correctly wrapped handlebars. There are several equally correct ways of wrapping. Tape should always be wrapped evenly without wrinkles, but with some overlap.

All tape should be wrapped evenly, without wrinkles with some overlap. One of the purposes of the tape is to cushion the rider's hands. Tight wrapping may cause tape to rip more easily and wear out quicker than smooth relaxed wrapping. Tape that is too loose, especially non-adhesive type, will not stay in position. Sufficient tension is important.

Wrapping from ends of handlebars toward center causes edge of tape to face away from direction of hand pressure. Tape will be smoother and may be easier on rider's hands. Handlebars equipped with shift controls in handlebar ends should always be wrapped from ends toward center. It is necessary to use adhesive backed tape to hold the end at middle of bar. Tape of a contrasting color may be used to hold the end down and make the job more attractive.

If necessary **to remove old wrapping, cut longitudinally** so that shorter pieces can be removed. Additional handlebar padding is possible if new tape can be wrapped over existing old tape; however, the old tape should be even and in reasonably good condition for best results. It is sometimes possible to repair old wrapping sufficiently to permit covering with new tape. It is also possible to install tape over closed cell foam handlebar covering for a good cushiony grip.

If wrapping tape from center of bar toward ends, begin about 3 inches from center and attach end of tape to bar with adhesive tape. Wrap tape tightly toward center of handlebar to anchor end of tape firmly and to cover the cut end. Pull tape tight and begin wrapping toward end of handlebar, overlapping tape evenly. The correct amount of overlap will depend upon length of tape and rider's preference. Tape that is left over at end of bar does nothing for rider comfort; however, about 1 inch of tape should be pushed into end of bar, then anchored by inserting plug into end of handlebar.

BRAKES

The brakes should be checked for proper operation and should be adjusted or repaired, if necessary, each time before the bicycle is ridden. **Back pedaling brakes should be disassembled, cleaned, inspected, repaired and lubricated at least once each year.** Refer to the SERVICE SECTION appropriate to the brake type.

Caliper and other **hand operated brakes may only need to be adjusted.** Brake shoes, on caliper brakes, should begin to contact the wheel rim soon after beginning to squeeze the control lever. Shoes should not rub on rim when released and the shoes should align with the rim. Different adjustment procedures are necessary for different types of brakes but the following outlines a generally accepted method for caliper type brakes.

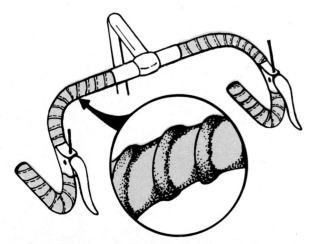

Fig. 2-14 — Wrapping tape from ends of handlebars toward the center is slightly more difficult, but positions the rough edge of tape away from hand pressure.

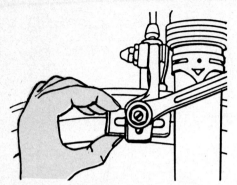

Fig. 2-16 — Brake pads should be aligned with wheel rim. Check to be sure that pads contact rim correctly when engaged.

ADJUSTMENT. Check condition of the brake pads before attempting any adjustment. It may be impossible to properly adjust brakes if pads are worn out.

Align brake pads with wheel rim. If not correctly aligned, loosen clamp nut or screw and relocate brake pad. It may be necessary to install a new brake pad if brake has operated for some time with pad not aligned with wheel rim.

EQUALIZE BRAKE PAD CLEARANCE. Check and be sure that the two brake shoes are equal distance from the rim (Fig. 2-17) with the brake released. If one shoe is closer to the rim than the other, rotate the wheel to make sure that the wheel is straight. Align the rim, if bent, before proceeding. Lubricate brake pivot points to assure freedom of movement. Make sure oil does not accidentally get on wheel rim or brake pads.

On center pull brakes, loosen the center mounting nut (12 – Fig. 2-18), move the brake mounting bridge (10) as required, then tighten mounting nut. Be sure

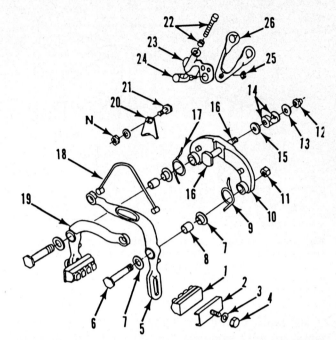

Fig. 2-18 — Exploded view of typical center pull brake assembly. Unit shown is for rear wheel, but front unit is similar.

1. Brake shoe	14. Seating pads
2. Holder	15. Spacer washer
3. Washer	16. Center bolt
4. Nut	17. Left side release
5. Inner brake arm	spring
6. Pivot bolt	18. Connecting cable
7. Delrin bushing	19. Outer brake arm
8. Metal bushing	20. Cable carrier
9. Right side release	21. Cable connector
spring	22. Cable adjuster
10. Brake arm bridge	23. Outer barrel
11. Nut	24. Stud
12. Nut	25. Nut
13. Washer	26. Cable hanger

that bridge doesn't move when tightening the mounting nut.

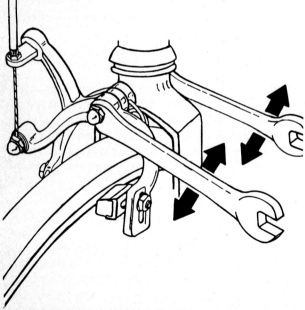

Fig. 2-17 — When brake is released, clearance between brake shoes and rim should be the same on both sides.

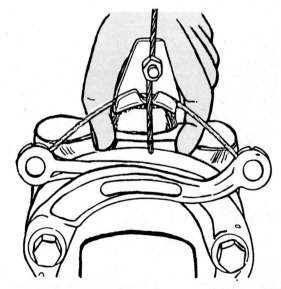

Fig. 2-18A — The brake arm bridge (10 – Fig. 2-18) can be moved after loosening nut (12). Hold bridge while tightening the nut.

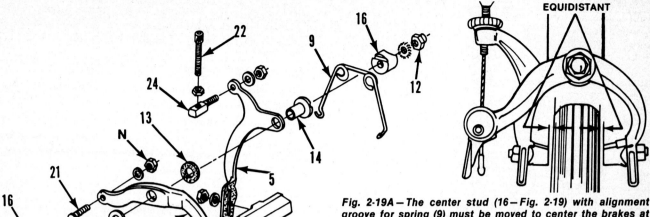

Fig. 2-19—Exploded view of typical side pull brake assembly. Several variations will be noticed.

1. Brake shoe	14. Bushing
2. Housing	15. Washer
3. Washer	16. Center stud &
4. Nut	spring alignment
5. Inner brake arm	groove
6. Nut	19. Outer brake arm
9. Release spring	21. Cable connector
11. Nut	22. Cable adjuster
12. Nut	24. Stud
13. Washers	

On side pull brakes, loosen the center pivot mounting nut (12–Fig. 2-19), move the center pivot (16) as required, then tighten the mounting nut. Be sure that center pivot doesn't move when tightening the mounting nut. The center pivot is also the center anchor for the release spring (9).

On cantilever brakes, apply brakes several times to center the cable carrier (20–Fig. 2-20). Loosen the mounting screw (4) of the brake pad closest to the wheel rim, begin to apply brakes gently until both the loosened and tightly mounted pads just touch wheel rim, then tighten the mounting screw of the loosened pad. If careful, pad alignment should not change.

TOE-IN. Brake noise or grabbing may be caused by improper toe-in of the brake pads. The front edge of brake pads should touch the wheel rim before the rear of pad. The brake pads can be sanded to provide toe-in or the caliper arms can be bent slightly. Some cantilever brakes use a wedge-shaped washer for adjusting toe-in.

WARNING: Do not reverse brake pads for any reason. The closed end of the pad holder must be toward front to keep the pad from pulling out when brake is engaged.

PAD CLEARANCE. Adjustment can be accomplished after making certain that brake is centered

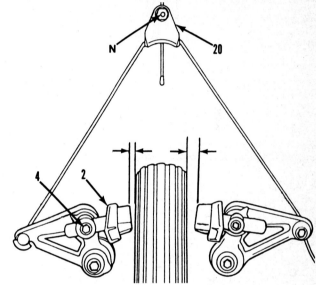

Fig. 2-19A—The center stud (16—Fig. 2-19) with alignment groove for spring (9) must be moved to center the brakes at sides of rim. It will be necessary to hold stud in some way while tightening mounting nut (12).

Fig. 2-20—Cantilever brakes are centered by correct positioning of the cable carrier (20); however, pads must also be correctly positioned. Refer to text for adjustment.

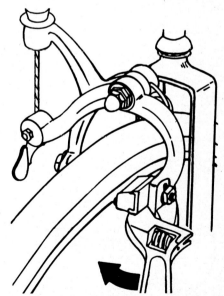

Fig. 2-21—Brake pads should toe-in slightly. The brake arm can be bent slightly as shown if necessary to cause front of pads to touch first.

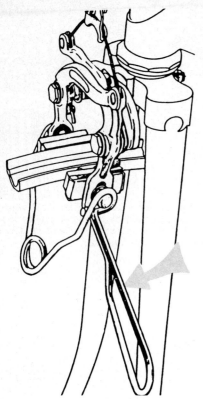

and shoes are aligned with rim. Squeeze shoes together at wheel, using a special tool (Fig. 2-22), a clamp or by hand. Loosen the cable clamp nut (N – Fig. 2-18, Fig. 2-19 or Fig. 2-20) and pull cable through the clamp screw. Tighten nut (N), release the brake shoes and check operation of the brake. Fine adjustment is accomplished by turning adjusters (22 – Fig. 2-18 or Fig. 2-19) if provided.

Other types of brakes are adjusted in different ways. Most cable operated brakes are adjusted by turning the cable adjusting screw.

BEARINGS

ADJUSTMENT. Bearings located in the wheel hubs, steering head and crank set must be cleaned, repacked and adjusted regularly to extend the life of the bearing and to assure safe operation. It is possible to adjust these bearings without disassembly, but complete disassembly, cleaning and inspection is recommended, when adjustment is necessary.

Parts of the bearing will almost always be damaged if operated while out of adjustment, even if only for a short time. Refer to the appropriate SERVICE section for correct procedure to disassemble, clean, in-

Fig. 2-22 — A special tool similar to the one shown is helpful for holding pads against rim while adjusting.

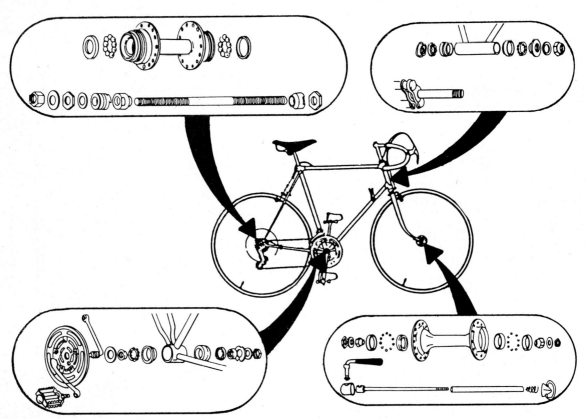

Fig. 2-23 — Bearings are used extensively on bicycles. All must be properly lubricated and adjusted to ensure long trouble free service.

spect, repair, lubricate, reassemble and adjust the bearings.

Check steering head bearings by turning handlebars from side to side. Movement should be smooth and little effort should be necessary. Lift handlebars and check for any play in steering head bearing. If play is noticed when lifting handlebars, bearings should be adjusted as described in the SERVICE section. Check for roughness again after adjusting bearings. If any roughness is noticed, refer to SERVICE section and disassemble, clean, inspect, repair, lubricate, reassemble, then adjust the steering head bearings.

Check bearings of wheel hubs, by raising wheel off the ground, then rotating the wheel. The wheel should rotate freely and smoothly. Problems in the rear hub, free-wheeling unit or back pedalling brake assembly may be indicated if the pedals turn when the rear wheel is rotated in the normal forward direction. Move wheel rim from side to side gently and check for side play at wheel hub. Only very slight side play is permissible. If play is noticed, bearings can be adjusted as described in the appropriate SERVICE section. Check for roughness again after adjusting the bearings. If any roughness is noticed, refer to the SERVICE section and disassemble, clean, inspect, repair, lubricate, reassemble, then adjust the wheel bearings. Wheel hubs should be disassembled and serviced at least once each year when subjected to normal use. More than "normal" mileage, unusually dusty or wet conditions, use over rough terrain and other similar adverse operation will require more frequent wheel bearing (and other) service.

Check the crank assembly for looseness by trying to move the pedal crank arms from side to side. Also check bearings for smooth rotation. The crank should turn freely in the bearings with no noticeable roughness and only very slight side play. On three piece crank assemblies, check to be sure that crank arms

are secured tightly to the crankshaft. Refer to the appropriate PERIODIC MAINTENANCE or SERVICE section for lubricating or repair. Special tools are sometimes required.

CHAIN

TENSION ADJUSTMENT. A drive chain that is well lubricated, in good condition and properly tightened, should move smoothly around the chainwheel and rear sprocket. Tension is adjusted in several ways as shown in Fig. 2-24, Fig. 2-25 and Fig. 2-26.

Some bicycles use a bushing assembly (B – Fig. 2-15) bolted to the frame. Loosen nuts (N) and move the bushing to tighten the chain. There should be only a small amount of free play (P – Fig. 2-27) after adjustment is accomplished.

Most bicycles without derailleurs are adjusted by moving the rear axle within slots in the rear frame lug. Refer to Fig. 2-25. Loosen the axle retaining nuts on both sides of axle and move axle toward rear of bicycle to reduce free play (P) in chain. Center the rear wheel between frame members before tighten-

Fig. 2-25 — Adjust chain tension on bicycle shown by moving rear wheel after loosening axle nuts. Be sure to center wheel as well as tighten chain while tightening axle nuts.

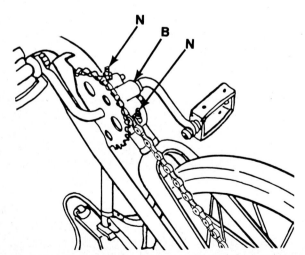

Fig. 2-24 — Chain tension (free play) is adjusted on bicycle shown by moving crank bracket (B) after loosening nuts (N).

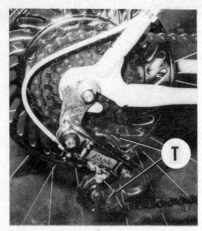

Fig. 2-26—*Derailleur equipped bikes and some single speed racing units are equipped with automatic tensioner (T).*

Fig. 2-27—*Chain free play (P) is measured between rear sprocket and chain wheel.*

ing the axle nuts. On bicycles with multi-speed rear hubs, check and adjust controls after moving the axle.

Bicycles with derailleur system and some racing single speed bicycles are equipped with a tensioner device (T–Fig. 2-26). Operation of the tensioner is automatic as long as the chain is the correct length and tensioner has enough range to compensate for size of sprockets and chainwheels. Adjustment should align the wheel with the frame and center the wheel between frame stays.

MULTI-SPEED HUB

ADJUSTMENTS. Multi-speed rear hubs are available which provide 2, 3, 4 and 5 different drive ratios. Control of some units is automatic, while others are cable operated by remote mounted controls. Controls may be a twist grip or a movable lever, but both types move a control rod in center of the axle. Refer to the appropriate paragraphs in the SERVICE section for details of adjusting controls for the individual units. The controls should be adjusted before internal parts of hub are damaged because of improper control settings.

DERAILLEURS

ADJUSTMENT. The derailleur moves the chain from one chainwheel or sprocket to another and correct operation is important. Improper operation or adjustment can damage parts, but can also cause injury or damage to the rider. Improper or unexpected operation of derailleur or controls is dangerous.

Derailleur adjustments are limited to setting cable lengths and positioning stop screws. Derailleur cable should be adjusted to permit full operation and stops should be set to limit movement of derailleur cages. Location of the stops and method of adjusting cables will be different for the various types. A full description and illustrations of adjustments are included in the SERVICE section for each specific unit.

The controls and the cables should not limit movement of the derailleur cages. Lack of lubrication, rusted cables or other problems, which may restrict movement, should be serviced before attempting to adjust controls.

Stop screws should be set to stop the derailleur just before it moves the chain off the side of the chainwheels or sprocket cluster. If screw is turned too far in, the chain will not be able to move onto some of the sprockets or chainwheels. If screw is too far out, the chain will come off sprocket or chainwheel and will probably wedge between wheel and frame, spokes and inner sprocket, chainwheel and frame or between chainwheel and chain guard.

Check for correct operation, especially with chain at extremes of travel. It is dangerous for chain to slip or come off sprockets while riding. Careful checks and adjustments should be done with wheel off ground, before attempting to ride bicycle.

TIRES AND PRESSURE

Tires with a large (approximately 2⅛ inches or 54-67 mm) cross section are often called **Balloon type.** Correct air pressure for balloon tires is approximately 40 psi. Balloon tires give the smoothest ride, but have the greatest rolling friction. Some later balloon tires may be designed for higher air pressure which will reduce rolling friction.

Tires with a nominal cross section of approximately 1¾ inches (47 mm) are called **middleweight type.** Correct air pressure for middleweight tires is approximately 50 psi. Middleweight tires provide less rolling resistance than balloon tires (of similar overall diameter), but also less comfort and less impact resistance.

Tires with a nominal cross section of approximately 1⅜-1⅝ inches (37-44 mm) are called **lightweight type** and usually require approximately 75 psi air pressure. Lightweight tires have less rolling resistance than middleweight tires, but provide a harsher ride on firm terrain. The narrow tire sinks into soft ground easily making its use very limited except on paved surfaces.

Tires with a narrow cross section of 1⅛-1¼ inches (28-32 mm) are called **high pressure type** and usually require approximately 95-100 psi of air pressure. Tires with a nominal cross section of 1 inch (22-25 mm) or less are called **extra-high pressure type.** Though lightest in weight and lowest in rolling friction, high pressure and extra-high pressure type tires are harsh riding on any but the smoothest of surfaces and are most susceptible to tire or tube damage.

Tread pattern and size of tire must be matched to the type of riding and to the size of the rim.

Refer to the following chart for cross reference of new ISO metric tire sizes to the older metric and inch markings.

NEW ISO	OLD SIZES	
28 – 622	28 x 1⅝ x 1⅛	700 x 28 C
	28 x 1⅝ x 1¼ x 1⅛	700 C Carrera
28 – 630	27 x 1¼ fifty	
28 – 636		700 B
28 – 642	28 x 1⅜ x 1⅛	700 x 28 A
32 – 239	12 x 1⅜ x 1¼	300 x 32
32 – 248	12 x 1¼	300 x 32 A
32 – 288	14 x 1⅜ x 1¼	350 x 32
32 – 296	14 x 1¼	350 x 32 A
32 – 340	16 x 1⅜ x 1¼	400 A
		400 x 32
32 – 349	16 x 1¼ NL	400 x 32 A
32 – 367	17 x 1¼	
32 – 369	16 x 1¼	
32 – 390	18 x 1⅜ x 1¼	450A
		450 x 32
32 – 400	18 x 1¼	450 x 32 A
32 – 438		500 x 32 ANL
32 – 440	20 x 1⅜ x 1¼	500 A
		500 x 32
32 – 451	20 x 1¼	500 x 32 A
32 – 489		550 x 32 ANL
32 – 490	22 x 1⅜ x 1¼	550 A
		550 x 32
32 – 501	22 x 1¼	550 x 32 A
32 – 508	22 x 1¼ x 1	
32 – 540	24 x 1⅜ x 1¼	
32 – 541	24 x 1⅜ x 1¼ NL	600 A
		600 x 32 A
32 – 547	24 x 1¼	

NEW ISO	OLD SIZES	
32 – 590	26 x 1⅜ x 1¼	650 x 32 A
32 – 597	26 x 1¼	
	28 x 1⅝ x 1¼	700 x 32 C
32 – 622	28 x 1¼ x 1¾	700 C Course
32 – 630	27 x 1¼	
32 – 635	28 x 1½ x 1⅛	700 x 28 B
		700 B Course
37 – 288		350 A Comfort
		350 A ½ Balloon
37 – 296	14 x 1⅜	
37 – 337	16 x 1⅜ ANL	
37 – 340	16 x 1⅜ NL	400 A Comfort
		400 A ½ Balloon
		400 x 42 A
		400 x 35 A
37 – 349	16 x 1⅜	
37 – 387	18 x 1⅜ NL	
37 – 390		450 A Comfort
		450 A ½ Balloon
37 – 400	18 x 1⅜	
37 – 438	20 x 1⅜ NL	
37 – 440		500 A Comfort
		500 A ½ Balloon
37 – 451	20 x 1⅜	
37 – 489	22 x 1⅜ NL	
37 – 490		550 A Comfort
		500 A ½ Balloon
37 – 498	22 x 1⅜ x 1¼ NL	
37 – 501	22 x 1⅜	
37 – 540	24 x 1⅜	
37 – 541		600 A Comfort
		600 A ½ Balloon
		600 x 35 A
37 – 584	26 x 1½ x 1⅜	
	26 x 1⅜ x 1½	
		650A
37 – 590	26 x 1⅜	
		650 x 35 A
37 – 622	28 x 1⅝ x 1⅜	700 x 35 C
	28 x 1⅜ x 1⅝	
37 – 642	28 x 1⅜	700 x 35 A
40 – 279	14 x 1½	350 x 38 B
40 – 288	14 x 1½ NL	350 x 38
40 – 330	16 x 1½	400 x 38 B
40 – 432	20 x 1½	

NEW ISO	OLD SIZES	
40 – 440	20 x 1½ NL	500 x 38
40 – 534	24 x 1½	
40 – 540	24 x 1⅜ x 1½	
	24 x 1½ x 1⅜	
40 – 571	26 x 1½ C.S.	
	26 x 1⅝ x 1½ NL	
40 – 584	26 x 1½	650 x 35 B
		650 x 38 B
40 – 590	26 x 1⅜ x 1½ NL	
40 – 622	28 x 1⅝ x 1½ NL	700 x 38 C
40 – 635	28 x 1½ x 1⅜	700 B Standard
		700 x 35 B
	28 x 1½	700 x 38 B
44 – 194	10 x 1⅝	
44 – 288	14 x 1⅜ x 1⅝	350 A
		350 x 42 A
44 – 340	16 x 1⅝	
44 – 428	20 x 1⅝ x 1½	
44 – 484	22 x 1⅝ x 1½	
44 – 531	24 x 1⅝ x 1½	
44 – 584	26 x 1½ x 1⅝	650 B Semi-Comf.
	26 x 1⅝ x 1½	650 B ½ Balloon
	26 x 1¾ x 1½	650 x 42 B
44 – 622	28 x 1⅝	700 x 42 C
44 – 635	28 x 1⅝ x 1½	
	28 x 1½ x 1⅝	
47 – 203	12½ x 1.75 x 2¼	
47 – 222	11 x 1¾	
47 – 305	16 x 1.75 x 2	
47 – 317	16 x 1¾	
47 – 355	18 x 1.75 x 2	
47 – 406	20 x 1.75 x 2	
	20 x 1.75	
47 – 419	20 x 1¾	
47 – 501 T	24 x 1¾ R	600 x 45 C

NEW ISO	OLD SIZES	
47 – 507	24 x 1.75 x 2	
	24 x 1.75	
47 – 520	24 x 1¾	
47 – 559	26 x 1.75 x 2	
	26 x 1.75	
47 – 571	26 x 1¾	650 x 45 C
	26 x 1⅝	650 C S.C.
47 – 584	26 x 1.75 x 1½	650 x 45 B
	26 x 1½ x 1¾	
47 – 622	28 x 1¾	700 x 45 C
	28 x 1.75	
	28 x 1⅝ x 1¾	
54 – 298	14 x 2 x 1¾	
54 – 305	16 x 2	
54 – 400	20 x 2 x 1¾	
	20 x 2 F 4 J	
54 – 406	20 x 2.00	
54 – 428	20 x 2	
54 – 559	26 x 2.00	
54 – 571	26 x 1¾ x 2	650 x 50 C
	26 x 2 x 1¾	
	26 x 2	
54 – 584	26 x 2 x 2½	
	26 x 1½ x 2	
54 – 609	28 x 2	
57 – 239		300 x 55 A
57 – 251 T		315 x 55
57 – 390		450 x 55 A
57 – 406	20 x 2.125	
	2 x 2.125 x 2	
62 – 203	12½ x 2¼	320 x 57
62 – 305	16 x 2.125	
67 – 203	13 x 2½	330 x 65
67 – 381	20 x 2½	

Inspection

Some troubles are just too big to overlook. A flat tire is obvious, but not enough or too much air in a tire might be ignored. Inspect the condition of the bicycle each time before riding. The inspection need not be difficult or time consuming, but the rider should be aware of the condition of the bicycle.

TIRES

All pneumatic tires require a certain, correct amount of air pressure for long tire life and safety to the rider. Not enough air pressure will weaken or damage sidewalls of the tire and the tire may slip on the rim. An excessive amount of pressure will cause the tire to wear faster than normal and it will be more vulnerable to blowout. Check the side of the tire for the manufacturer's recommended pressure. Check the pressure with a gage and, if necessary, inflate tire carefully. Bicycle tires contain a very small volume of air and can be blown up very easily and quickly. A hand tire pump is recommended. Large volume, high pressure air systems such as used by many gasoline service stations should only be used with extreme care by experienced personnel. The following lists approximate recommended tire pressures:

Size - Inches	Pressure - psi
16 x 1-3/8	35-45
16 x 1.75	30-40
20 x 1-3/8	35-45
20 x 1.75	30-40
20 x 2.125	30-35
24 x 1-3/8	40-45
24 x 1.75	30-40
24 x 2.125	35-45
26 x 1-3/8	45-50
26 x 1.75	30-40
26 x 2.125	35-45
27 x 1-1/4	75-85
27 Tubular Touring	
Front	75-90
Rear	85-100
27 Tubular Road Racing	
Front	65-90
Rear	75-100

BEARINGS

Bicycles use many bearings to reduce the effort required to move the bicycle. Any of these bearings can fail and result in personal injury and damage to the bicycle. **Check all bearings carefully for free movement and for looseness.** Bearings may require periodic adjustment and lubrication, but should be checked often between normal service intervals.

To check the head set bearing, lift up on the handlebar by the hand grips. There should not be any play of the stem and fork in the frame head tube. Turn handlebar from side to side. Refer to the PERIODIC MAINTENANCE Section for lubricating and adjusting the head set bearings.

Pedals are usually equipped with ball bearings. Some pedal bearings can be disassembled, cleaned, lubricated and adjusted;

Fig. 3-1—Tire pressure should be checked frequently. Air should be added to increase pressure by using an air pump that fits valve stem correctly.

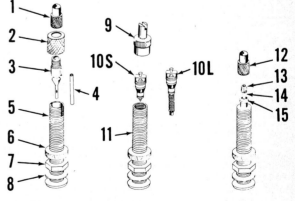

Fig. 3-2—Exploded views of three most popular types of valve stems. Type shown in center is most popular and is used on most tubes for clincher type tires. Type at right is most common type used on tubular (sew-up) tires. Type on left is used on some (usually older) British and Japanese tubes.

1. Dust cap
2. Valve retainer
3. Valve body
4. Valve tubing
5. Stem
6. Lock nut
7. Nut
8. Washer

9. Schrader type valve cap
10L. Long (exposed spring) valve core
10S. Short (internal spring) valve core

11. Valve stem
12. Cap
13. Lock
14. Valve core
15. Valve and stem

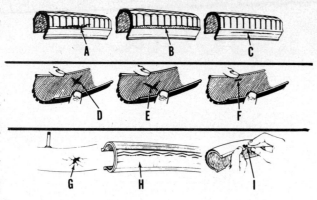

Fig. 3-3—Drawings of some common tire and tube failures.

A. Cut in sidewall caused by running over glass or other sharp object.
B. Chafing caused by tire rubbing against fork or other object.
C. Rim cut caused by rusty rims, low tire pressure or too much weight on bicycle.
D. Star break as shown is evidence of collision with pointed object such as a sharp rock. Often there is no evidence of break on outside of tire.
E. Rupture is often caused by collision with object like curb, stones, holes in pavement.
F. Rim bruise or cut is caused by collision with curb, rocks, etc. when tires are

low on air pressure.
G. Blowout caused by weakening of tube. Often this damage is result of improper installation or size of tube. Folding or sticking stretched tubes are likely to blowout.

H. Uneven wear may be caused by locking wheel with brake.
I. Broken beads are often result of improper mounting tools. Sharp objects such as screwdrivers may pinch holes in tube as well as break the tire bead.

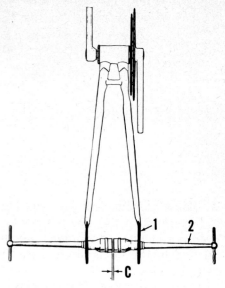

Fig. 3-5—Special tools (2) or an extra axle that is sawed in two is used to check alignment of fork ends (1). Clearance (C) should be even and straight.

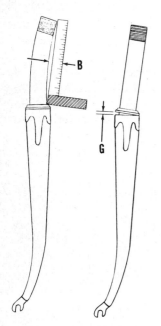

Fig. 3-4—Front fork may be very obviously bent, broken or otherwise damaged. Small bends in stem tube (B) or between stem tube and fork (G) may be harder to notice. Usually these problems will first be noticed by erratic head set bearing operation or difficulty in adjusting head set bearings.

while others must be renewed if damaged.

Crank set should be inspected for bent crank arms. Check the fit of the crank arms on the spindle of three piece crank sets. Check crank bearings by turning the crank and by pulling the crank spindle from side to side. The crank should turn easily and should have only a trace of side play. Refer to the PERIODIC MAINTENANCE Section for lubrication and adjustment of the crank bearings.

Try to wiggle the wheels from side to side with your fingers. The wheels should not be loose. A loose wheel can be caused by loose axle bolts, bearings that need adjustment or service, loose or damaged spokes or some other problem. Discover the cause and correct the trouble before beginning to ride.

Check the rims for straightness by spinning the wheel with the wheel off the ground. Be sure spokes are tight and not broken. Check operation of the brakes. The handlebars should be aligned with the front wheel and the handlebar clamp and stem wedge bolts should be tight. Check all bolts, nuts and quick release clamps for tightness.

FRAME

The original design and geometry of the frame and front fork is carefully planned by the manufacturer. Frame modifications are most often the result of an accident and are not planned at all. Measurements for checking frame alignment are seldom available, but certain special tools are available for checking some types of damage. Ride the bicycle and see if it tracks comfortably. A bicycle with a bent frame or front fork will usually wander from side to side or may pull to one side. A close visual inspection may also reveal some obvious frame damage. Check for broken welds and bent tubes. Be sure to check any wrinkled, loose or missing paint carefully since these conditions often accompany a bent frame tube. Frame damage is seldom repairable except by installing a new frame. Straightening and painting will visually only hide the damage, not correct it. Missing paint will permit steel frames to rust which isn't desirable.

Periodic Maintenance

Regular maintenance should include cleaning, lubrications, inspection and adjustment. Damaged parts may be found during regular maintenance and, of course, should be repaired or renewed. The SERVICE Section will further outline the procedures for repairing specific components.

Frequency of periodic maintenance will depend upon the type and amount of riding. Bicycles are not commonly equipped with an indicator which records the distance traveled and it is difficult to determine just what an average rider is. Bicycles, like other vehicles, are very often maintained incorrectly. The fastest, most expensive, most precision bicycles will probably require careful and constant service in order to maintain the high quality of performance that is expected. Slower, heavier, less expensive bicycles are often considered expendable and are many times maintained with much less care. Unfortunately the less expensive bicycles are often ridden by less experienced riders (children) under severe conditions and should require more frequent service.

Fig. 4-2—Cleaning will offer an opportunity to inspect bicycle carefully as well as extend usefulness of the finish.

CLEANING

Reflectors and lights are installed to increase the visibility and therefore safety. Dirty or damaged parts cannot be seen and may therefore defeat the purpose for which they were installed.

Painted and plated surfaces should be clean and dry. Wipe dirt, moisture and oil from all parts with a clean, soft cloth. **High pressure cleaners, solvents and harsh soaps should not be used; because they might wash the grease and oil out of the bearings.** Painted and plated surfaces may also be damaged by solvents or soaps.

LUBRICATION

All of the bearings should be clean, lubricated and properly adjusted at all times. Ideally, bearings should be disassembled, cleaned, inspected, lubricated, assembled and adjusted just before it becomes necessary. It is naturally difficult to identify at which time this is. Seldom will all of the bearings require service at

Fig. 4-3—Brakes can melt lubricant from hub of some models.

the same time. Different types of riding, different weather conditions and many other variables will affect the condition of the bearings and the lubricant. Lubricant can be quickly melted out of the rear hub of models with back pedaling brakes by prolonged use of the brake. **A high pressure car wash can wash all of the lubricant out of nearly all of the bearings.** Dust and dirt can contaminate the grease and make the grease more like sandpaper than lubricant. Shock loads like pounding the cotter pins into the crank

Fig. 4-1—Less experienced riders often use poor quality, inadequately maintained bicycles and may not be capable of reacting correctly to problems that are likely to occur.

Fig. 4-5—Dust can mix with lubricant to create an abrasive that can quickly wear parts.

Fig. 4-7—Improper use can damage parts easily.

Fig. 4-8—Grease and oil specifically formulated for use on bicyle components is available.

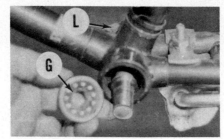

Fig. 4-11—Crank set bearings can be lubricated with grease (G) while assembling or with oil through fitting (L) after bicycle is assembled.

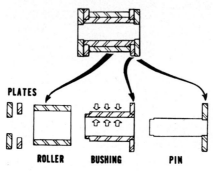

Fig. 4-12—Drawing showing parts of typical chain. White arrows indicate area that should be coated with lubricant.

ing with new grease (G-Fig. 4-11). Refer to Fig. 4-9 for common lubrication points. Bicycle grease is normally used at locations (1, 2, 3, 4, 6 & 7). Light oil should be used only at locations (5, 8, 9, 10 & 11) unless otherwise specified. Refer to the following adjustment paragraphs for adjusting the bearings.

Bicycle chain should be kept lubricated at all times. Stiff or rusty chain may sometimes be lubricated and worked loose, but installation of a new chain is recommended. Improper maintenance and neglect of the chain not only shortens chain life but also contributes to sprocket and chainwheel wear.

Several commercial chain lubricants are available which can be applied to chain while chain is installed on the bicycle. Lubricant for the bushing area (White Arrows - Fig. 4-12) must work into bushing between the close fitting side plates. Immersion in cleaning solvent, then in lubricant, is a most satisfactory method of assuring complete lubrication. Some commercal chain grease requires heating to thin the grease and permit the lubricant to enter all surfaces of chain.

Brake and gear change cables and controls should be lubricated. Several methods of oiling cables are commonly used including the method shown in Fig. 4-13. A hose is fitted over cable housing and filled with oil. Air pressure is then introduced into open end of

arms or riding over curbs can split bearing balls or dent the bearing races.

Until experience indicates the correct interval for lubrication and adjustment, it is better to check bearings too often than not often enough. Refer to specific SERVICE sections for type of lubricant and method used for lubricating multi-speed hubs.

Bearings for some specialized racing bicycles are lubricated with oil. Manufacturers of most

bicycles and components suggest using special bicycle bearing grease. This grease is available in tubes and several sizes of cans. NOTE: Heavy (thick) grease will **probably prevent coaster brakes, freewheeling hubs and multi-speed hubs from operating properly.** Some manufacturers recommend a mixture of petroleum jelly and oil. Some wheel hubs are equipped with an oil opening and should be lubricated with a few drops of light weight oil. Bearings must be disassembled, cleaned and inspected before coat-

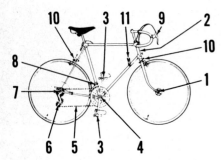

Fig. 4-9—Indicated points require lubrication.

1. Front hub bearings
2. Steering head bearings
3. Pedal bearings
4. Crank set bearings
5. Chain
6. Rear derailleur
7. Rear hub bearings
8. Front derailleur
9. Brake controls and cables
10. Brake pivot bushings
11. Shift controls and cables

Fig. 4-13—Oil can be forced into cable housing with air pressure. The aerosol product and the adaptor are available from Ashland Chemical Company, Santa Fe Springs, Ca. 90670, specifically for lubricating cables.

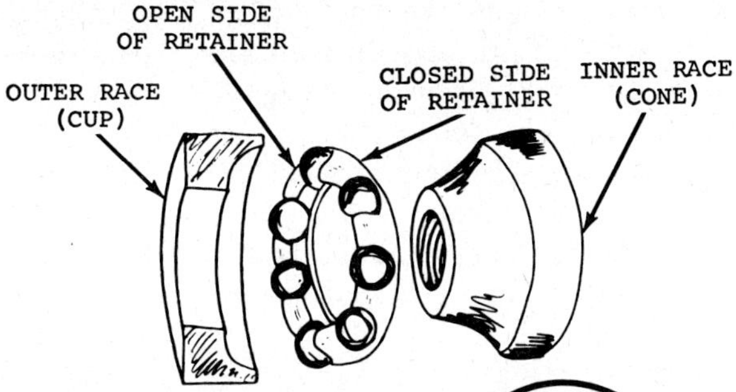

Fig. 4-25—Drawing of ball bearing typical of type used on many bicycles. The location that the bearing is installed will not change the names of the parts.

OPEN SIDE OF RETAINER
OUTER RACE (CUP)
CLOSED SIDE OF RETAINER   INNER RACE (CONE)

Fig. 4-27—Bearing balls may be loose or may be installed in retainer. Be sure that correct type is installed.

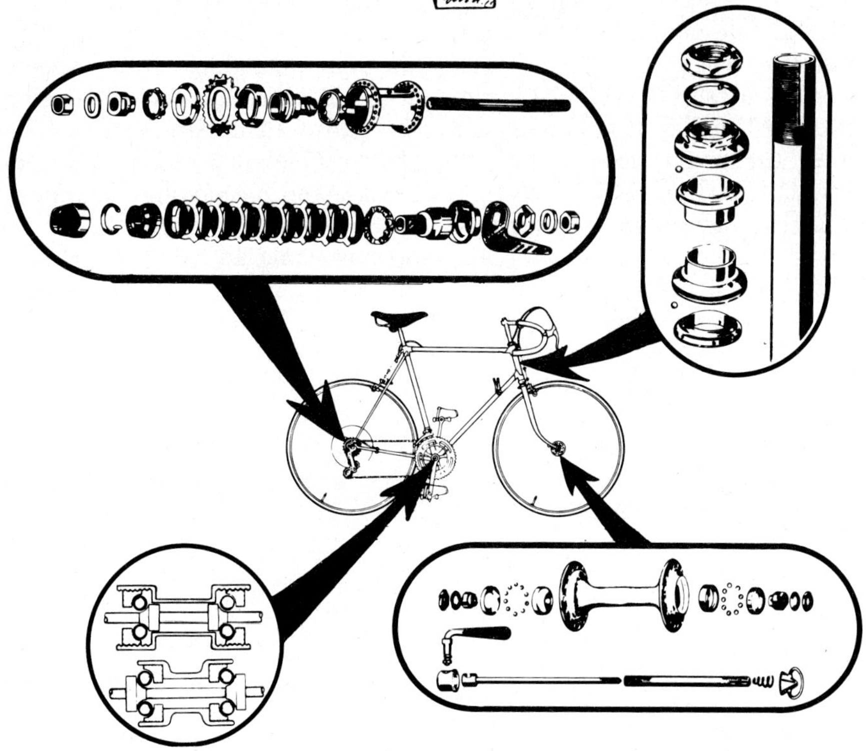

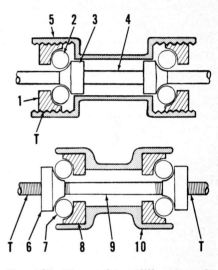

Fig. 4-26—View showing typical bearing installations. All bearings must be maintained to insure long trouble free service.

Fig. 4-28—Views of two different methods of assembling ball bearings. The cup may be adjustable as shown at top or cone may be adjustable as shown in lower view.

T. Threads	4. Axle	7. Ball
1. Cup	5. Housing	8. Cup
2. Ball	6. Cone	9. Axle
3. Cone		10. Housing

hose which blows oil into the cable housing. Lack of cable lubrication will permit cable to rust, become stiff and stick in housing. All of these conditions can and probably will prevent the brake or gear selector from operating.

BEARING ADJUSTMENTS

Bearings used in specific components such as multi-speed hubs should be adjusted as outlined in the appropriate SERVICE section. Most bicycles use ball type bearings which consist of the basic parts shown in Fig. 4-25. Bearing may be located in a steering head, crank, wheel hub or pedal. All bearings are NOT the same size and some bearings are adjusted differently than others (Fig. 4-26). Bearing balls may

be contained in a retainer or they may be installed loose between the cup and cone (Fig. 4-27). The cone may be made as part of the shaft or the cup may be manufactured as part of the pedal or wheel hub (Fig. 4-28). Adjustment of all bearings should remove all play from the bearing, but should permit the shaft to turn freely. Most bearings use a lock washer and a lock nut to prevent bearing

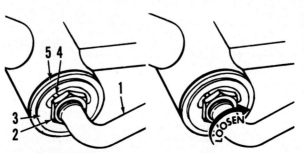

adjustment from changing accidentally. Lock nut (2-Fig. 4-29) and bearing cone (4) on left side of one piece crank assembly (1) are usually provided with left hand threads. These threaded parts are loosened or removed by turning clockwise. Other bearing

Fig. 4-29—Crank set bearings are adjusted by turning cone (4) on many models with one piece crank. Threads may be left hand thread on left side as indicated.

1. Crank
2. Lock nut
3. Tab Washer
4. Adjustable cone
5. Bearing cup

cones or cups are usually provided with the normal right hand threads that require parts to be turned counterclockwise to loosen. Be sure to recheck adjustment after lock nut is tightened. Tightening the lock nut will often cause the bearing to be too tight (bind).

BRAKES

All types of brakes should be checked for proper operation and should be adjusted or repaired if necessary, each time before the bicycle is ridden. Back pedaling brakes should be disassembled, inspected and repaired as outlined in the individual SERVICE section. Caliper and other hand operated brakes can often be adjusted. Brake shoes, on caliper brakes, should begin to contact the wheel rim soon after beginning to squeeze the control lever. Shoes should not rub on rim when released and the shoes

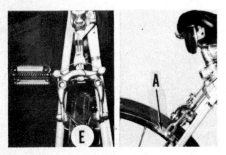

Fig. 4-30—Brake shoes should be same distance from wheel rim (E) and aligned with rim (A).

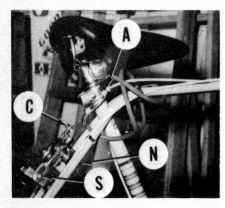

Fig. 4-31—View of typical rear caliper brake installation.

A. Cable adjuster   N. Centering nut
C. Clamp screw   S. Shoe

should align with the rim. Different adjustment procedures are necessary for different types of brakes but the following outlines a generally accepted method for caliper type brakes.

Check and be sure that the two brake shoes are equal distance from the rim (E-Fig. 4-30) with the brake released. If one shoe is closer to the rim than the other, rotate the wheel to make sure the wheel is straight. Align the rim before proceeding if it is bent. To center the brake, loosen nut (N-Fig. 4-13 or Fig. 4-31) and turn mounting screw as required to center brake. Be certain that brake remains centered after nut (N) is tightened. Check the alignment of brake shoes with rim (A-Fig. 4-30). Loosen attaching nut and move the brake shoe (S-Fig. 4-31 or Fig. 4-32) as necessary to align it with the wheel rim, then tighten nut.

Adjustment can be accomplished after making certain that brake is centered and shoes are aligned with rim. Squeeze shoes

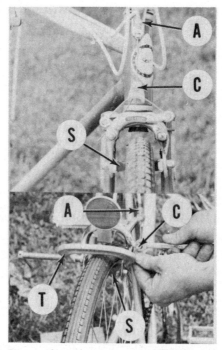

Fig. 4-32—Views showing center pull caliper brake (Top) and side pull caliper brake (Bottom). Clamp (T) is used to hold calipers together while relocating cable in clamp (C). Fine adjustment can be accomplished by turning adjuster (A). Shoes (S) should not drag on rim.

together at wheel, using a special tool, clamp or by hand. Loosen the cable clamp (C-Fig. 4-31 or Fig. 4-32) and pull the cable through clamp screw. Tighten clamp (C), release the brake shoes and check operation of the brake. Fine adjustment is accomplished by turning adjusters (A).

Other types of brakes are adjusted in different ways. The internal expanding brake shown in Fig. 4-33 is adjusted by turning the cable adjusting screw. The disc brake shown in Fig. 4-34 can be adjusted by moving the end of brake cable in clamp (4) and by turning cable adjuster (3). Examine other types of brakes to determine method of adjustment.

Fig. 4-33—Hub brakes are used on front wheel of some bicycles. Cable adjustment is similar to other installations.

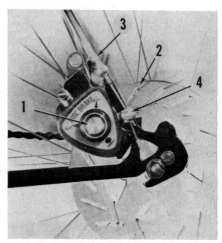

Fig. 4-34—Disc brakes operate similar to other caliper brakes except that a disc (2) is held instead of the rim. Cable can be relocated in clamp (4) and fine adjustment is accomplished by turning adjuster (3).

Service

Each bicycle is composed of many different parts. These parts are usually manufactured by several different companies. Some companies specialize in crank sets, others specialize in producing multi-speed rear hubs. Refer to the appropriate following paragraphs for servicing standard component parts.

Front Wheel and Hub

REMOVE AND REINSTALL THE ASSEMBLY

Support the bicycle, loosen nuts (1-Fig. 5-1) and pull wheel down away from fork ends. On models with caliper brakes, remove one brake pad (B) or in some other way provide clearance between the wheel rim and the brake pads. Some models are provided with quick release brake controls and quick release hubs to speed removal of front wheel.

Install the front wheel assembly as follows: Position axle in slots of fork ends, install washers (28-Fig. 5-2) and nuts (1). Tighten the two nuts (1) carefully and evenly. Be sure that wheel rim is centered in fork when tightening nuts. On models with caliper brakes, check to be sure that brake pads are aligned with rim. Closed end of brake pad holder should be toward front of both brake pads (Fig. 5-1).

Service to front hubs with hub mounted front brake (Fig. 5-3) will be slightly different than standard models. Detach brake controls and anchor strap before removing wheel. Oil brake cam lever shaft (18) lightly. Be sure that brake drum (9) and brake shoes (17) are dry and free of oil and grease.

Fig. 5-1—Axle retaining nuts (1) must be loosened or removed to release axle from fork ends. Procedure for removal will be different on different bicycles. Wing nuts (W) are used on some models. One brake shoe (B) should be removed to gain clearance for some models. Special plates (P) are hooked into fork ends of some models and these plates must be released before axle will slide out of fork ends.

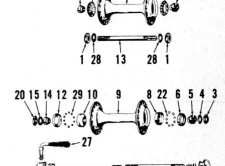

Fig. 5-2—Exploded view of some typical front wheel hubs. Other variations are also used.

1. Nut	13. Axle
3. Lock nut	14. Bearing cone
4. Lock washer	15. Lock washer
5. Bearing cone	20. Lock nut
6. Dust shield	22. Bearing balls
7. Bearing and retainer	23. Adjuster
8. Bearing cup	24. Spring
9. Hub	25. Quick release skewer
10. Bearing cup	26. Housing
11. Bearing and retainer	27. Release lever
12. Dust shield	28. Lock washers
	29. Bearing balls

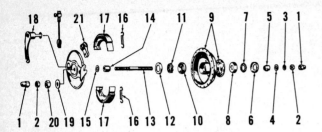

Fig. 5-3—Exploded view of internal expanding brake that is used on front wheel of some DBS bicycles.

1. Nut
2. Nut
3. Lock nut
4. Lock washer
5. Bearing cone
6. Dust shield
7. Bearing and retainer
8. Bearing cup
9. Hub and brake drum
10. Bearing cup
11. Bearing and retainer
12. Dust shield
13. Axle
14. Bearing cone
15. Washer
16. Return springs
17. Brake shoes
18. Cam lever
19. Washer
20. Lock nut
21. Brake anchor strap

CLEAN, INSPECT AND LUBRICATE AXLE BEARINGS

Remove the wheel and hub assembly. Clamp one end of axle in a soft jawed vise. Use care not to damage threads on axle. Remove lock nut (3-Fig. 5-2) and lock washer (4) from free end of axle. Remove bearing cone (5) from axle by turning cone counterclockwise. Lift bearing balls carefully out of bearing cup. NOTE: Bearing balls (22) may be contained in a retainer or may be loose. Carefully release axle from vise while holding axle into hub, then remove axle (13), bearing cone (14) and bearing (11) or balls (29) from hub (9). CAUTION: Do not drop or lose bearing balls. Clean all parts with a suitable solvent and inspect for any visible damage. Renew any parts that are nicked or rough. On some models, bearing cups (8 & 10) may be separately renewable pieces, but on many models, the hub (9) is integral with bearing

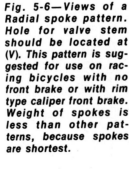

Fig. 5-5—Cone wrench (4) is used to hold bearing cone (2) while tightening lock nut (3).

cups and must be renewed if cups are damaged. Check the axle to see if it is bent or if threads are damaged.

Be sure that correct size of bearing and that correct number of bearing balls are installed. Bearings that use a retainer to hold balls will be marked for identification. Refer to Fig. 5-4.

Loose bearing balls will usually be one of the following diameters: 1/8-inch, 5/32-inch, 3/16-inch, 7/32-inch or 1/4-inch.

Grease the bearing surface of cups (8 & 10-Fig. 5-2) and position loose bearing balls in cup. Grease should also be packed into retainer of bearings that use a retainer to hold the bearing balls (7 & 11). A sufficient amount of grease should be used to hold the bearings in place while assembling. Position axle (13), with one of the bearing cones (14) installed, through hub (9). Turn remaining bearing cone (5) onto end of axle by hand until bearing cones are finger tight against bearings. Loosen bearing cone slightly and install lock washer (4) and lock nut (3) if so equipped. Check to be sure that bearing is free to turn without any apparent looseness.

NOTE: Special thin wrenches (cone wrenches) are available to permit holding bearing cone (2-Fig. 5-5) while tightening lock nut (3). Adjustment may be extreme-

Fig. 5-4—Loose bearing balls are available in several diameters (D). Locate bearing code number (N) on retainer of bearings that use a retainer.

Fig. 5-6—Views of a Radial spoke pattern. Hole for valve stem should be located at (V). This pattern is suggested for use on racing bicycles with no front brake or with rim type caliper front brake. Weight of spokes is less than other patterns, because spokes are shortest.

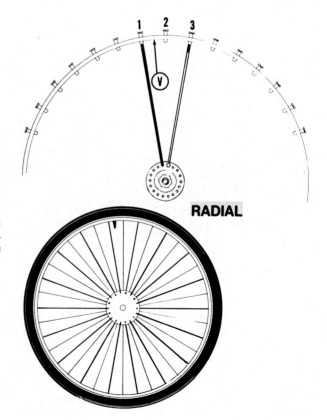

RADIAL

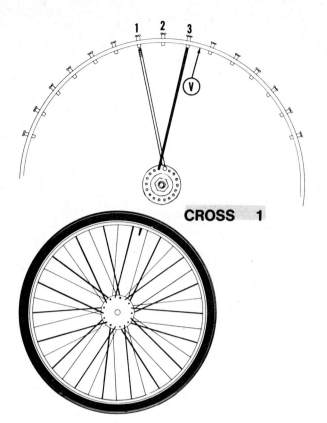

CROSS 1

CROSS 2

Fig. 5-7—Views of Cross 1 spoke pattern. Hole for valve stem should be located at (V). This pattern can be used on front wheel of bicycles with rim type caliper brake or no front brake. Spokes are longer than radial pattern, shorter than Cross 2 pattern.

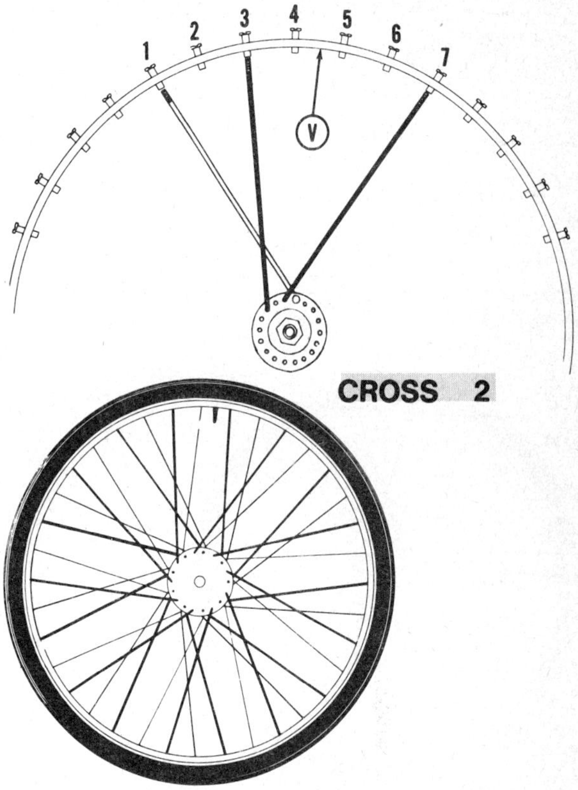

Fig. 5-8—Views of Cross 2 spoke pattern. Hole for valve stem should be located at (V). Pattern can be used for front wheel of bicycles with rim type caliper brake or no front brake. Spokes are longer than Cross 1 pattern, shorter than Cross 3 pattern.

ly difficult without these special cone wrenches.

Install the wheel assembly on bicycle and check hub bearings for looseness or binding. Final inspection of bearing cone should be accomplished with wheel installed in fork. Be critical of bearing adjustment. Improper adjustment can easily damage the bearings and correct adjustment is not difficult to achieve.

RENEW HUB, SPOKES OR RIM

Identify the spoke pattern currently used (Fig. 5-6 through Fig. 5-10). Shorter (therefore lighter) spokes can be laced in radial pattern to the front wheel of some bicycles. A cross three pattern is recommended for front wheels with a hub brake. Many models use a cross three pattern for both front and rear wheels.

A single new spoke (or just a few spokes) can be installed and the wheel aligned as outlined in the following paragraphs. Be sure that new spoke is the same as others in both length and diameter.

All of the spokes attach the hub to wheel rim. To install a new wheel rim, it is necessary to remove wheel from the bicycle, remove tire from rim and remove all of the spoke nipples from end of spokes. To install a new hub, it is necessary to also remove spokes from hub. It may be necessary to change the length of all spokes or to change the pattern of lacing if a different type or size of rim or hub is installed.

The necessary steps to install new parts will depend upon what parts need to be renewed as well as the manufacturer of the parts. It is often easier to install new parts made by the same manufacturer as the original parts. Changing rim type, spoke lacing pattern, hub flange diameter, etc., will make the job harder.

The procedure for assembling the hub, spokes and rim will be evident. The following notes may help assemble the various parts into a usable front wheel unit.

Be sure that rim and hub are equipped with the same number of spoke holes. Spokes are made in a variety of wire sizes (diameters). It is important that holes in rim and in hub are both the correct size for the spokes and nipples used. Beveled side of hole in hub flange (B-Fig. 5-11) should be near bend in spoke, NOT against head of spoke. Begin assembly by locating the valve stem hole. Correctly locating valve stem hole (V-Fig. 5-6 thru Fig. 5-10) will position valve stem at opening of spokes. Incorrect location will cause spokes to cross near stem. Truing (aligning) the wheel and tightening the spokes will be much easier if wheel is assembled carefully and slowly.

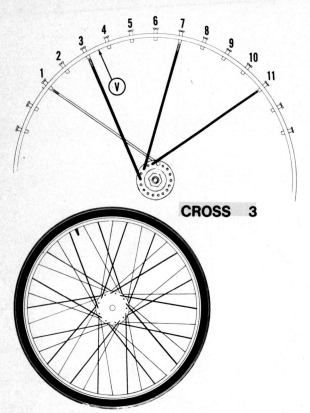

CROSS 3

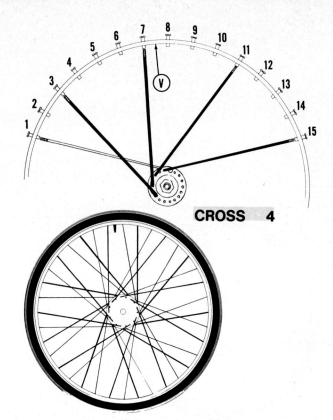

CROSS 4

Fig. 5-9—View of Cross 3 spoke pattern. Hole for valve stem should be located at (V). This is the most popular pattern for lacing and can be used on front or rear wheels with various types of brakes.

Fig. 5-10—Views of Cross 4 spoke pattern. Hole for valve stem should be located at (V). Pattern requires longer spokes than Cross 3. The drive [rear] wheel for tandem bicycles is sometimes laced as shown because of added strength.

To begin assembling the hub, spokes and rim, insert one spoke through hole in hub, with bend next to bevel around hole. Refer to the appropriate drawing (Fig. 5-6 thru Fig. 5-10) and locate the correct position for valve stem hole (V) in rim. Insert spoke through correct hole in rim and start nipple on threaded end of spoke. Starting with one installed spoke, install spokes the same direction through every other hole in hub flange and through every fourth hole in rim. This first set of spokes will be ¼ of the total number used. The hub will be held loosely in center of rim. Insert spokes through the remaining holes in flange in opposite direction from the first. The bend in this second set (¼ total) of spokes should also be against bevels of holes in hub. Hold rim and turn hub so that the installed spokes radiate clockwise from center (hub) to the rim. Insert threaded end of one loose spoke

in hole of rim after crossing the correct number of installed spokes. Install nipple on the first cross spoke and position the remaining cross spokes and nipples. This will locate ½ of the total number of spokes and the hub should hang at center of rim. Turn wheel over and install the other two sets of spokes in other flange of hub. With all spokes installed loosely, hub should be free to flop from side to side. Position wheel in test fixture or bicycle fork and gradually and evenly tighten all spokes. Tighten all spokes just enough for all nipples to contact the rim and to center the wheel (D-Fig. 5-13). Tighten spokes and align wheel as outlined in the following paragraphs.

TIGHTENING SPOKES AND ALIGNING WHEELS

Ideally, if every spoke is tightened alike, the wheel will be

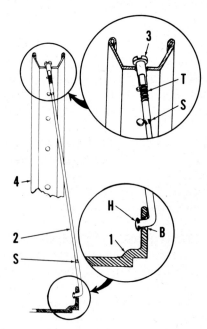

Fig. 5-11—View of hub (1), spoke (2), nipple (3) and rim (4). Swaged (S) spoke is shown. Head (H) of spoke should be away from bevel (B).

exactly centered and aligned. The weight of the bicycle and rider will be supported by the top spokes and this weight will be evenly transmitted to successive spokes as the wheels turn. Actually it isn't that easy. Spokes are attached to the rim by nipples (3-Fig. 5-11). The nipple might break, pull the rim down, pull the rim to one side, break the spoke or any of several things if spoke is too tight. A spoke won't carry its share of the load if it is too loose and the spokes around it will have to carry more weight.

The procedure for tightening and aligning spokes is best learned by doing it several times. Rim should be concentric with axle and should not wobble from side to side. Alignment test fixtures or a fork can be used to hold the axle while checking. Two reference points should be used, one for checking out-of-round or eccentricity (E-Fig. 5-13), and the second for checking side to side movement or wobble (W). Often both conditions exist at the same point (B) and several different

conditions may exist at various locations around the rim.

First, center the rim. Locate the low (closest to the center) areas of rim and loosen the spoke nipples. Tighten the spokes to move the rim in toward the center in high sections. Be sure that all spoke nipples are tight enough to contact the rim firmly, but not too tight, or the rim, spoke hub or nipple may be damaged. Check

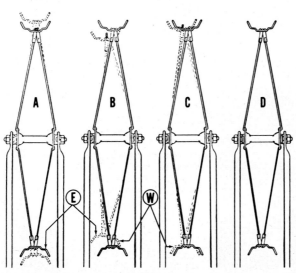

Fig. 5-12—A combination of tightening and loosening spokes is necessary to move the rim when aligning.

movement of rim from side to side (wobble). To move the rim toward left as shown in Fig. 5-12, loosen the spokes on right and tighten spokes on left.

As noted before, spokes should all be tightened the same amount. Be sure that no spoke is loose after centering and aligning the rim. Spokes may all be too tight if the rim suddenly jumps out of alignment when nearly finished. Check to make certain that rim is centered in fork or alignment fixture. Aligning the tire off center (B-Fig. 5-14), then centering

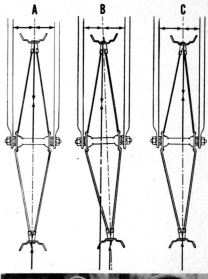

Fig. 5-14—Centerline of wheel should be in center of axle as shown in "A". View "B" shows wheel incorrectly laced off center, then installed on an angle to center wheel between fork tubes. Wheel shown in view "C" is incorrectly laced off center and may rub side of fork tube.

Fig. 5-13—Eccentricity (E) and side to side wobble (W) should be removed by adjusting spokes. Measurement is usually accomplished with pointer or grease pencil, but racing models are often checked with a dial indicator.

the tire between fork tubes will cause the weight of the bicycle to be on side of wheel. This condition will cause the bicycle to pull to one side when riding and will quickly loosen spokes, bend the rim or do other similar damage.

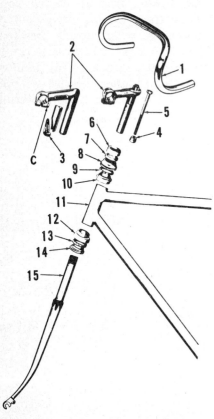

Fig. 5-15—Exploded view of a typical front fork and head set.

1. Handlebar	8. Adjustable race
2. Stems	9. Bearing
3. Wedge block	10. Fixed race
4. Expansion block	11. Frame
5. Stem bolt	12. Fixed race
6. Lock nut	13. Bearing
7. Lock washer	14. Fork race
	15. Fork

Front Fork, Stem and Handlebars

REMOVE AND REINSTALL HANDLEBARS AND STEM

To remove the handlebars from the stem clamp, proceed as follows: Disconnect all handlebar mounted controls (brake, shift, light, horn, etc.), then remove everything (grip, tape, controls) from one side. Loosen stem clamp bolt (C-Fig. 5-15) and slide handlebars out of stem.

Refer to HANDLEBAR AND LEVERS paragraph in the GENERAL ADJUSTMENT Section for installation and adjustment. Handgrips can be removed several different ways including cutting. Air pressure can be used to blow the grips off without damaging them. Direct air pressure into end of grip while plugging other end of handlebar. The grip will swell up away from handlebar and will press back against air source. Move the air supply back slowly and the grip will follow (Refer to Fig. 5-16).

The stem (2-Fig. 5-15) can be removed after loosening the wedge. Loosen bolt (5) about four turns, then tap the bolt down to dislodge wedge (3) or expansion block (4). Check the stem for being bent as well as broken. Stems of different heights and offsets are available.

REMOVE AND REINSTALL FORK AND HEADSET BEARINGS

Disconnect all handlebar mounted controls, loosen stem

wedge bolt, then tap the bolt down to dislodge wedge. Withdraw stem with handlebars attached and set this assembly aside. Support bicycle and remove the front wheel assembly from the fork. Remove or detach any lights, horns, cables, controls or brake parts that would interfere with removal of the front fork. Remove lock nut (6-Fig. 5-15) and lock washer (7). Hold the front fork up in position and remove the top adjustable race (8). This adjustable race may be a cone or a cup, but is threaded onto the fork stem to adjust the headset bearings. CAUTION: Use care to prevent losing bearing balls when race (8) is removed. Grease may hold balls in position, but probably will not. NOTE: A magnet can sometimes be useful in retaining the bearing balls. Some headset bearings are contained in retainers but many use loose balls. The loose balls may fall into the frame head tube along side of the fork stem. Be sure to count the number of bearing balls removed from each race (top and bottom). Carefully catch the balls from the lower bearing when withdrawing the fork from the frame head tube. The headset bearings are usually not sealed or protected well and all of the grease may be gone when disassembling. The bearings may be rusted if not lubricated often. High pressure, soap, water or solvent can easily wash all grease from headset bearings.

Headset bearing races (10 & 12) are piloted in frame head tube (11). Lower race (14) is piloted on fork stem. These races can be removed from their respective bores and tube by tapping (Fig. 5-17). The piloted races must fit tightly when assembling.

Clean all parts of bearing and inspect for nicks, cracks, rough

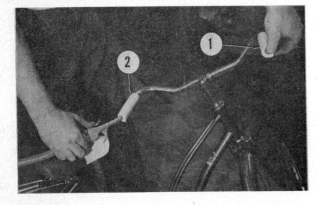

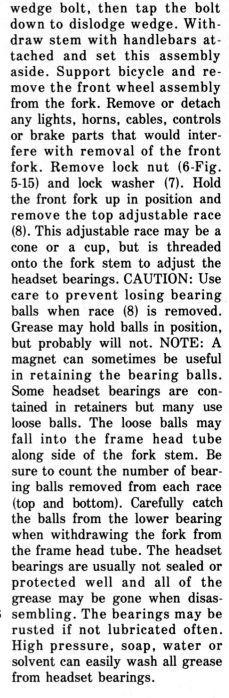

Fig. 5-16—Hand grips can sometimes be removed using air pressure as shown. Blow grip (1) off, then cover end of handlebar with hand and blow grip (2) off.

surfaces or any other defect which would require renewal. Loose bearing balls will usually be 1/8-inch, 5/32-inch, or 3/16-inch diameter. NOTE: Be sure to

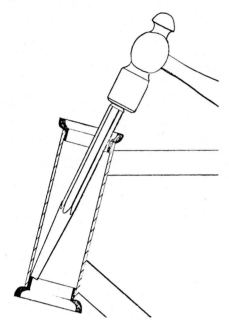

Fig. 5-17—Bearing races can be driven from frame head tube by carefully tapping, completely around bearing. Special drivers are available that facilitate removal.

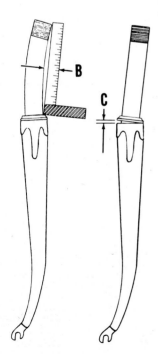

Fig. 5-18—Two of the easier places to check for a bent fork are at (B & C) as shown. Lower bearing race should be flat against shoulder of fork and should not have clearance at (C). Fork stem tube can be checked for bend (B) using a straight edge.

install the correct size and number of loose balls when assembling. Bearings which use balls held by a retainer are marked with an identification number stamped on the retainer. Be certain to use correct bearing.

Damage to the fork is usually evident before disassembly. Inspect for bent fork stem by checking for clearance under the installed lower bearing race (C-Fig. 5-18). The bearing race should seat flat against shoulder of fork stem. Check for bent fork stem using a straight edge as shown at (B-Fig. 5-18).

Install bearing races (10, 12 & 14-Fig. 5-15), grease bearing surfaces and position loose bearing balls in the cups. NOTE: Be sure to install correct number and size. Grease should also be packed into

retainer of bearings equipped with retainer to hold the balls. Use a sufficient amount of grease to hold bearings in place while assembling. Position the fork stem in frame head tube and install the upper race (8) on threaded end of the fork stem. Adjust the position of the upper race to remove all play from bearing without causing the bearings to bind. Install tabbed lock washer (7) and lock nut (6). Check adjustment of bearings again after lock nut (6) is tight. The upper race (8) can be adjusted by turning after lock nut (6) is loosened a small amount. Be sure lock nut is tightened after adjustment is complete. Reinstall handlebars and stem assembly and the front wheel assembly. Attach and install controls or other parts if they were disturbed when disassembling.

Pedals, Crank and Chainwheels

PEDAL REPAIR AND LUBRICATION

Some pedals are manufactured in such a way that they can be easily disassembled, cleaned, inspected, repaired, lubricated, assembled and adjusted. Individual

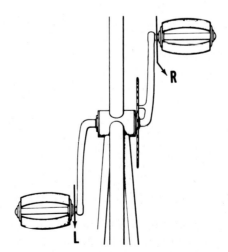

Fig. 5-19—Left and right pedals are not the same. Turn pedal on right side (viewed from top) in standard counter-clockwise direction to remove as shown at (R). Turn pedal on left side of bicycle in clockwise direction (L) to remove.

repair parts are available for these pedals. The bearings are to be serviced regularly in the same way as other bearings used at the axles and crank. Pedals that are riveted or welded together should be considered NOT REPAIRABLE.

The pedal shafts are threaded into the crank arms. The pedal on right side uses a standard right hand thread and is removed using a thin wrench by turning in normal counter-clockwise direction. Refer to Fig. 5-19. The pedal on left side of bicycle has left hand thread and is removed by turning in clockwise direction. The ends of pedal axles are marked to indicate left or right. Standard English marking is "L" for left, "R" for right. Italian marking is "S" for left; "D" for right side.

Repairable pedals are generally constructed similarly to the one shown in Fig. 5-20. Remove dust cap (1), lock nut (2) and lock washer (3). Unscrew adjustable

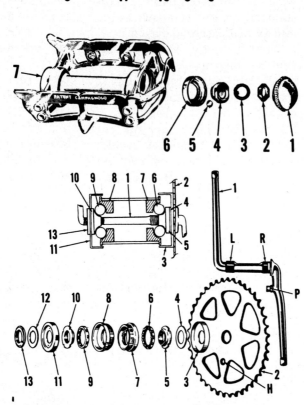

Fig. 5-20—Exploded view of typical repairable pedal. Bearing balls (5 & 9) are usually alike and are often loose.

1. Dust cap
2. Lock nut
3. Lock washer
4. Adjustable cone
5. Bearing ball
6. Bearing race (cup)
7. Platform and housing
8. Bearing race (cup)
9. Bearing ball
10. Dust seal
11. Pedal shaft

Fig. 5-21—Exploded and cross sectional views of typical one piece crank and associated parts. Threads (R) for fixed cone (5) are standard right hand threads. Threads (L) for adjustable cone (10) are smaller in diameter and are left hand (opposite) to prevent tightening when riding.

1. Ashtabula crank	6. Bearing balls and retainer	10. Adjustable bearing cone
2. Sprocket	7. Bearing cup	11. Dust shield
3. Dust shield	8. Bearing cup	12. Tab (lock) Washer
4. Washer	9. Bearing balls and retainer	13. Lock nut
5. Fixed cone		

bearing cone (4) and carefully catch bearing balls (5 & 9). Inner dust seal (10) and bearing cups (6 & 8) can be removed if necessary for cleaning or renewal. Clean and carefully inspect bearing balls (5 & 9), bearing cups (6 & 8), fixed bearing cone (C) on shaft (11) and the adjustable bearing cone (4). Renew bearing components if nicked, worn or otherwise damaged. NOTE: Pedal hub can be heated to facilitate removal and installation of bearing cups (6 & 8).

Install bearing cups (6 & 8) in pedal hub if removed. Grease bearing surface of cups and position bearing balls in cups. NOTE: Be sure to install the correct number and size of bearing balls. Use a sufficient amount of grease to hold bearings in place while assembling. Install inner dust seal (10) with cupped side in. Position hub over pedal shaft and install adjustable cone (4). Tighten the cone enough to remove all play from bearings without causing pedals to bind. Install tabbed lock washer (3) and lock nut (2). Be sure adjustment is correct after lock nut is tightened. Install dust cap (1) after bearings are correctly adjusted and lock nut (2) is tightened.

CRANK AND CRANK BEARING LUBRICATION AND REPAIR

Because of differences in construction, refer to the appropriate following section for service procedures. A typical one piece (Ashtabula) crank is shown in Fig. 21. Three piece Cottered Crank is shown in Fig. 5-23; and three

piece Cotterless Crank is shown in Fig. 5-25. The crank rotates on bearings that require lubrication, the crank arms may be bent, the bearings may be damaged or the chain wheel may just be changed for another with a different number of teeth. Regardless of the reason, care should be used when servicing these parts.

One Piece Crank

Remove the pedal from left side and frame mounted chain guard from right side of models so equipped. CAUTION: Do not turn the bicycle upside down when disassembling the crank. Parts may fall into frame tubes and be lost and dirt normally located in bottom bracket may not be evident or easily removed. Remove lock nut (13-Fig. 5-22) by turning nut clockwise. NOTE: Lock Nut (13-Fig. 5-21) and adjustable bearing cone (10) on left side are usually equipped with left hand threads. These parts are installed on left hand threads (L) of the crank (1). Remove lock washer (12) and dust cover (11). Remove the adjustable bearing cone (10) and ball bearing (9). Turn the crank until the left crank arm is up, then withdraw the crank out right side. Chainwheel (2), dust cap (3), washer (4), fixed bearing cone (5) and bearing (6) will be removed with the crank. Bearing cups (7 & 8) may be screwed into the crank

Fig. 5-22—View of one piece (Ashtabula) crank installed. Lock nut is visible at (13) and bearing cup at (8).

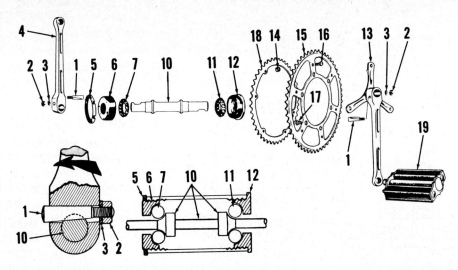

Fig. 5-23—*Exploded and cross sectional views of typical cottered three piece crank and associated parts. Large end of tapered cotter pins (1) should be toward direction of travel as shown in cross sectional drawing.*

1. Cotter pin	6. Adjustable bearing cup	11. Bearing balls and retainer
2. Nut	7. Bearing balls and retainer	12. Fixed bearing cup
3. Washer	10. Crank shaft	13. Right crank arm
4. Left crank arm		14. Nut
5. Lock ring		15. Large (fast) chainwheel
		16. Screw
		17. Screw
		18. Small (slow) chainwheel

bracket, but are usually pressed into place. Bearing cone (5) is threaded onto crank at (R). Cone (5) holds washer (4), dust cover (3) and chainwheel (2) firmly against flange on crank. Pin (P) should enter hole (H) to drive the chainwheel (2).

Clean and inspect all parts very carefully. The complete bearing (cup, balls and cone) should usually be renewed at the same time. Damage to one part will quickly damage the other parts of bearing.

Position the chainwheel (2) over crank (1) with pin (P) engaging drive hole (H). Slide dust shield (3) and washer (4) against

sprocket, then install bearing cone (5). Tighten the bearing cone by turning in standard (clockwise) direction. Install bearing cups (7 & 8) in bottom bracket. Pack grease into bearings (6 & 9) and in bearing surfaces of cups (7 & 8). Locate the right side bearing (6) in cup (7) with closed side of retainer toward outside (cone). Insert crank through the bearing (6) and bearing cups (7 & 8). Install bearing (9) in left side cup (8) with closed side of retainer toward outside (cone). Turn adjustable cone (10) counter-clockwise onto threads (L) by hand until bearings are tight. Back the cone (10) off about 1/8-turn, install dust shield (11), lock washer (12) and lock nut (13). Check adjustment of bearings after tightening lock nut (13) and readjust cone (10) if necessary. The crank should not be loose in bearings but bearings should not bind.

Three Piece Cottered Crank

CAUTION: The crank bearings are often damaged by pounding the cotter pins (1-Fig. 5-23) when attempting to tighten or remove the cotter pins. A clamp type

special tool (Fig. 5-24) for removing and installing the cotter pins is the only recommended method.

Remove both cotter pins and both crank arms. Loosen the lock nut or ring (5-Fig. 5-23) and unscrew the adjustable bearing cup (6) from left side of bottom bracket. NOTE: The lock nut and left side (adjustable) bearing cup may have left hand thread. Carefully catch bearing balls as the cup is removed. NOTE: Hold the crank toward right side to keep bearing balls for right side from falling out and being mixed with those from the left. CAUTION: Do not turn the bicycle upside down when disassembling the crank. Parts may fall into the frame tubes and be lost. Also, dirt normally located in bottom bracket may not be evident or easily removed. Withdraw crank shaft (10) and remove fixed bearing cup (12). Be careful to catch the bearing balls for right side when shaft is removed.

Clean and inspect all parts very carefully. Damage to one part of bearing will quickly damage the other parts of bearing. If any of the bearing parts (cup, balls or cone) are damaged, be especially critical when inspecting the matching parts of the bearing. NOTE: Pounding the cotter pins will usually result in dented surfaces on bearing cones and cups which is evident by rough (lumpy) feel when turning crank.

Apply grease to bearing surface of the fixed cup (12) and stick the loose bearing balls in the cup. On models so equipped, pack grease in bearing retainer and position bearing in cup with the closed side of retainer toward bearing cone (away from the cup). Use enough grease to be sure that bearings will stay in cup while assembling. Install the fixed bearing cup in right side of bottom bracket and tighten firmly in place. Insert the crank shaft through bearing and cup. Grease the bearing surface of the adjust-

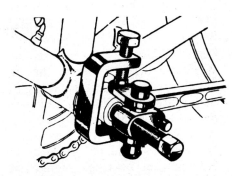

Fig. 5-24—*View of special tool used to remove and install cotter pins. Unit will also pull crank arms from crank shaft.*

Fig. 5-25 — Exploded and cross sectional views of typical cotterless crank assembly. Crank arms (4 & 13) are usually made of light metal that can be easily damaged by hammering.

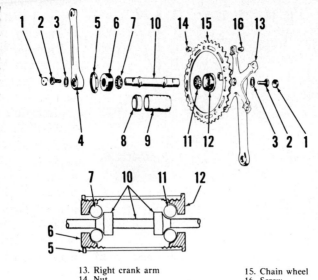

1. Cover
2. Retaining screw
3. Washer
4. Left crank arm
5. Lock ring
6. Adjustable bearing cup
7. Bearing balls and retainer
8. Sleeve cone
9. Protection sleeve
10. Crank shaft
11. Bearing balls and retainer
12. Fixed bearing cup
13. Right crank arm
14. Nut
15. Chain wheel
16. Screw

able cup and stick loose bearing balls in the cup. On models so equipped, pack grease in bearing retainer and position bearing in cup with the closed side of retainer toward bearing cone (away from the cup). Use enough grease to be sure that bearings will stay in cup while assembling. Install adjustable cup in left side of bottom bracket. Screw the adjustable cup in until hand tight, then install and tighten lock nut. Check crank bearing adjustment and reposition if necessary. The crank should not be loose in bearings but bearings should not bind. Install crank arms and secure with cotter pins. Cotter pins are usually 8, 8.5 or 9 MM in diameter. Be sure that correct size is installed.

Three Piece Cotterless Crank

CAUTION: The crank arms are usually made from a light weight metal that can be easily damaged by incorrect service procedures. Be sure all parts that are threaded into the light weight material are correctly installed and have the proper matching thread size.

Remove covers (1-Fig. 5-25), retaining screws (2) and washers (3) from both sides. NOTE: Special wrenches or metric size Allen wrenches are sometimes neces-

sary to remove covers (1) and/or screws (2). Use the correct puller and remove crank arms from shaft. Refer to Fig. 5-26. Loosen lock nut or ring (5-Fig. 5-25) and unscrew the adjustable bearing cup (6) from left side of bottom bracket. NOTE: The lock nut and left side (adjustable) bearing cup may have left hand thread. Carefully catch bearing balls as the cup is removed. NOTE: Hold the crank toward right side to keep bearing balls in place on right. Don't mix used bearing balls from the left and right sides even if new balls are identical. CAUTION: Do not turn the bicycle upside down when disassembling the crank. Parts may fall into the frame tubes and be lost. Also, dirt normally located in the bottom bracket may not be evident or easily removed. Withdraw crank shaft (10) and remove fixed bearing cup (12). Be careful to

Fig. 5-26—Special pullers similar to type shown should be used to remove crank arms. Cotterless crank arms can be easily damaged if incorrect tools are used when removing.

catch the bearing balls for right side when shaft is withdrawn. All crank assemblies are not equipped with the protection sleeve (9) and cone (8).

Clean and inspect all parts very carefully. Damage to one part of bearing will quickly damage the other parts. If any of the bearing parts (cup, balls and cone) are damaged, be especially critical when inspecting the matching parts of the bearing. NOTE: Pounding on the crank arms when removing or installing will usually result in dented surfaces of the bearing cups and cones which is evident by rough (lumpy) feel when crank is turned.

Apply grease to bearing surface of the fixed cup (12) and stick the loose bearing balls in cup. On models so equipped, pack grease in bearing retainer (11) and position bearing in cup with the closed side of retainer toward bearing cone (away from the cup). Use enough grease to be sure that bearings will stay in cup while assembling. Install the fixed bearing cup in right side of bottom bracket and tighten firmly in place. Insert the crank shaft (10) through bearing and cup. Grease the bearing surface of the adjustable cup (6) and stick loose bearing balls in the cup. On models so equipped, pack grease in bearing retainer (7) and position bearing in cup with the closed side of retainer toward bearing cone (away from the cup). Use enough grease to be sure that bearings will stay in cup while assembling. Install adjustable cup in left side of bottom bracket. Screw the adjustable cup in until hand tight, then install and tighten lock nut (5). Check crank bearing adjustment and reposition if necessary. The crank should not be loose in bearings but bearings should not bind. Install crank arms (4 & 13), secure with screws (2) and install covers (1).

CRANK TRANSMISSIONS

Some manufacturers have transmission assemblies that are located on the crank shaft. Refer to Fig. 5-27 and Fig. 5-28. The construction of these units vary and some are serviced only as a complete exchange assembly. Front derailleur systems are included in a separate service section.

CHAINWHEEL REMOVAL AND INSTALLATION

Chainwheels are most often attached to the crank as shown in Fig. 5-21, Fig. 5-23 or Fig. 5-25.

Some models may be welded or riveted onto the crank arm and these types should be serviced by installing new assemblies as required. Chainwheels are available to fit various chain sizes, but should be selected to match the chain and rear sprocket size as well as fit the crank assembly. Sizes are generally listed as length of chain pitch (P-Fig. 5-29) and width (W) between the side plates. Chain with 25.4 MM (1 inch) pitch and 4.9 MM (3/16-inch) width is used on some bicycles, especially older models. Later one speed bicycles, models with multispeed rear hubs and three speed rear derailleur are most often equipped with chain that has 12.7 MM (1/2-inch) pitch and 3.3 MM (1/8-inch) witch. Nearly all bicycles with derailleur use chain with 12.7 MM (1/2-inch) pitch and narrow 2.38 MM (3/32-inch)

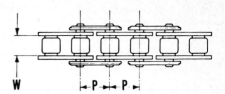

Fig. 5-29—Chain (chain wheel and sprocket) sizes are usually given as pitch (P) and width (W). Other specifications such as roller diameter etc. are important, but are somewhat standardized.

width. It is very important to use the correct length of chain, as well as the correct type and size of parts. NOTE: Bicycles with derailleur should not be equipped with a master link.

New chainwheels are usually installed because of wear or damage to the original parts or because a different drive ratio is desired. Different size chainwheels will probably require a change in the length of the drive chain. On derailleur equipped bicycles, be sure the chain tensioner has enough range to accommodate the sizes of chainwheel used. Wear is usually evidenced by hook shaped teeth (H-Fig. 5-30). The hooked teeth will probably be present all around the chainwheel, but may be more pronounced at certain areas. Broken teeth (B) can occur anywhere. Small burrs on teeth may prevent smooth shifting or cause overshifting on derailleur models. It is

Fig. 5-27—View of Hagen variable ratio drive installed on a bicycle with 3 speed rear hub. Unit is available from TCM New Products Division, Inc., 2201 Washington Avenue North, Minneapolis, Minnesota 55411.

Fig. 5-28—Views of Dana three speed transmission. Unit is available from Dana Cycle Systems, 8000 Yankee Road, Ottawa Lake, Michigan 49267.

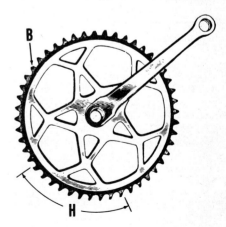

Fig. 5-30—Bent chain wheels can sometimes be straightened, but renew chain wheels if any teeth are hooked (H) or broken (B).

sometimes possible to polish rough surfaces of chainwheel teeth and to straighten or align chainwheels. The time and effort used to attempt a repair of a damaged part may be just wasted.

It is necessary to remove the crank assembly on models with one piece (Ashtabula) crank (Fig.

Fig. 5-31—Chain wheels may be riveted (R) onto crank arms or welded (W) as shown.

5-21). Refer to the appropriate preceding paragraph for CRANK AND CRANK BEARING LUBRICATION AND REPAIR. The pin (P) on crank arm should engage hole (H) in sprocket when assembling.

Most three piece cranks attach the chainwheel (or wheels) to the right crank arm. The chainwheel may be riveted or welded to the arm, in which case the arm and chainwheel should be renewed as a unit. The chainwheel may be removed from some units without removing the crank arm from the crank. Refer to Fig. 5-23 and Fig. 5-25.

CHAIN

CHAIN TIGHTENING

Bicycle chain should be kept lubricated and at correct tension all the time. Chain that has not

Fig. 5-32—Chain free play (P) is measured between rear sprocket and the chain wheel.

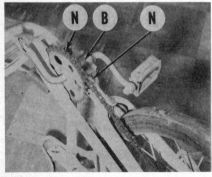

Fig. 5-33—Chain tension (free play) is adjusted on bicycle shown by moving crank bracket (B) after loosening nuts (N).

been lubricated properly will be stiff and tension cannot be correctly set.

A good (not worn out), well lubricated chain should move smoothly around the chainwheel and the rear sprocket with only a small amount of free play (P-Fig. 5-32). The tension of the chain is adjusted in several different ways.

On some bicycles (Fig. 5-33) the crank is located in a bushing assembly (B). The bushing is bolted to the bicycle frame and can be moved forward or backward to tighten or loosen the drive chain. Loosen nuts (N) and move the bushing (B) to tighten the chain, then tighten nuts (N).

On most single speed bicycles and models with multi-speed hubs, adjust chain tension by moving the rear wheel. Loosen the rear axle retaining nuts and move the wheel back to tighten the chain. Be sure to center the wheel in the frame before tightening the axle retaining nuts. On models with multi-speed hubs, it will be necessary to check and adjust remotely attached speed controls. Refer to appropriate

REAR WHEEL HUB section for adjustment procedures.

Bicycles with derailleur system and some racing single speed bicycles are equipped with a tensioner device. It is important that the chain tensioner has enough range of travel to compensate for the size of rear sprockets and chainwheels. Determine the correct length of chain by installing chain around largest rear sprock-

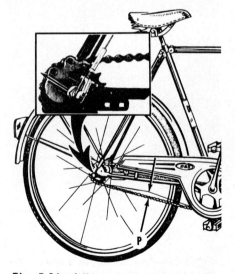

Fig. 5-34—Adjust chain tension on bicycle shown by moving rear wheel after loosening axle nuts. Be sure to center wheel as well as tighten chain while tightening axle nuts.

et and largest chainwheel. Chain should be located through the tensioner assembly and tensioner should be tight but should have some movement remaining.

CHAIN REPAIR

Sprocket tooth profile is precisely ground to fit the roller diameter and chain pitch. Refer to Fig. 5-36. When chain and sprocket are new, the chain moves around the sprocket smoothly with a minimum of friction, and the load is evenly distributed over several sprocket teeth. Wear on pins and bushings of a roller chain results in a lengthening or "stretch" of each individual chain pitch as well as a lengthening of the complete chain. The worn chain, therefore, no longer perfectly fits the sprocket. Each roller contacts the sprocket tooth higher up on the bearing area (C) and that tooth bears the total load until the next tooth and roller make contact. Chain wear will therefore quickly result in increased sprocket wear.

As a rule of thumb, the chain should be inspected periodically

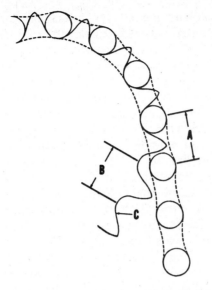

Fig. 5-36—Pitch of chain (A) and pitch of sprocket or chain wheel (B) must be the same. Worn chain increases in pitch and causes chain to contact tooth higher than normal (C).

and renewed whenever chain stretch exceeds 2% (or ¼-inch per foot). Check sprockets carefully for wear if chain wear is substantially greater than 2%, and renew sprockets if in doubt. Sprocket wear usually shows up as a hooked tooth profile. A good test is to fit the sprocket to a new chain. If sprockets must be renewed because of wear, always renew the chain. Early failure can be expected if a new chain is mated with worn sprockets or new sprockets with a worn chain.

Individual sections of the chain are available and may be renewed, but installation of a complete new chain is recommended in most cases of worn or damaged links. Be sure that chain is cor-

rect length and that free play (tension) is correct after installation is complete.

CHAIN REMOVE AND INSTALL

Rear chain on many bicycles without derailleur is equipped with a master (connecting) link to facilitate removal. Refer to Fig. 5-37. The master link is identified by straight side plates (2) and often by spring clip (1). Remove the clip, then pry the side plate off of the master link using a small screwdriver or similar tool. The pins of master links without the spring clip are notched and the removable side plate fits into these notches. Hold chain on both sides of master link and bend chain slightly to release notched pins from master link side plate. The plate can be withdrawn while notches are not holding side plate.

Rear chain used on bicycles with a derailleur must be smooth on the sides. Any projection such as a master link would cause the chain to catch on the guide mechanism. Chain used on bicycles with derailleur, racing single speed bicycles and some other types are riveted together to become a constant one piece unit. Removal of the chain necessitates that the chain be "broken" and a special tool (Fig. 5-38) is required.

The necessary length of new chain is usually easily determined by the length of the old chain. The chain should be long enough to be installed around the rear

Fig. 5-35—An automatic tensioner device (T) is incorporated into the design of most rear derailleurs.

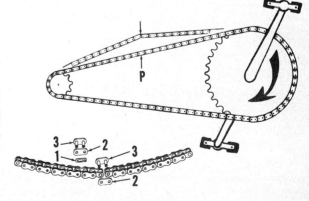

Fig. 5-37—Removable plate (2) for master link should be toward outside. Spring clip (1), if used, should have closed end toward direction of chain travel as shown. Free play (P) should be measured midway between rear sprocket and chain wheel.

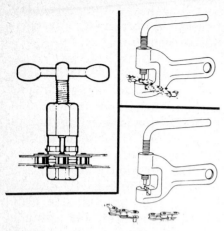

Fig. 5-38—View of special tools available for removing and installing rivets in chain.

sprocket and the front chainwheel. Check length of chain with adjustment (rear axle or crank bracket) in center of travel on models without derailleur. On de-

railleur models, chain should be guided through tensioner, around largest rear sprocket and around largest chainwheel. The tensioner should be in a tight position but should still have some movement.

On chain with master link, be sure that loose side plate is toward outside. Installation of master link is easier if ends of chain are located on each side of one tooth of chainwheel. Slip master link pins through ends of chain from the back side of chain. Turn chainwheel until master link is at bottom between sprocket and chainwheel and complete assembly of side plate and spring clip. On models with spring clip (1-Fig. 5-37), closed end of clip should be toward normal direction of travel as shown. The special tool (Fig. 5-38) is also used to install the rivet on one piece chain.

Install the rear wheel assembly as follows: Position chain around sprocket and slide axle into slots of frame drop outs. On models with back pedaling brake, install the brake arm to left chain stay clamp strap (S-Fig. 5-40). Center the wheel between the chain and seat stays with chain tight, then install and tighten axle retaining nuts.

CLEAN, INSPECT AND LUBRICATE AXLE BEARINGS

Models With Coaster Brake Or Multi-Speed Hub

Service procedures for these units will vary depending upon manufacturer of the hub. Refer to the appropriate paragraphs for servicing the particular unit.

Models With Only Freewheeling Hub

Remove the wheel assembly from the bicycle frame, then service the axle bearings in manner similar to that used for front wheel axle bearings. Refer to Fig. 5-2 and the preceding service notes for front wheel. The freewheeling unit and the sprocket cluster are shown at 1 thru 5-Fig. 5-41. Most freewheeling units and sprockets can be disassembled. Refer to Fig. 5-42 and Fig. 5-43 for exploded and cross sectional views of typical units. Bearings (B-Fig. 5-42) in freewheeling unit

Rear Wheel Assembly

REMOVE AND REINSTALL THE ASSEMBLY

Removal procedure will vary depending upon what type of brake and what type of hub is used. Support the bicycle and

disconnect or remove clamps and/or controls which will interfere with removal of the wheel. On models with caliper type brakes it may be necessary to remove one brake pad to provide clearance for removing the wheel. Remove axle retaining nuts or clamps and pull wheel down away from drop outs.

Fig. 5-40—Clamp strap (S) should hold brake arm close to left chain stay as shown.

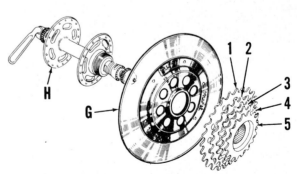

Fig. 5-41—View of typical rear hub for use with derailleur. Hub (H) is similar to most front hubs, except that right side is threaded to accept sprocket and freewheeling unit. Low speed sprocket (1) is usually toward inside and high speed sprocket (5) is often toward outside. Guard (G) is sometimes used to protect spokes in case chain comes off low speed sprocket.

are only used when sprocket is turning slower than hub and does not carry the weight of the bicycle.

RENEW HUB, SPOKES OR RIM

Identify the spoke pattern currently used (Fig. 5-44 or Fig. 5-45) for the rear wheel. Shorter (therefore lighter) spokes can be laced in radial (Fig. 5-6), cross 1 (Fig. 5-7) and cross 2 (Fig. 5-8) patterns. These patterns may be used on the front wheel of some bicycles, but should NOT be used on the rear. Most bicycles use a cross 3 pattern and some tandem models use a cross 4 pattern.

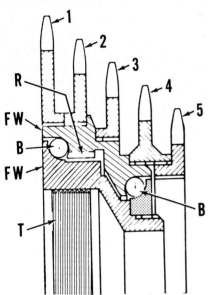

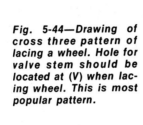

Fig. 5-42—Cross section of typical freewheeling hub and five sprockets. Ratchet assembly (R) causes sprockets to drive the hub of freewheeling unit, while also permitting hub to coast.

B. Bearing
FW. Freewheeling hub
R. Ratchet
T. Threads
1. Low speed sprocket
2. Second speed sprocket
3. Third speed sprocket
4. Fourth speed sprocket
5. Fifth (fast) sprocket

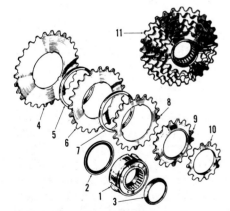

Fig. 5-43—View of sprockets exploded from freewheeling hub. Construction is different but similar for units manufactured by other companies.

1. Freewheeling hub
2. Seal
3. Seal
4. Low speed gear
5. Spacer
6. Second speed gear
7. Spacer
8. Third speed gear
9. Fourth speed gear
10. Fifth speed gear
11. Sprockets and freewheeling hub hub unit

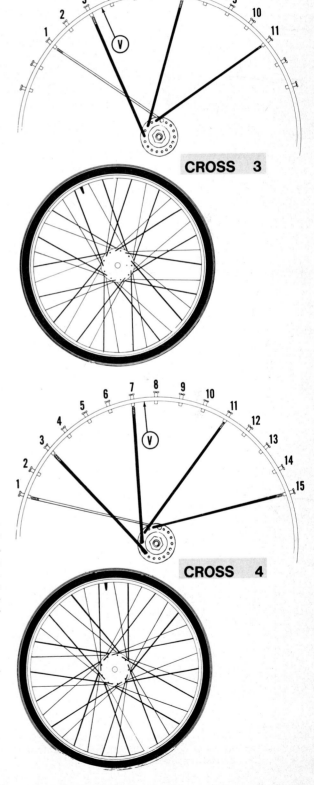

Fig. 5-44—Drawing of cross three pattern of lacing a wheel. Hole for valve stem should be located at (V) when lacing wheel. This is most popular pattern.

CROSS 3

Fig. 5-45—Drawing of cross four pattern of lacing a wheel. Hole for valve stem should be located at (V) when lacing wheel. This pattern is sometimes recommended for tandem bicycles.

CROSS 4

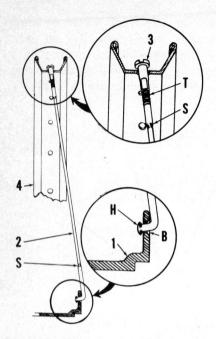

Fig. 5-46—Cross section showing correctly assembled spoke. Head (H) of spoke should be away from bevel (B) of hub. Bevel is for clearance at bend. Some spokes are swaged (S) while others may be straight. Be sure that enough threads (T) engage nipple (3). Hub is shown at (1), spoke at (2) and rim at (4).

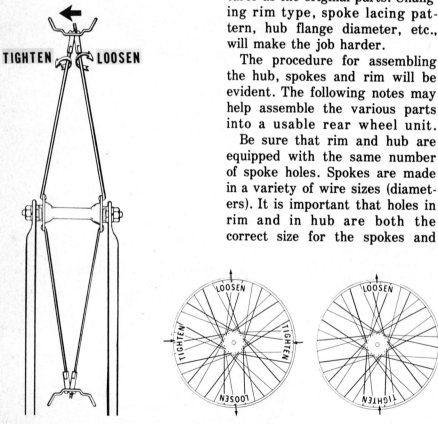

Fig. 5-47—Tighten or loosen spokes as required to move wheel rim to desired location. Patience and correct combination of tightening and loosening will center and align rim as well as tighten all of the spokes.

A single new spoke (or just a few spokes) can be installed and the wheel aligned as outlined in the following paragraphs. Be sure that new spoke is the same as other similar spokes in both length and diameter.

All of the spokes attach the hub to the wheel rim. To install a new wheel rim, it is necessary to remove the wheel from the bicycle, remove tire from the rim and remove all of the spoke nipples from the end of the spokes. To install a new hub, it is necessary to also remove the spokes from the hub. It may be necessary to change the length of all of the spokes or to change the pattern of lacing if a different type or size of rim or hub is installed.

The necessary steps to install new parts will depend upon what parts need to be renewed as well as the manufacturer of the parts. It is often easier to install new parts made by the same manufacturer as the original parts. Changing rim type, spoke lacing pattern, hub flange diameter, etc., will make the job harder.

The procedure for assembling the hub, spokes and rim will be evident. The following notes may help assemble the various parts into a usable rear wheel unit.

Be sure that rim and hub are equipped with the same number of spoke holes. Spokes are made in a variety of wire sizes (diameters). It is important that holes in rim and in hub are both the correct size for the spokes and

nipples used. The beveled side of hole in hub flange (B-Fig. 5-46) should be near bend in spoke, NOT against head of spoke. Begin assembly by locating the valve stem hole. Correct locating of the valve stem hole (V-Fig. 5-44 or Fig. 5-45) will position the valve stem at opening of spokes. Incorrect location will cause spokes to cross near the stem. Truing (aligning) the wheel and tightening the spokes will be much easier if the wheel is assembled carefully and slowly.

To begin assembling the hub, spokes and rim, insert one spoke through hole in hub, with bend next to the bevel around the hole. Refer to the appropriate drawing (Fig. 5-44 or Fig. 5-45) and locate the correct position for valve stem hole (V) in rim. Insert spoke through correct hole in rim and start nipple on threaded end of spoke. Starting with one installed spoke, install spokes the same direction through every other hole in hub flange and through every fourth hole in rim. This first set of spokes will be ¼ of the total number used in the wheel. The hub will be held loosely in the center of the rim. Insert spokes through the remaining holes in the flange the opposite direction from the first. The bend in this second set (¼ total) of spokes should also be against bevels of holes in hub. Hold the rim and turn hub so that the installed spokes radiate clockwise from the center (hub) to the rim. Insert the threaded end of one loose spoke in hole of rim after crossing the correct number of installed spokes. Install nipple on the first cross spoke and position the remaining cross spokes and nipples. This will locate ½ of the total number of spokes and the hub should hang at center of rim. Turn the wheel over and install the other two sets of spokes in the other flange of hub. With all of the spokes installed loosely, the hub should be free to flop from side to side. Position wheel in test fixture or the bicycle and gradually and evenly tighten all of the spokes. Tighten all spokes just enough for all nipples to contact the rim and to center the wheel. Tighten spokes and align wheel as outlined in the following paragraphs.

TIGHTENING SPOKES AND ALIGNING WHEELS

Ideally, if every spoke is tightened alike, the wheel will be exactly centered and aligned. The weight of the bicycle and rider will be supported by the top spokes in the wheel and this weight will be evenly transmitted to successive spokes as the wheel turns. Actually it isn't that easy. Spokes are attached to the rim by nipples (3-Fig. 5-46). The nipple might break, pull the rim down, pull the rim to one side, break the spoke or any of several things if the spoke is too tight. The spoke won't carry its share of the load if it is too loose and the spokes around it will have to carry more weight.

The procedure for tightening and aligning spokes is best learned by doing it several times. The rim should be concentric with the axle and should not wobble from side to side. Alignment test fixtures or a fork can be used to

hold the axle while checking. Two reference points should be used, one for checking out-of-round or eccentricity (E-Fig. 5-48) and the second for checking side to side movement or wobble (W). Often both conditions exist at the same point (B) and several different conditions may exist at various locations around the rim.

First, center the rim. Locate the low (closest to the center) areas of the rim and loosen the spoke nipples. Tighten the spokes to move the rim in toward the center in high sections. Be sure that all spoke nipples are tight enough to contact the rim firmly, but not too tight or the rim, spoke hub or nipple may be damaged. Check movement of rim from side to side (wobble). To move the rim toward the left as shown in Fig. 5-47, loosen the spokes on the right and tighten spokes on the left.

As noted before, the spokes should all be tightened the same amount. Be sure that no spoke is loose after centering and aligning the rim. The spokes may all be too tight if the rim suddenly jumps out of alignment when nearly finished. Check to make certain that the rim is centered in the fork or alignment fixture. On most bicycles with derailleur sprockets and freewheeling hub located on right side of hub, the

spokes should be shorter on the right. Instead of using different lengths of rear spokes, the spoke nipples are usually threaded further onto the spokes for the right. The wheel will appear similar to drawing (C-Fig. 5-49). Regardless of hub design, be sure that center line of rim is aligned with frame. Do not install wheel off center as shown at (B). This condition will cause the bicycle to pull to one side when riding and will quickly loosen spokes, bend the rim or other similar damage.

Fig. 5-49—Wheel should be laced so that rim is centered between fork tubes. Some coaster brake and multi-speed hubs should be centered as shown at (A). Models with derailleur sprockets mounted on right side of hub must be assembled similar to drawing (C) to compensate for sprockets.

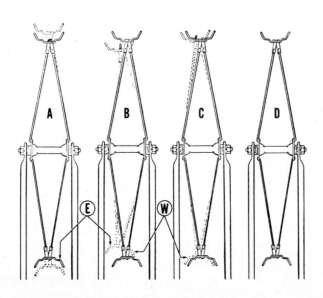

Fig. 5-48—Drawings of wheel showing conditions of eccentricity (E) and wobble (W).

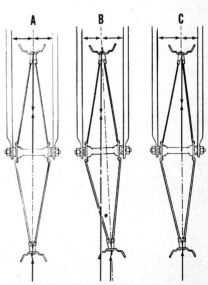

Coaster Brake Rear Hubs

COASTER BRAKE

Bendix

Several different variations of Bendix brake units have been manufactured. Repair kits are available which up-date early units. Also, some individual parts from late units can be installed in early hubs which sometimes make identification difficult. NOTE: Some parts will not interchange. Refer to Fig. B1 through B6 for exploded views.

The original (old) Bendix brake unit is shown in Fig. B1 and can be identified by the smooth hub (15). Sprocket (19) is threaded onto driving screw (17) and held in position with lock nut (24).

Bearings (7 & 16) are identical and have 10 balls each.

The RB model (Fig. B2) is similar to the original model except that sprocket (19) is splined to the driving screw (17) and held in position with snap ring (20). Hub can be identified by the red band around the center.

The RB-2 model (Fig. B3) is similar to the RB model. Sprocket is attached to driving screw (17) with three lugs. The same repair kit (part number BB-121) is used for RB, RB-2 and Junior brakes, so the internal parts of these three brakes may be overhauled to be like the RB-2.

The Junior brake (Fig. B4) uses a brake shoe (9) with less area than RB and RB-2 models. The

Junior (or later 70-J) brake is recommended for use on 16 and 20 inch sidewalk bikes. The repair kit used for RB and RB-2 brakes can be installed in the hub of Junior model. The repair kit includes the brake shoes and cam and will change the brake to be like the RB-2 shown in Fig. B3.

The 70-J brake (Fig. B5) can be identified by the knurled hub and the 70J stamped on the brake arm. This brake is recommended, like the earlier Junior model, to be used on 16 and 20 inch sidewalk bikes. Bearings (7 & 21) each have 9 balls and cannot be interchanged with bearings for original Bendix RB, RB-2 or Junior models which have 10 balls.

The Bendix 70 brake (Fig. B6) can be identified by the 70 stamped on the brake arm (5) and by the knurled hub. Repair kit (part number BB-521) is available which includes all parts except hub (15) and sprocket (19). This kit can be installed in hub of 70-J models, but the brake shoe used is the large type (9).

There are many other differences and some will be noted in the REPAIR section. The preceding are differences which can be used for ready identification.

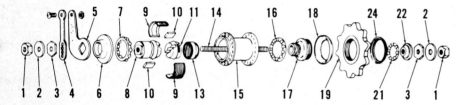

Fig. B1—Exploded view of original Bendix brake. Some parts of this unit are no longer available for service, however, most are available and some are the same as used in later type brakes. Sprocket (19) is threaded onto driving screw (17) and locked with nut (24).

1. Axle retaining nuts	7. Bearing (10 balls)	13. Driving clutch
2. Washers	8. Anchor end	14. Axle
3. Lock nuts	expander	15. Hub (smooth)
4. Brake arm	9. Brake shoes	16. Bearing (same as 7)
retaining strap	10. Brake shoe keys	17. Driving screw
5. Brake arm	11. Expander &	(threaded for
6. Dust cap (large	retarder assembly	sprocket)
diameter)		

18. Dust cap	
19. Sprocket (1 inch	
pitch chain)	
21. Bearing (7 balls)	
22. Bearing cone	
24. Sprocket retaining	
nut	

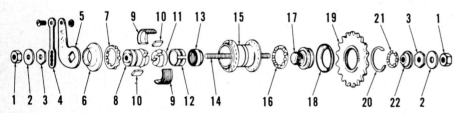

Fig. B2—Exploded view of RB type coaster brake. Retarder spring (12) is also used on all models except original Bendix. Expander (11), driving clutch (13) and driving screw (17) are different than other models. Unit can be up-dated to the RB-2 type by using repair kit number BB-121. Original sprockets (19) are splined to driving screw (17).

1. Axle retaining nuts	7. Bearing (10 balls)	13. Driving clutch
2. Washers	8. Anchor end	14. Axle
3. Lock nuts	expander	15. Hub (one groove)
4. Brake arm	9. Brake shoes	16. Bearing (same as 7)
retaining strap	10. Brake shoe legs	17. Driving screw
5. Brake arm	11. Expander	(splined for
6. Dust cap (large	12. Retarder spring	sprocket)
diameter)		

18. Dust cap (large	
diameter)	
19. Sprocket (splined)	
20. Sprocket retaining	
ring	
21. Bearing (7 balls)	
22. Bearing cone	

MAINTENANCE. The hub should be disassembled, cleaned, inspected and reassembled when difficulty is noticed or approximately every one or two years. Bearings (7, 16 & 21-Fig. B1, B2, B3, B4, B5 and B6) can be lubricated with oil without disassembling. NOTE: Do not use gasoline, kerosene or similar solvent which will cause grease to be removed from the brake hub. Disassemble the unit if cleaning and inspection is necessary. Be sure to lubricate with grease before and during assembly. Refer to the REPAIR section for disassembly and assembly instructions.

Hub bearings should always be correctly adjusted and the axle retaining nuts (1-Figs. B1, B2, B3, B4, B5 & B6) should be tight. Adjust bearings as follows: Loosen axle retaining nut (1) at right end of axle, then loosen lock nut (3). Turn the bearing cone (22) onto axle against the bearing with fingers, loosen the bearing cone slightly, then tighten lock nut (3). Tighten chain and center the wheel in frame, then tighten both axle retaining nuts (1).

REPAIR. Remove the wheel and hub assembly from bicycle, then proceed as follows: Remove axle nuts (1-Figs. B1, B2, B3, B4, B5 & B6) from both ends of axle. Remove washers (2) and lock nut (3) from the sprocket side of axle. Unscrew bearing cone (22), then lift bearing (21) from race in driver (17). Turn sprocket (19) and driver (17) out of the driving clutch (13 or 23). The remaining parts can then be withdrawn from left side of hub. Disassemble parts from axle if cleaning and inspection is necessary.

Repair kits are available, but must be installed in the correct hub.

If hub (15 – Figs. B2, B3 & B4) has a smooth shell with one groove, kit part number BB-121 can be used. The kit includes the brake parts which will change the Junior and the RB brake into the RB-2 type brake. Parts included are shown at (1, 2, 3, 4, 5, 6, 7, 8, 9, 14, 16, 17, 18, 20, 21, 22 & 23 – Fig. B3).

Use repair kit part number BB-721 hub is knurled as on 70 and 70-J models (Fig. B5 & B6). Installation of this kit will change the 70-J model into a standard 70 type. Parts included are shown at (1, 2, 3, 4, 5, 6, 7, 8, 9, 14, 16, 17, 18, 20, 21, 22 & 24 – Fig. B5).

Use repair kit part number BB721 for 76 model brakes which have four brake shoes (9 – Fig. B6). Installation of this kit in model 70 or 70-J hub will effectively change the earlier brake to a later 76 type.

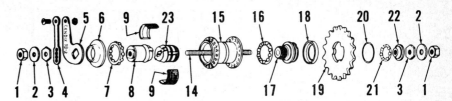

Fig. B3—Exploded view of RB-2 brake. Installation of repair kit in RB or Junior brake will change unit to this type. Original driving screw for RB brake has three starting threads. Driving screw (17) in repair kit and in RB-2 models has six starting threads and is used with bearing (16) which has ten balls. The similar driving screw used on brakes with knurled hub uses bearing with nine balls and is identified by a groove.

1. Axle nuts	7. Bearing (10 balls)	17. Driving screw (NO identification groove)	20. Retaining ring
2. Washers	8. Anchor end expander		21. Bearing (7 balls)
3. Lock nuts	9. Brake shoes	18. Dust cap (large diameter)	22. Bearing cone
4. Brake arm retaining strap	14. Axle		23. Retarder sub-(expander, retarder spring & drive cone)
5. Brake arm	15. Hub (one groove)	19. Sprocket (3 drive lugs)	
6. Dust cap (large diameter)	16. Bearing (same as 7)		

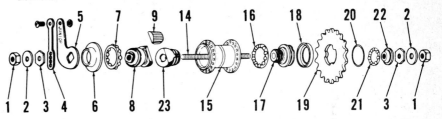

Fig. B4 — Exploded view of Junior brake assembly. Bendix 70-J brake is similar. The small brake shoe (9) is recommended for use with small (16-20 inch) sidewalk bicycles. Refer to Fig. B3 for legend.

Disassemble and clean all parts that are to be reinstalled. Inspect all bearings and bearing races carefully. Renew brake shoes (9-Fig. B1, B2, B3, B4, B5 or B6) if worn below the depth of the grooves. Check the square hole in brake arm (5) and the square lug on anchor end expander (8). Check condition of threads on axle (14), lock nuts (3) and axle retaining nuts (1). Refer to the appropriate exploded view for assembly order.

To reassemble, proceed as follows: Screw expander (8) onto axle until approximately 1-1/8 inch of the axle extends out beyond the square lug end of expander. Grease bearing (7) and push over the expander using dust cap (6). Closed side of bearing retainer should be toward dust cap (Fig. B7). NOTE: Expander, bearings and dust cap are different for models with knurled hub than for models with single grooved hub. Install brake arm (5-Fig. B1, B2, B3, B4, B5 & B6) and lock in position with lock nut (3). Clamp axle in a soft jawed

vise with brake arm down and complete assembly of hub. Coat parts with grease, then install the retarder sub-assembly (10, 11, 12 & 13 or 23) and brake shoes (9). Coat inside of hub with grease, hold brake shoes in position and install hub over the parts assembled on axle. Be sure that hub bearing (7) is seated in race of hub. Grease bearing (16) and locate in race of hub. Turn driving screw (17) into driving clutch. NOTE: Bearing (16) is same as bearing (7), but should not be interchanged if old units are reinstalled. Closed side of retainer for bearings (16 & 21) should be toward outside of hub (15). Grease bearing (21) and install in race of driving screw (17). Screw bearing cone (22) onto axle until finger tight, then back cone up approximately ¼-turn. Hold bearing cone (22) in this position while tightening lock nut (3). Install dust shield and sprocket on driving screw if these were removed.

Install the assembled wheel and hub on bicycle. Strap (4) should hold brake arm against bottom of

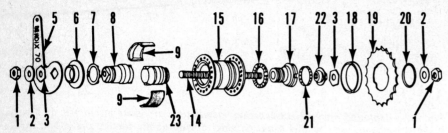

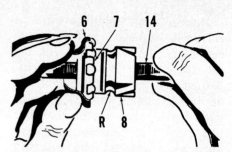

Fig. B5 — Exploded view of 70 brake assembly. Parts (5, 6, 7, 8, 16, 17, 18, & 23) are different than similar parts for installation in hubs with one groove.

Fig. B7 — Drawing showing installation of bearing (7). Push bearing over expander (8) using dust cap (6). Closed side of bearing retainer should be toward dust cap (6) and bearing balls should be in race (R).

1. Axle nut	7. Bearing (9 balls)
2. Washer	8. Anchor end
3. Lock nut	expander
4. Brake arm strap	9. Brake shoes
5. Brake arm	14. Axle
6. Dust cap (stamped	15. Hub (knurled)
BENDIX)	16. Bearing (same as 7)

17. Driving screw	20. Retaining ring
(Identification	21. Bearing (7 balls)
groove at largest	22. Bearing cone
O.D.)	23. Retarder sub-
18. Dust cap (Stamped	assembly
BENDIX)	(expander, retarder
19. Sprocket (3 drive	spring & drive
lugs)	cone

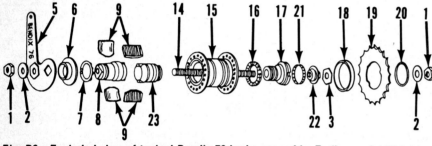

Fig. B6 — Exploded view of typical Bendix 76 brake assembly. Earlier model 70 brakes may be converted to use the four narrow braking shoes (9) instead of the two previously used. Refer to Fig. B5 for legend.

frame tube. Adjust position of wheel to tighten chain and center wheel in frame, then tighten both axle nuts (1).

TROUBLE SHOOTING. The following list some troubles and possible remedies. Refer to MAINTENANCE or REPAIR section for additional adjustment and disassembly procedures.

1. Slippage when bicycle is pedaled forward.
   a. Insufficient retarder pressure. Disassemble and bend fingers of retarder spring (12) in slightly. Install new parts if worn excessively.
   b. Excessive wear on tapered surfaces of driving clutch (13). Renew parts as necessary, if small end of driving clutch extends 1/16-inch beyond tapered shoulder of hub.

2. Pedals rotate backward excessively when brake is applied (indicating slippage).

   a. Insufficient retarder pressure. Refer to item 1-a.
   b. Mismatched, damaged or dirty detents on driving clutch (13) or expander (11). Clean or renew parts as necessary

3. Poor braking or failure to stop as quickly as desired.
   a. Check for highly polished surfaces on inside of hub and outside of brake shoes. Roughen surfaces slightly with coarse emery paper or renew parts. NOTE: Be sure that abrasive is cleaned off of parts before assembling.

4. Brake does not release after being applied or drags when bicycle is pedaled forward.
   a. Bearing cone is adjusted too tight. Refer to MAINTENANCE paragraphs for bearing adjustment.
   b. Axle bent. Disassemble and check axle for straightness.

5. Cracking or grinding noises.
   a. Chain dirty, broken or adjusted too tight. Inspect chain and clean, renew or adjust as required.
   b. New sprocket used with old chain or old sprocket used with new chain. It is best to renew chain when it is necessary to install new sprocket because the old sprocket is worn out. Check condition of old sprockets when installing a new chain.
   c. Dust caps rubbing on hub. Check dust caps and renew if bent. Be sure that dust caps are correctly assembled.
   d. Hub bearing is damaged. Disassemble and check condition.

6. Excessive lost motion between forward and backward (braking) position of pedals.
   a. Incorrect bearing cone adjustment. Refer to MAINTENANCE paragraphs and adjust bearings.
   b. Brake shoes worn out. Refer to REPAIRS paragraphs, disassemble and renew brake shoes.

7. Squealing noises when brake is applied.
   a. Lack of lubrication or incorrect type of lubricant. Disassemble and lubricate.

Centrix K

The Centrix brake unit is manufactured in Germany. A repair kit is available which includes all parts except hub shell (9-Fig. C1), brake arm (14) and sprocket (2). Sprocket (2), used on early models, is threaded onto driver (6). On later units, the sprocket is equipped with driving lugs which engage notches in driver and retaining ring (19) holds sprocket on driver.

MAINTENANCE. Hub should be disassembled, cleaned, inspected and reassembled when difficulty is noticed or approximately every one or two years. Bearings (5, 7 & 7L-Fig. C1) and brake shoe (11) should be continuously lubricated with heat resistant grease. Clutch (10) and threaded end of driver (6) should only be lubricated with oil. Slippage may result if grease is on thread between parts (6 & 10).

Durex

The Durex brake unit is manufactured in Germany and is available with either Metric or American threads. Be sure that threaded repair parts match the existing parts. Sprocket (18-Fig. D1) is threaded onto driver (16) and lock ring (19) holds the sprocket in position.

MAINTENANCE. Hub should be disassembled, cleaned, inspected and reassembled when difficulty is noticed or approximately every one or two years. Bearings (8, 8L & 23-Fig. D1) and brake shoes (10) may be lubricated with grease when assembling. Rollers in cage (15) should be lubricated with oil only and should not be stuck with heavy grease. Frequent oiling through filler (L) will provide necessary lubrication.

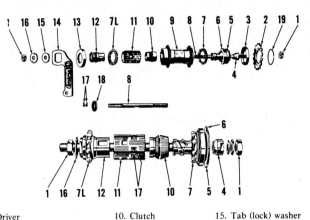

Fig. C1 — Exploded drawing of Centrix coaster brake rear hub. Some models have sprocket (2) threaded onto driver (6).

1. Axle nuts
2. Sprocket
3. Dust cap
4. Adjusting cone
5. Small bearing
6. Driver
7. Right side bearing
7L. Left side bearing
8. Axle
9. Hub
10. Clutch
11. Brake shoe
12. Expander
13. Dust cap
14. Brake arm
15. Tab (lock) washer
16. Lock nut
17. Brake shoe clips
18. Dust seal
19. Retaining ring

Elgin

Refer to the following service section for Musselman coaster brake while repairing Elgin brake. Design and even some parts are identical to the Musselman brake assembly.

Excel

Refer to the following service section for Perry B-100 coaster brake while repairing Excel brake. Design and even some parts are identical to the Perry B-100 brake assembly.

Hawthorne

Refer to the following service section for Nankai coaster brake while repairing Hawthorne brake. Design and even some parts may be identical to the Nankai brake assembly.

J.C. Higgins

Refer to the following service section for Musselman coaster brake while repairing J.C. Higgins brake. Design and even some parts are identical to the Musselman brake assembly.

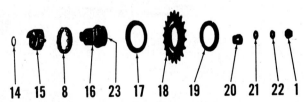

Fig. D1—Exploded view of Durex coaster brake rear hub. Lubrication fitting is shown at (L).

1. Axle nuts
2. Lock nut
3. Washer
4. Brake arm strap
5. Brake arm
6. Dust cap
7. Arm side cone
8. Right side bearing
8L. Left side bearing
9. Dust washer
10. Brake shoe
11. Brake actuator
12. Hub
13. Axle
14. Spring (snap) ring
15. Roller cage
16. Driver
17. Dust cap
18. Sprocket
19. Lock ring
20. Adjusting cone
21. Lock washer
22. Lock nut
23. Bearing (10 balls)

Mattatuck-Musselman Brakes

Mattatuck

Service repair procedures for the model D are similar to those for the E model shown. Parts (5, 6, 7, 8, 9, 10, 14, 15 & 16–Fig. M1) are different for D model.

MAINTENANCE. Hub should be disassembled, cleaned, inspected and reassembled if difficulty is noticed or approximately every one or two years. Be especially careful to check the seventeen alternate bronze and steel brake discs (17–Fig. MA1) and the brake clutch (15). Bearings (8, 11 & 11L) should be packed with grease when assembling. Other parts including the brake discs (17) should be oiled.

Morrow

MAINTENANCE. Disassemble, clean inspect and reassemble the unit if difficulty is noted in operation or at approximately one year intervals. Use exploded drawing (Fig. M1) as a guide when disassembling or reassembling. Closed side of retainer for all three bearings (4, 9 & 9L) should be toward outside. Bearings (9 & 9L) are not identical.

Musselman

MAINTENANCE. Brake should be disassembled, cleaned, inspected and reassembled if difficulty is noticed or approximately every one or two years. Check condition of clutch (9) and thread on driver (6) if unit slips while pedaling. The brake is operated by pushing clutch (9) to the left on thread of driver (6). The clutch pushes spool (18) toward left which pushes the wedge (19). The wedge expands brake shoe (17) against inside of hub (8). Only the bearings (3, 7 & 7L) should be greased; other parts should be lubricated with oil.

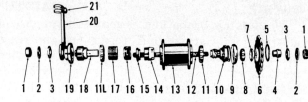

Fig. MA1 — Exploded view of Mattatuck model "E" coaster brake rear hub. Model "D" is similar.

1. Axle nuts
2. Washers
3. Lock nuts
4. Adjustment cone
5. Snap ring
6. Sprocket
7. Dust cap
8. Small bearing (7 balls, 1/4-inch)
9. Dust cap
10. Driver
11. Right side bearing (10 balls, 1/4-inch)
11L. Left side bearing (10 balls, 1/4-inch)
12. Axle
13. Hub
14. Clutch sleeve
15. Brake clutch
16. Transfer spring
17. Brake discs
18. Disc support sleeve
19. Dust cap
20. Brake arm
21. Brake arm strap

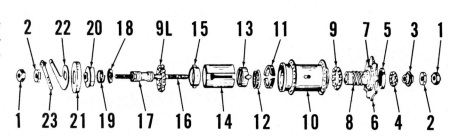

Fig. M1—Exploded view of Morrow coaster brake. Closed side of retainer for bearings (4, 9 & 9L) should be toward outside. Bearings (9 & 9L) are not the same.

1. Axle nuts
2. Lock nuts
3. Bearing cone (adjustable)
4. Small bearing (8 balls, 1/4-inch)
5. Sprocket lock nut
6. Sprocket
7. Dust cap
8. Driving screw
9. Bearing (11 balls, 1/4-inch)
9L. Bearing (12 balls, 1/4-inch)
10. Hub
11. Clutch ring halves
12. Clutch retaining ring
13. Nut and sleeve expander
14. Brake sleeve
15. Sleeve expander with teeth
16. Axle
17. Axle bushing
18. Retarder washer
19. Retarder spring
20. Cone (brake arm side)
21. Dust cap
22. Brake arm
23. Brake arm strap

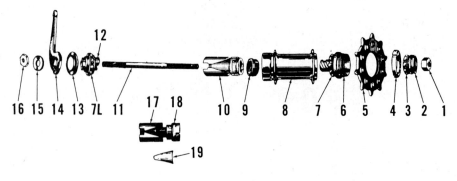

Fig. MU1—Exploded view of Musselman coaster brake rear hub.

1. Axle nut
2. Adjusting cone
3. Bearing with retainer
4. Retaining nut
5. Sprocket
6. Driver
7. Bearings with retainer
7L. Bearings with retainer
8. Hub
9. Clutch
10. Brake assembly
11. Axle
12. Expander
13. Dust cap
14. Brake arm
15. Washer
16. Lock nut
17. Brake shoes
18. Spool and drag
19. Wedge

Nankai NK 75

This brake is similar to the American made New Departure brake.

MAINTENANCE. Hub should be disassembled, cleaned, inspected and reassembled when difficulty is noticed or approximately every one or two years. Check condition of clutch band (13-Fig. N1) and brake discs (15 & 16) carefully. Be sure that band (13) is wrapped around cone (14) in direction shown. Check brake holder (17) and slots in hub (10) for wear notches caused by brake discs (15 & 16). Renew brake discs (15 & 16) if damaged in any way. Nine steel internal lugged discs (15) are used and eight bronze external lugged discs (16). Alternate steel and bronze discs (15 & 16) when assembling. Bearings (4, 9 & 9L) should be greased when assembling. Other parts should be assembled with oil. Lubricate hub frequently with oil through fitting (L).

New Departure

MAINTENANCE. Hub should be disassembled, cleaned, inspected and reassembled aproximately once every year or when unit is not operating properly. Check condition of brake discs (16-Fig. ND1) and transfer spring (14).

To disassemble, remove rear wheel assembly from bicycle and proceed as follows: Remove axle nut (1), washer (2) and lock nut (3) from right end of axle. Remove cone (4) and bearing (7). Turn driver assembly (5, 6, 8 & 9) counter-clockwise and lift driver assembly and bearing (10) away from hub. Hub (12) can be lifted away from the remaining brake parts and parts can be removed as required.

Check disc support sleeve (17) and slots in hub (12) for wear notches caused by brake discs (16). Renew brake discs (16) if damaged in any way. Inspect transfer spring (14) and renew if

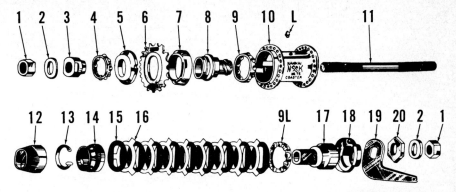

Fig N1—Exploded view of Nankai No. 75 coaster brake rear hub.

1. Axle nuts
2. Washers
3. Adjustment cone
4. Small bearing
5. Retaining nut
6. Sprocket
7. Dust cap
8. Driver
9. Right side bearing
9L. Left side bearing
10. Hub
11. Axle
12. Screw cone
13. Clutch band
14. Clutch cone
15. Internal (steel) discs
16. External (bronze) discs
17. Brake disc holder
18. Dust cap
19. Brake arm
20. Lock nut

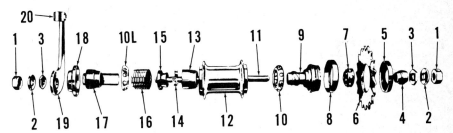

Fig. ND1—Exploded view of New Departure coaster brake rear hub.

1. Axle nuts
2. Washers
3. Lock nuts
4. Small bearing cone
5. Retaining nut
6. Sprocket
7. Small bearing
8. Dust cap
9. Driver
10. Right side bearing
10L. Left side bearing
11. Axle
12. Hub
13. Screw cone
14. Clutch band
15. Clutch cone
16. Brake discs (steel internal, bronze external)
17. Brake disc holder
18. Dust cap
19. Brake arm
20. Brake arm strap

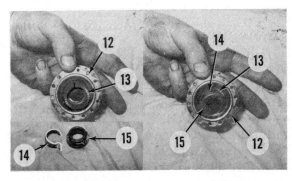

Fig. ND2—View showing method of assembling New Departure brake. Refer to Fig. ND1 for legend.

tab is bent or broken or if band doesn't grip brake clutch (15) tightly. Grease bearings (7, 10 & 10L) when reassembling and oil the remaining parts.

Install transfer spring (14-Fig. ND2) onto brake clutch (15) in direction shown. Tang on end of spring should be located in slot of clutch sleeve (13). Install one

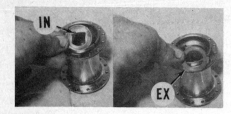

Fig. ND3—Internal discs (IN) are steel, external discs (EX) are bronze on New Departure brake.

Fig. ND4—Bearings should be lubricated with grease. Refer to Fig. ND1 for legend.

steel brake disc (IN-Fig. ND3), then one external lugged bronze disc (EX). Alternate steel and bronze discs until all seventeen are installed. Thread support sleeve (17-Fig. ND4) onto axle, position the left bearing (10L) in bore of hub with closed side of retainer toward outside. Install axle and support sleeve through hub, brake discs and clutch assembly. Position the large right side bearing (10) in bearing cup with closed side of retainer toward outside. Turn driver (9), clockwise to screw the large thread into the clutch sleeve. Position the small bearing (7-Fig. ND1) into cup of driver with closed side of retainer toward outside. Screw bearing cone (4) onto axle until bearings are correctly adjusted. Bearings should not bind when turning the hub, but hub should have only a very small amount of side play. Install lock nuts (3) after adjustment is complete. Be sure to recheck bearing adjustment after lock nuts are tightened.

Fig. P1—Exploded view of Perry B-100 coaster brake rear hub. Oversize rollers (9) are available to compensate for wear.

1. Axle nuts
2. Retaining nut
3. Sprocket
4. Axle
5. Dust cap
6. Bearing cone
7. Driving sleeve
8. Right side bearing
8L. Left side bearing
9. Driving rollers
10. Roller guide ring
11. Brake actuator
12. Brake cylinder
13. Hub
14. Dust cap
15. Brake cone
16. Brake arm
17. Tab washer
18. Lock nut

Perry B-100

Some models use threaded lock ring (2-Fig. P1) while others are equipped with a snap ring to hold sprocket onto driver (7). This brake is sometimes called "2 Star".

MAINTENANCE. Disassemble, clean, inspect and reassemble the unit if difficulty is noted in operation or at approximately one or two year intervals. End of axle (4-Fig. P1) that is toward right (sprocket) side is equipped with a square end to facilitate disassembly and reassembly.

Hold axle (4) by the square end and remove lock nut (18), washer (17) and brake arm (16). Unscrew brake cone (15) from axle, pry seal (14) out of hub (13) and lift out bearing (8L). Lift hub (13) off, away from axle. Remove brake (shoe) cylinder (12) and actuator (11). Remove driver assembly (2, 3, 5, 7, 7R, 8, 9 & 10). Separate guide ring (10), rollers (9) and bearing (8) from driver (7) after removing retaining ring (7R).

Lubricate bearings with grease while reassembling. Rollers (9), guide ring (10) and driver (7) should be lubricated with oil. Adjust axle bearings by turning cone (15). Install brake arm (16), tab washer (17) and lock nut (18) after adjustment is complete.

Perry B-500

MAINTENANCE. Hub should be disassembled, cleaned and lubricated approximately once each year or whenever operation is not satisfactory. Refer to the following REPAIR paragraphs for disassembly instructions. Hub bearings should always be adjusted to permit wheel to rotate freely without excessive play. Hub bearings can be adjusted by turning brake cone (13-Fig. P5).

REPAIR. Remove wheel and hub assembly from bicycle, then proceed as follows: Remove axle nuts (1-Fig. P5), lock nut (17) and washers (2 & 16). Unscrew cone (13) from axle and remove brake arm (15), dust shield (14), cone (13) and bearing (9L). Withdraw brake cylinder (12) and driving cone (11) from left side of hub (10) after unscrewing drive cone (11) from driver (8).

Clean and inspect all parts. Bearings (9 & 9L) are identical but should not be interchanged if old bearings are reinstalled. Inner race (cone) for bearing (9L) is integral with brake cone (13). Outer races for bearings (9 & 9L) are both integral with hub (10). Outer race for small bearing and inner race (cone) for bearing (9) is integral with driver (8). Fixed cone (7) is located on axle (6).

Sprocket (4) can be withdrawn from driver (8) after removing retaining ring (3). Sprockets are available for standard 1/2 x 1/8-inch roller chain with 16, 18 or 20 teeth.

Coat driving cone (11) with oil and insert into end of brake cylinder (12). Coat outside surface of brake cylinder with grease and pack additional grease inside brake cylinder. Position driving cone (11) and brake cylinder (12) in hub (10). Coat bearing (9L) with oil or grease and locate bearing over brake cone (13).

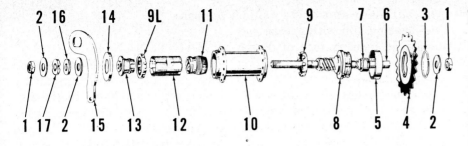

Fig. P5—Exploded view of Perry B-500 coaster brake rear hub.

1. Axle nuts	7. Bearing cone	12. Brake cylinder
2. Washers	8. Driver	13. Brake cone
3. Retaining ring	9. Right side bearing	14. Cover
4. Sprocket	9L. Left side bearing	15. Brake arm
5. Dust cap	10. Hub	16. Washer
6. Axle	11. Traveler (actuator) and	17. Lock nut
	drag spring	

Pixie

Refer to the following service section for Sachs coaster brake while repairing Pixie brake. Design and even some parts are identical to the Sachs brake assembly. Bearing (13–Fig. 51) is ten loose bearing balls, not a bearing with retainer as shown.

Renak

Refer to the following service section for Perry B-100 coaster brake while repairing Renak brake. Design and even some parts are identical to the Perry B-100 brake assembly.

Resilion

Refer to the following service section for Perry B-100 coaster brake while repairing Resilion brake. Design and even some parts are identical to the Perry B-100 brake assembly.

Sachs (Jet, Komet, Komet Super and Torpedo Boy)

MAINTENANCE. Hub should be disassembled, cleaned and lubricated at least once each year. Refer to the REPAIR paragraphs for disassembly instructions. Hub bearings should always be adjusted to permit wheel to rotate freely without excessive play. Hub bearings can be adjusted by turning brake cone (6-Fig. S1).

NOTE: Closed side of retainer for bearing (9L) should be toward outside (brake arm). Position brake cone (13) and bearing (9L) against hub, making sure that slots in brake cone (13) engage lugs on brake cylinder (12). Bearing (9L) should be contacting races on both cone (13) and hub (10) when parts are correctly assembled. Lubricate bearing (9) with oil or grease and locate bearing in race at right side of hub (10). NOTE: Closed side of retainer for bearing (9) should be toward outside. Lubricate driver (8), then locate driver assembly through bearing (9) and turn the assembly into driving cone (11). NOTE: Turn driver assembly (8) clockwise as viewed from sprocket and driver side. Pack small bearing with grease and position in bearing race of driver (8) with closed side of retainer toward outside. Grease fixed hub (7) on axle, then insert axle through the assembled hub. Screw axle through brake cone (13) until bearings are correctly adjusted. Bearings should not bind when turning driver (8), but hub should have only a small amount of side play. After adjustment is complete, install dust cap (14), brake arm (15), washers (2 & 16) and lock nut (17). Be sure to recheck bearing adjustment after tightening lock nut (17). Dust cap (5) and sprocket (4) are attached to driver (8) by retaining ring (3).

REPAIR. Remove the wheel and hub assembly from bicycle, then proceed as follows: Remove axle nut (1-Fig. S1), lock nut (2) and washers (3), then unscrew cone (6) from axle (15). Bearing (7), brake cylinder (8) and driving cone (9) can be withdrawn from left side of hub (10) after unscrewing driving cone (9) from driver (12).

Clean and inspect all parts. Bearings (7 & 11) are identical but should not be interchanged if

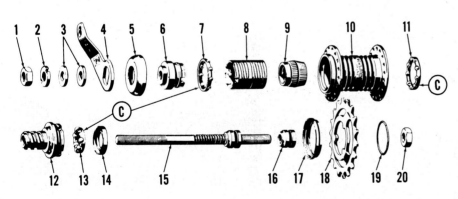

Fig. S1—Exploded view of Sachs Jet hub. Closed sides of bearing carriers should be toward side indicated by (C).

1. Axle nut	6. Brake cone	11. Ball bearing	16. Fixed cone
2. Lock nut	7. Ball bearing	12. Driver assembly	17. Dust cap
3. Washers	8. Brake cylinder	13. Ball bearing (S519)	18. Sprocket
4. Brake arm	9. Driving cone	14. Dust cap	19. Retaining ring
5. Dust cap	10. Hub	15. Axle	20. Axle nut

old bearings are reinstalled. Inner race (cone) for bearing (7) is integral with brake cone (6). Outer races for bearings (7 & 11) are both integral with hub (10). Outer race for bearing (13) and inner race (cone) for bearing (11) is integral with driver (12). Fixed cone (16) is located on axle (15).

Hub (10) is available with 16, 20, 24, 28 or 36 spoke holes. Sprocket (18) can be withdrawn from driver (12) after removing retaining ring (19). A threaded retaining nut is used in place of ring (19) on some models. Sprockets are available for standard 1/2 x 1/8-inch roller chain with 12, 14, 15, 16, 17, 18, 19, 20, 21 or 22 teeth. Flat and dished sprockets are available depending upon application. Rear sprocket (18) should align with chainwheel (large sprocket on pedal crank). Axle (15) is provided with American bicycle thread (3/8-24 UNF-2A).

Coat driving cone (9) with oil and insert into end of brake cylinder (8). Coat outside surface of brake cylinder with grease and pack additional grease inside brake cylinder. Position driving cone (9) and brake cylinder (8) in hub (10). Coat bearing (7) with oil or grease and locate bearing over brake cone (6). NOTE: Closed side (C) of carrier for bearing (7) should be toward outside brake arm (4). Position brake cone (6) and bearing (7) against hub, making sure that slots in brake cone (6) engage lugs on brake cylinder (8). Bearing (7) should be contacting races on both cone (6) and hub (10) when parts are correctly assembled. Lubricate bearing (11) with oil or grease and locate bearing in race at right side of hub (10). NOTE: Closed side (C) of carrier for bearing (11) should be toward outside. Lubricate driver (12), then locate driver assembly through bearing (11) and turn the assembly into driving cone (9). NOTE: Turn driver assembly (12) clockwise as viewed

from sprocket and driver side. Pack bearing (13) with grease and position in bearing race of driver (12) with closed side (C) of carrier toward outside.

On some models, 10 loose bearing balls are used instead of bearing with retainer (13). Install dust cap (14) firmly in bore of driver. Grease fixed hub (16) on axle, then insert axle through the assembled hub. Screw axle through brake cone (6) until bearings are correctly adjusted. Bearings should not bind when turning driver (12), but hub should have only a small amount of side play. After adjustment is complete, install dust cap (5), brake arm (4), washers (3) and lock nut (2). Be sure to recheck bearing adjustment after tightening lock nut (2). Dust cap (17) and sprocket (18) are attached to driver (12) by retaining ring (19) or by a threaded lock ring.

Schwinn Approved

Refer to the preceding service section for Sachs coaster brake while repairing early Schwinn approved brake or to the Perry B-100 section while repairing later Schwinn approved Mark IV brake.

Shimano

MAINTENANCE. The hub should be disassembled, cleaned and lubricated approximately once each year. Refer to the REPAIR paragraphs for disassembly instructions. Hub bearings should always be adjusted to permit wheel to rotate freely without excessive play. Adjust bearings by turning adjusting cone (4-Fig. SH1).

REPAIR. Remove rear wheel assembly from bicycle, then proceed as follows: Remove axle nuts (1-Fig. SH1), washers (2) and lock nut (3) from right end of axle (16). Remove bearing cone (4) and small bearing (5). Turn the driver assembly (6, 7, 8, 9 & 10) counterclockwise to release threaded end from clutch (12) and lift assembly out of hub. Lift hub (11) off of remaining brake parts. Disassembly procedure for remaining parts will be evident.

Be sure that clutch spring (13) is wrapped around clutch (12) in the direction shown. Tang or end of clutch spring should correctly engage slot in brake shoes (14). Grease all parts of brake while assembling except the large thread between clutch (12) and driver (9). Oil this thread.

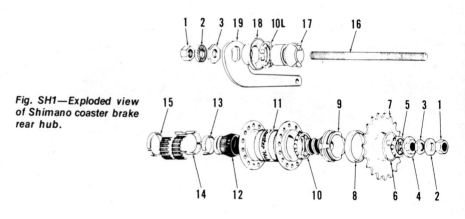

Fig. SH1—Exploded view of Shimano coaster brake rear hub.

1. Axle nuts	6. Retaining ring
2. Washers	7. Sprocket
3. Lock nuts	8. Dust cap
4. Bearing cone	9. Driver
5. Bearing with retainer	10. Right bearing with retainer

10L. Left bearing with retainer	14. Brake shoes
11. Hub	15. Spring
12. Driving clutch	16. Axle
13. Clutch spring	17. Brake expander
	18. Dust cap
	19. Brake arm

Assembly bearing (10L) onto expander (17), with closed side of retainer toward outside (brake arm). Screw axle (16) into expander (17), locate dust cap (18) and brake arm (19) over end and install lock nut (3) onto left end of axle. Install spring (15) over brake shoes (14), then position brake shoes over clutch (12) and clutch spring (13). Locate brake shoes and clutch assembly over axle and position over lugs of expander (17). Install hub over the assembled parts. Position bearing in race of hub with closed side of retainer out, then position driver (9) into right side of hub and turn the driver clockwise to engage clutch (12). Position small bearing (5) in driver (9) with closed side of retainer out, then screw cone (4) onto axle until bearings are correctly adjusted. Bearings should not bind, when turning hub, but hub should have only a very small amount of side play. After adjustment is complete, lock bearing adjustment with nut (3). Be sure to recheck bearing adjustment after tightening lock nut. Install dust cap (8), sprocket (7) and retaining ring (6) if they were removed.

Sturmey Archer

MAINTENANCE. Disassemble, clean, inspect and reassemble the unit if difficulty is noted in operation or at approximately one or two year intervals. End of axle (6-Fig. SA1C) that is toward right (sprocket) side is equipped with a square end to facilitate disassembly and reassembly.

Hold axle (6) by the square end and remove lock nut (18), washer (17) and brake arm (16). Unscrew brake cone (15) from axle, pry seal (14) out of hub (13) and lift out bearing (8L). Lift hub (13) off, away from axle. Remove brake (shoe) cylinder (12) and actuator (11). Remove driver assembly (2, 3, 5, 7, 7R, 8, 9, 10 & 22). Separate guide ring (10), rollers (9) and bearing (8) from driver (7) after removing retaining ring (7R).

Lubricate bearings with grease while reassembling. Rollers (9), guide ring (10) and driver (7) should be lubricated with oil. Adjust axle bearings by turning cone (15). Install brake arm (16), tab washer (17) and lock nut (18) after adjustment is complete.

Styre

Refer to the preceding section for Perry B-100 coaster brake while repairing Styre brake. Design and even some parts are identical to the Perry B-100 brake assembly.

Swift (100 & 2 Star)

Refer to the preceding service section for Perry B-100 coaster brake while repairing Swift brake. Design and even some parts are identical to the Perry B-100 brake assembly.

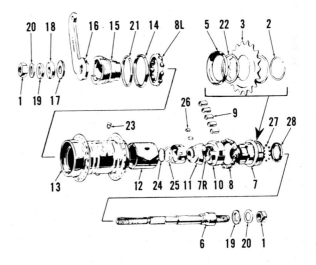

Fig. SA1C—Exploded view of Sturmey-Archer coaster brake hub.

1. Axle nut	11. Actuator	20. Washer
2. Retaining ring	12. Brake shoe	21. Dust cover
3. Sprocket	13. Hub	22. Spacers (2 used)
5. Dust cap	14. Dust cap	23. Lubricating fitting
6. Axle and fixed race	15. Brake cone	24. Actuator snap ring
7. Driver	16. Brake arm	25. Roller retaining washer
7R. Snap ring	17. Washer	26. Actuator washers (2 used)
8. Bearing balls with retainer	18. Lock nut	27. Bearing balls
9. Drive rollers (5 used)	19. Washer	28. Dust cap
10. Drive roller retainer		

Two Speed Rear Hubs

Bendix 2-Speed Automatic

Three variations have been manufactured and each is slightly different than the others. All three units are equipped with a back pedal brake and are shifted by back pedaling a small amount. Gears automatically change from low to high and from high to low.

The standard "Automatic 2-Speed" hub can be identified by the **three painted yellow bands** around center of hub. High speed is a direct drive and rear sprocket and hub rotate at the same speed. Low gear is accomplished by disengaging the high speed clutch from the hub shell and the slower turning driver will engage the low speed clutch with the hub shell. The hub shell will rotate 32 per cent slower than the sprocket in low gear. The standard (yellow) hub is equipped with shoe type brakes and is shown in Fig. B11.

The "2-Speed Automatic Overdrive" hub can be identified by the **three painted blue bands** around the center of the hub. Low speed is direct drive and the rear sprocket turns the hub at the same speed. Overdrive is accomplished by engaging the high speed slutch. The faster moving hub shell will override the low speed driver. The hub shell will rotate 47 per cent faster than the sprocket in overdrive. The overdrive hub is equipped with shoe brakes.

The "2-Speed Automatic" hub with disc brakes can be identified by the **three painted red bands** around center of hub. Low speed and direct drive are like the standard; however, brake discs are used instead of shoes. Operation and service are similar to the standard model, but many of the parts are different.

It is important to correctly identify the unit so that correct

Fig. B11—Exploded view of the standard "2 Speed Automatic". Unit can be identified by three yellow bands around hub (15). A retarder spring is located on high speed clutch assembly (14).

1. Axle nut
2. Washer
3. Lock nut
4. Brake arm
5. Brake arm clip
6. Dust cap
7. Bearing (Do not use No. 68 bearing)
8. Anchor end expander
9. Brake shoes (4 used)
10. Retarder spring (low speed clutch)
11. Drive end expander
12. Low speed clutch
13. Retarder coupling
14. High speed clutch with retarder spring
15. Hub
16. Axle
17. Special bearing (same as 7)
18. Indexing spring
19. High speed driving screw and sprocket
20. Bearing balls 1/4-inch (11 used)
21. Low speed driving screw
22. Pin (3 used)
23. Planet gear (3 used)
24. Bearing (small retainer)
25. Adjusting cone and sun gear
26. Dust cap
27. Retaining ring
28. Lock nut
29. Washer (same as 2)
30. Axle nut (same as 1)

service procedures can be used. It is even more important when obtaining new parts, because some parts that will not interchange are similar in appearance.

Bendix Yellow Band

MAINTENANCE. Hub should be disassembled, cleaned, inspected and reassembled when difficulty is noticed or approximately every one or two years. Bearings (7, 17, & 27-Fig. B11) can be lubricated with oil without disassembling. NOTE: Do not use gasoline, kerosene or similar solvent which will cause grease to be removed from the brake hub. Disassemble the unit if cleaning and inspection is necessary. Be sure to lubricate with grease before

and during assembly. Refer to the REPAIR section for disassembly and assembly instructions.

Hub bearings should always be correctly adjusted and axle retaining nuts (1 & 30) should be kept tight. Adjust bearings as follows: Remove wheel and hub assembly from the bicycle, then loosen lock nut (28). Turn adjusting cone and sun gear (25) onto axle threads until tight while turning the sprocket in opposite direction (counter - clockwise). Back the sun gear out 1/8-turn and tighten lock nut (28). Rim of wheel should have slight play, but bearings should not be loose. Tighten chain and center the wheel in frame, then tighten both axle retaining nuts (1 & 30).

Fig. B12—Special tool (T) is used to remove lock nut shown at (28-Fig. B11).

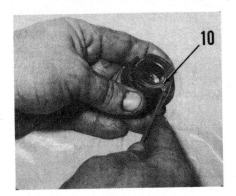

Fig. B13—Retarder spring (10) is also shown in Fig. B11. Do not bend or otherwise damage spring when removing.

Fig. B14—All bearings should be thoroughly packed with grease before assembling. Dust cap can be used to properly assembly bearing (7-Fig. B11) and anchor end expander (8).

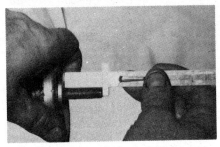

Fig. B15—Approximately 1 1/8 inches of axle should extend beyond expander or support as shown. Lock position by installing lock nut (3-Fig. B11).

REPAIR. Remove wheel and hub assembly from bicycle, then refer to the following paragraphs.

Shift the hub into the lowest speed and clamp brake arm end of axle in a soft jawed vise. Hub can be shifted by turning the sprocket counter-clockwise slightly by hand. Check to be sure of correct gear engagement by turning sprocket clockwise. The wheel should turn slower than the sprocket. CAUTION: Coupling (13-Fig. B11), may be damaged if unit is not shifted to low gear when disassembling. Remove lock nut (28) while holding the adjusting cone and sun gear (25) stationary. NOTE: Special tool (part number AB-102) is available for turning the lock nut and special tool (part number BB-100) is used for holding the adjusting cone and sun gear.

Turn the sprocket clockwise while unscrewing the adjusting cone and sun gear (25) from the axle. Remove ball bearing (24). Turn sprocket counter-clockwise and lift out of hub. NOTE: Turning the sprocket will disengage it from the high speed clutch (14) and low speed driving screw (21) from low speed driving clutch (12). NOTE: Bearings (7 & 17) should be reinstalled in original location to preclude unnecessary wear, but they are the same part. Bearing (24) uses the same number (twelve) of ¼-inch bearing balls as the other bearings, but the retainer is different. This bearing (24) is smaller in diameter than the other two bearings.

Remove bearing (17), then lift hub (15) from axle. CAUTION: Cup hand around bottom of hub when removing, to catch the four brake shoes (9). Clutches and expander subassembly (10, 11, 12, 13 and 14) can be lifted from axle.

Disassemble by first unhooking coupling (13) from low speed driving clutch (12), then unhooking coupling from ends of the retarder spring on high speed clutch (14). To separate low speed clutch (12) and drive end expander (11), pry up retarder spring (10) using a small screwdriver as shown in Fig. B13. Remove lock nut (3-Fig. B11), brake arm (4) and dust cap (6). Bearing (7) should be removed and installed from squared end of expander (8). Planet gears (23) can be removed by driving pins (22) out of driving screw (21).

Inspect parts for wear, breakage or other damage. Lubricate all parts except high speed clutch (14) and indexing spring (18) with grease such as Texaco Regal Starfac No. 2 or equivalent. These two parts (14 & 18) should be oiled when assembling. Bore of driving screws (19 & 21) should be filled with grease when assembling.

Assemble unit as follows: Grease bearing (7) and push onto anchor end of expander (8) using dust cap (Fig. B14). Screw axle into expander until axle protrudes approximately 1-1/8 inches from square drive end of expander (Fig. B15). Install dust cap (6-Fig. B11), brake arm (4) and lock nut (3). Position drive end expander (11) on hub of low speed clutch (12) with notched surfaces together. Locate bottom hook of retarder spring (10) in cut-out of expander and push the retarder spring into groove of low speed clutch (12). Retarder spring (10) will hold expander (11) and low speed clutch (12) together. Notice that the retarder spring, installed in groove of high speed clutch (14), is larger than spring (10) and identification is not difficult. Hook coupling (13) over ends of retarder spring on high speed clutch (14). NOTE: Lower window in coupling should be over lower end of retarder spring as

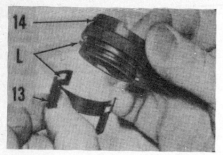

Fig. B16—Lower window in coupling (13) should be assembled over end of retarder spring.

Fig. B17—View of assembled clutch subassembly. Unit should be lubricated with grease (except inner bore of high speed clutch) before installing.

Fig. B18—View showing installation of the clutch subassembly and brake shoes. Lubricate parts before assembling; parts are shown dry for clarity.

CAUTION: Be careful when installing to prevent damaging indexing spring (18) or losing bearing balls (20). Grease bearing (24) and insert in race with closed side of retainer out. Screw adjusting cone and sun gear (25) onto axle until sun gear just contacts the planet gears, then continue turning sun gear while turning sprocket counter-clockwise. Tighten adjusting cone and sun gear (25) down until seated, then loosen approximately 1/8-turn. Wheel should turn freely with only a slight amount of play at wheel rim.

TROUBLE SHOOTING. The following list some troubles and possible remedies. Refer to MAINTENANCE or REPAIR section for additional adjustment and disassembly procedures.

1. Unit will not shift. Disassemble hub and inspect indexing spring (18-Fig. B11) and bore of clutch (14).

shown at (L-Fig. B16). Hook coupling (13-Fig. B11) over edge of low speed clutch (12). Clutch and expander subassembly (Fig. B17) is now assembled. Coat the subassembly with grease except for bore in end of high speed clutch (14-Fig. B11) and install in hub. Refer to Fig. B18. Grease hub and brake shoes and assemble shoes into hub. Insert the previously assembled axle, anchor end expander, bearing and brake arm into hub. Lugs on expander must fit into spaces between the brake shoes. Turn the unit over and clamp brake arm end of axle in a soft jawed vise.

Position indexing spring (18-Fig. B11) over sleeve on high speed driving screw. NOTE: Install indexing spring carefully, with short lugs (L-Fig. B19) toward bearing race of drive screw. Internal springing pieces will engage cut-outs in sleeve of the high speed driving screw. Grease bearing race in the high speed driving screw, locate the eleven loose bearing balls (20) in the race, then install the low speed

driving screw as shown. Grease bearing (17-Fig. B11) and install in hub race. NOTE: Closed side of bearing retainer should be out with bearing balls down, against the race in the hub. Hold driving screws (19 and 21) together and carefully insert into hub while turning clockwise until seated.

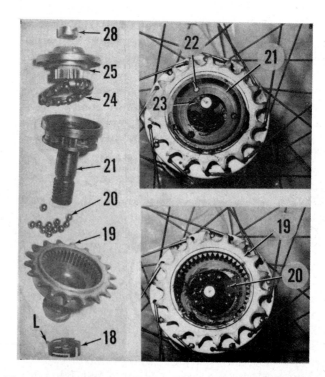

Fig. B19—Views of drive parts used in standard models. The three short protruding lugs (L) should be toward bearing race of drive screw as shown. Refer to Fig. B11 for legend.

a. Make certain that perpendicular lugs on indexing Spring are not bent or broken. Renew spring (18) if damaged.

b. Check for wear on external prongs of indexing spring (18) which drag on notches in bore of clutch (14). The prongs should have turned up ends. Renew spring (18) and/or clutch (14) if damaged.

c. Assemble clutch (14) and indexing spring (18) on driving screw (19). Rotate clutch back and forth and notice that indexing spring (18) is shifting. Renew damaged parts as necessary.

2. Slips when pedaling forward.

a. Insufficient retarder pressure. Disassemble and check retarder springs. Pressure of retarder spring (10 - Fig. B11) should be greater than retarder for high speed clutch (14). Turn clutch subassembly (Fig. B17) onto driving screw (19-Fig. B11). Hold the driving screw with one hand and turn anchor end expander (11) clockwise with other hand. The retarder spring on high speed clutch (14) will slip. Renew retarder spring (10) if it slips with this check.

b. Engaging clutches worn out. Disassemble and check condition of clutches (12 and 14-Fig. B11). Renew clutches and retarder springs if condition is questionable.

3. Pedals rotate backward excessively when brake is applied (indicating slippage).

a. Insufficient retarder pressure. Renew retarder spring (10-Fig. B11).

b. Mismatched, damaged or dirty detents on driving clutch (12) or expander (11). Clean or renew parts as necessary.

4. Poor braking or failure to stop as quickly as desired.

a. Check for highly polished surfaces on inside of hub and outside of brake shoes. Roughen surfaces slightly with coarse emery paper or renew parts. NOTE: Be sure that abrasive is cleaned off of parts before assembling.

5. Brake does not release after being applied or drags when bicycle is pedaled forward.

a. Bearing cone is adjusted too tight. Refer to MAINTENANCE paragraphs for bearing adjusting.

b. Axle bent. Disassemble and check axle for straightness.

6. Cracking or grinding noises.

a. Chain dirty, broken or adjusted too tight. Inspect chain and clean, renew or adjust as required.

b. New sprocket used with old chain or old sprocket used with new chain. It is best to renew chain when it is necessary to install new sprocket because the old sprocket is worn out. Check the condition of old sprockets when installing a new chain.

c. Dust caps rubbing on hub. Check dust caps and renew if bent. Be sure that dust caps are correctly assembled.

d. Hub bearing is damaged. Disassemble and check condition.

7. Excessive lost motion between forward and backward (braking) position of pedals.

a. Incorrect bearing cone adjustment. Refer to MAINTENANCE paragraphs and adjust bearings.

b. Brake shoes worn out. refer to REPAIRS paragraphs, disassemble and renew brake shoes.

8. Squealing noises when brake is applied.

a. Lack of lubrication or incorrect type of lubricant. Disassemble and lubricate.

9. Unit binds, detent noise.

a. Check frame plates to be sure they are parallel. Straighten plates (frame) if necessary. Axle attaching plates on frame are bent if noise disappears when axle attaching nuts are loosened.

b. Bent axle. Install new axle if bent. Do not attempt to straighten.

Bendix Blue Band

MAINTENANCE. Hub should be disassembled, cleaned, inspected and reassembled when difficulty is noticed or approximately every one or two years. Bearings (7, 17 & 24-Fig. B20) can be lubricated with oil without disassembling. NOTE: Do not use gasoline, kerosene or similar solvent which will cause grease to be removed from brake hub. Disassemble the unit if cleaning and inspection is necessary. Be sure to lubricate with grease before and during assembly. Refer to the REPAIR section for disassembly and assembly instructions.

Hub bearings should always be correctly adjusted and axle retaining nuts (1 & 30) should be kept tight. Adjust bearings as follows: Remove wheel and hub assembly from bicycle, then loosen lock nut (28). Turn adjusting

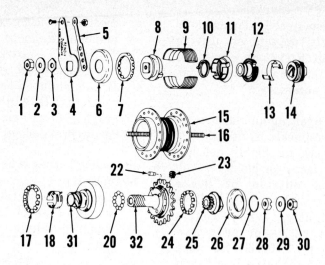

Fig. B20—Exploded view of the "2 Speed Overdrive" hub. Unit is identified by three blue bands around hub (15). A retarder spring is located on the high speed clutch assembly (14).

1. Axle nut
2. Washer
3. Lock nut
4. Brake arm
5. Brake arm clip
6. Dust cap
7. Bearing (Do not use No. 68 bearing)
8. Anchor end expander
9. Brake shoes (4 used)
10. Retarder spring (low speed clutch)
11. Drive end expander
12. Low speed clutch
13. Retarder coupling
14. High speed clutch with retarder spring
15. Hub
16. Axle
17. Special bearing (same as 7)
18. Indexing spring
20. Bearing balls 1/4-inch (11 used)
22. Pin (3 used)
23. Planet gear (3 used)
24. Bearing (small retainer)
25. Adjusting cone and sun gear
26. Dust cap
27. Retaining ring
28. Lock nut
29. Washer (same as 2)
30. Axle nut (same as 1)
31. High speed driving screw
32. Low speed driving screw and sprocket

sun gear (25) from axle. Remove ball bearing (24). Hold both driving screws (31 and 32) together and lift them both out of hub. CAUTION: Loose bearing balls (20) will fall if the two driving screws are not held together while removing.

NOTE: Bearings (7 and 17) should be reinstalled in original location to preclude unnecessary wear, but they are the same part. Bearing (24) uses the same number (twelve) of 1/4-inch bearing balls as the other bearings, but the retainer is different. This bearing (24) is smaller in diameter than the other two bearings.

Remove bearing (17), then lift hub (15) from axle. CAUTION: Cup hand around bottom of hub when removing, to catch the four brake shoes (9). Clutches and expander subassembly (10, 11, 12, 13 and 14) can be lifted from axle. Disassemble by first unhooking coupling (13) from low speed driving clutch (12), then unhooking coupling from ends of the retarder spring on high speed clutch (14). To separate low speed clutch (12) and drive end expander (11), pry up retarder spring (10) using a small screwdriver as shown in Fig. B22. Remove lock nut (3-Fig. B20), brake arm (4) and dust cap (6). Bearing (7) should be removed and installed from squared end of expander (8). Planet gears (23)

cone and sun gear (25) onto axle threads until tight while turning the sprocket in opposite direction (counter-clockwise). Back the sun gear out 1/8-turn and tighten lock nut (28). Rim of wheel should have slight play, but bearings should not be loose. Tighten chain and center the wheel in frame, then tighten both axle retaining nuts (1 & 30).

REPAIR. Remove wheel and hub assembly from bicycle, then refer to the following paragraphs.

Shift the hub into the lowest speed possible and clamp brake arm end of axle in a soft jawed vise. Hub can be shifted by turning the sprocket counter-clockwise slightly by hand. Check to be sure of correct gear engagement by turning sprocket clockwise. On this overdrive model, direct drive is slowest speed and sprocket and hub will turn together. CAUTION: Coupling (13-Fig. B20) may be damaged if unit is

not shifted to low gear when disassembling. Remove lock nut (28) while holding adjusting cone and sun gear (25) stationary. NOTE: Special tool (part number AB-102) is available for turning the lock nut and special tool (part number BB-100) is used for holding the adjusting cone and sun gear.

Hold sprocket stationary while unscrewing adjusting cone and

Fig. B21—Special tool (T) is used to remove lock nut shown at (28-Fig. B20).

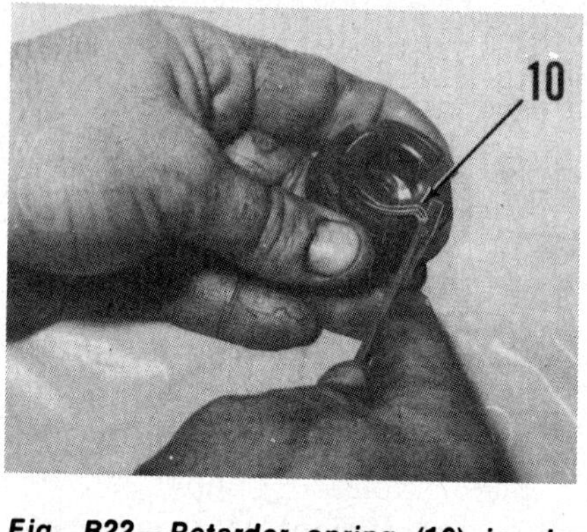

Fig. B22—Retarder spring (10) is also shown in Fig. B20. Do not bend or otherwise damage spring when removing.

can be removed by driving pins (22) out of driving screw (32).

Inspect all parts for wear, breakage or other damage. Lubricate all parts except high speed clutch (14) and indexing spring (18) with grease such as Texaco Regal Starfac No. 2 or equivalent. These two parts (14 and 18) should be oiled when assembling. Bore of driving screws (31 and 32) should be filled with grease when assembling.

Fig. B23—All bearings should be thoroughly packed with grease before assembling. Dust cap can be used to properly assemble bearing (7-Fig. B20) and anchor end expander (8).

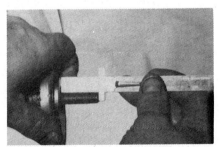

Fig. B24—Approximately 1 1/8 inches of axle should extend beyond expander or support as shown. Lock position by installing lock nut (2-Fig. B20).

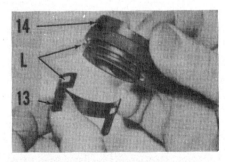

Fig. B25—Lower window in coupling (13) should be assembled over end of retarder spring.

Assemble unit as follows: Grease bearing (7) and push onto anchor end of expander (8) using dust cap (Fig. B23). Screw axle into expander until axle protrudes approximately 1-1/8 inches from square end of expander (Fig. B24). Install dust cap (6-Fig. B20), brake arm (4) and lock nut (3). Position drive end expander (11) on hub of low speed clutch (12) with notched surfaces together. Locate bottom hook of retarder spring (10) in cut-out of expander and push retarder spring into groove of low speed clutch (12). Retarder spring (10) will hold expander (11) and low speed clutch (12) together. Notice that retarder spring, installed in groove of high speed clutch (14), is larger than spring (10) and identification is not difficult. Hook

Fig. B26—View of assembled clutch subassembly. Unit should be lubricated with grease (except inner bore of high speed clutch) before installing.

Fig. B27—View showing installation of clutch subassembly and brake shoes. Lubricate parts before assembling; parts are shown dry for clarity.

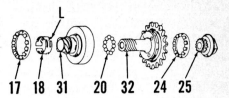

Fig. B28—Views of drive parts used. The three short protruding lugs (L) should be toward bearing race of drive screw (31) as shown. Refer to Fig. B20 for legend.

coupling (13) over ends of retarder spring on high speed clutch (14). NOTE: Lower window in coupling should be over lower end of retarder spring as shown (L-Fig. B25). Hook coupling (13-Fig. B20) over edge of low speed clutch (12). Clutch and expander subassembly (Fig. B26) is now assembled. Coat subassembly with grease except for bore in end of high speed clutch (14-Fig. B20) and install in hub. Refer to Fig. B27. Grease hub and brake shoes and assemble shoes into hub. Insert the previously assembled axle, anchor end expander, bearing and brake arm into hub. Lugs on expander must fit into spaces between the brake shoes. Turn the unit over and clamp brake arm end of axle in a soft jawed vise.

Position indexing spring (18-Fig. B20) over sleeve on high speed driving screw. NOTE: Install indexing spring carefully with short lugs (L-Fig. B28) toward bearing race of drive screw. Internal springing pieces will engage cut-outs in sleeve of high speed driving screw. Grease bearing race in the high speed driving screw, locate the eleven loose bearing balls (20) in the race, then install the low speed driving screw as shown. Grease bearing (17-Fig. B20) and install in hub race. NOTE: Closed side of bearing retainer should be out with bearing balls down, against the race in the hub. Hold the driving screws (31 and 32) together and carefully insert into hub while turning clockwise until seated. CAUTION: Be careful when installing to prevent damaging indexing spring (18) or losing bearing balls (20). Grease bearing (24) and insert in race with closed side of retainer out. Screw the adjusting cone and sun gear (25) onto axle until the sun gear just contacts the planet gears, then continue turning sun gear while turning sprocket counter-clockwise. Tighten adjusting cone and sun gear (25) down until seated, then loosen approximately 1/8-turn. Wheel should turn freely with only a slight amount of play at the wheel rim.

TROUBLE SHOOTING. Following is a list of some troubles and possible remedies. Refer to MAINTENANCE or REPAIR section for additional adjustment and disassembly procedures.

1. Unit will not shift. Disassemble hub and inspect indexing spring (18-Fig. B20) and bore of clutch (14).
   a. Make certain that perpendicular lugs on indexing spring are not bent or broken. Renew spring (18) if damaged.
   b. Check for wear on external prongs of indexing spring (18) which drag on notches in bore of clutch (14). Prongs should have turned up ends. Renew spring (18) and/or clutch (14) if damaged.
   c. Assemble clutch (14) and indexing spring (18) on driving screw (31). Rotate clutch back and forth and notice that indexing spring (18) is shifting. Renew damaged parts as necessary.

2. Slips when pedaling forward.
   a. Insufficient retarder pressure. Disassemble and check retarder springs. Pressure of retarder spring (10 - Fig. B20) should be greater than retarder for high speed clutch (14). Turn clutch subassembly (Fig. B26) onto driving screw (31 - Fig. B20). Hold driving screw with one hand and turn anchor end of expander (11) clockwise with other hand. Retarder spring on high speed clutch (14) will slip. Renew retarder spring (10) if it slips with this check.
   b. Engaging clutches worn out. Disassemble and check condition of clutches (12 and 14). Renew clutches and retarder springs if condition is questionable.

3. Pedals rotate backward excessively when brake is applied (indicating slippage).
   a. Insufficient retarder pressure. Renew retarder spring (10-Fig. B20).
   b. Mismatched, damaged or dirty detents on driving clutch (12) or expander (11). Clean or renew parts as necessary.

4. Poor braking or failure to stop as quickly as desired.
   a. Check for highly polished surfaces on inside of hub and outside of brake shoes. Roughen surfaces slightly with coarse emery paper or renew parts. NOTE: Be sure that abrasive is cleaned from parts before assembling.

5. Brake does not release after being applied or drags when bicycle is pedaled forward.
   a. Bearing cone is adjusted too tight. Refer to MAINTENANCE paragraphs for bearing adjustment.
   b. Axle bent. Disassemble and check axle for straightness.

6. Cracking or grinding noises.
   a. Chain dirty, broken or adjusted too tight. Inspect chain and clean, renew or adjust as required.
   b. New sprocket used with old chain or old sprocket used with new chain. It is best to renew chain when it is necessary to install new sprocket because the old sprocket is worn out. Check condition of old sprockets when installing a new chain.
   c. Dust cap rubbing on hub. Check dust caps and renew if bent. Be sure that dust caps are correctly assembled.
   d. Hub bearing is damaged. Disassemble and check condition.

7. Excessive lost motion between forward and backward (braking) position of pedals.
   a. Incorrect bearing cone adjustment. Refer to MAINTENANCE paragraphs and adjust bearings.
   b. Brake shoes or discs worn out. Refer to REPAIRS paragraphs, disassemble and renew brake shoes.

8. Squealing noises when brake is applied.
   a. Lack of lubrication or incorrect type of lubricant. Disassemble and lubricate.

9. Unit binds, detent noise.
   a. Check frame plates to be sure they are parallel. Straighten plates (frame) if necessary. Axle attaching plates on frame are bent if noise disappears when axle attaching nuts are loosened.
   b. Bent axle. Install new axle if bent. Do not attempt to straighten.

Bendix Red Band

MAINTENANCE. Hub should be disassembled, cleaned, inspected and reassembled when difficulty is noticed or approximately every one or two years. Bearings (7, 17 & 24-Fig. B29) can be lubricated with oil without disassembling. NOTE: Do not use gasoline, kerosene or similar solvent which will cause grease to be removed from brake hub. Disassemble the unit if cleaning and inspection is necessary. Be sure to lubricate with grease before and during assembly. Refer to REPAIR section for disassembly and assembly instructions.

Hub bearings should always be correctly adjusted and axle retaining nuts (1 & 30) should be kept tight. Adjust bearings as follows: Remove wheel and hub assembly from bicycle, then loosen lock nut (28). Turn adjusting cone and sun gear (25) onto axle threads until tight while turning the sprocket in opposite direction (counter-clockwise). Back the sun gear out 1/8-turn and tighten lock nut (28). Rim of wheel should have slight play, but bearings should not be loose. Tighten chain and center the wheel in frame, then tighten both axle retaining nuts (1 & 30).

REPAIR. Remove wheel and hub assembly from bicycle, then refer to the following paragraphs.

Shift the hub into lowest speed possible and clamp brake arm end of axle in a soft jawed vise. Hub can be shifted by turning the sprocket counter-clockwise slightly by hand. Check to be sure of correct gear engagement by turning sprocket clockwise. Wheel should be turning slower than sprocket. CAUTION: Coupling (13-Fig. B29) may be damaged if unit is not shifted to low gear when disassembling. Remove lock nut (28) while holding the adjusting cone and sun gear (25) stationary. NOTE: Special tool (part number AB-102) is available for turning the lock nut and special tool (part number BB-100) is used for holding the adjusting cone and sun gear.

Turn sprocket clockwise while unscrewing adjusting cone and sun gear (25) from the axle. Remove ball bearing (24). Turn sprocket counter-clockwise and lift out of hub. NOTE: Turning sprocket will disengage it from high speed clutch (14) and low speed driving screw (41) from low speed driving clutch (39).

NOTE: Bearings (7 and 17) should be reinstalled in original location to preclude unnecessary wear, but they are the same part. Bearing (24) uses the same number (twelve) of ¼-inch bearing

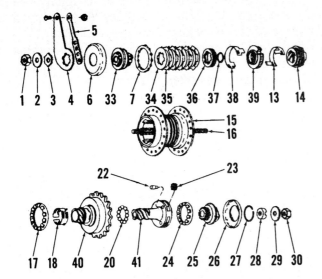

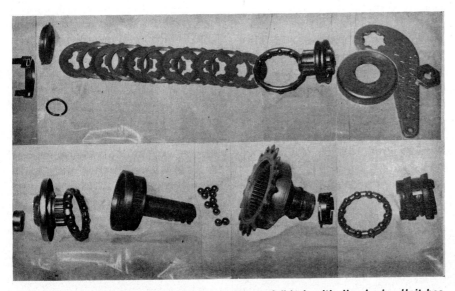

Fig. B29—Exploded view of the "2 Speed Automatic" hub with disc brake. Unit has three red bands around hub for identification.

1. Axle nut	16. Axle	35. External splined brass discs (5 used)
2. Washer	17. Special bearing (same as 7)	
3. Lock nut		36. Pressure plate with retarder spring
4. Brake arm	18. Indexing spring	
5. Brake arm clip	20. Bearing balls 1/4-inch (11 used)	37. Retaining ring
6. Dust cap		38. Retarder coupling
7. Bearing (Do not use No. 68 bearing)	22. Pin (3 used)	39. Low speed driving clutch
	23. Planet gear (3 used)	
13. Retarder coupling	24. Bearing (small retainer)	40. High speed driving screw and sprocket
14. High speed clutch with retarder spring	25. Adjusting cone and sun gear	41. Low speed driving screw
15. Hub	26. Dust cap	
	27. Retaining ring	
	28. Lock nut	
	29. Washer (same as 2)	
	30. Axle nut (same as 1)	
	33. Arm, disc and cone support	
	34. Internal splined steel disc (5 thin, 1 thick)	

balls as the other bearings, but the retainer is different. This bearing (24) is smaller in diameter than the other two bearings.

Remove bearing (17), then lift hub (15) from axle and brake discs. CAUTION: Hub may be difficult to remove or broken discs may fall off if the brake assembly is damaged. Clutches (14 and 39) can be separated by removing coupling (13). Remove retaining ring (37), then lift pressure plate (36), clutch discs (34 and 35) from cone, arm and disc support (33). Remove and install bearing (7) from inner (brake disc) side of support (33). Planet gears (23) can be removed by driving pins (22) out of the driving screw (41).

Inspect parts for wear, breakage or other damage. Lubricate all parts except high speed clutch (14) and indexing spring (18) with grease such as Texaco Regal Starfac No. 2 or equivalent. These two parts (14 and 18) should be oiled when assembling. Bore of driving screws (40 and

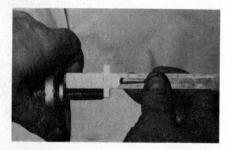

Fig. B30—Approximately 1 1/8 inches of axle should extend beyond expander or support as shown. Lock position by installing lock nut (2-Fig. B29).

41) should be filled with grease when assembling.

Assemble the unit as follows: Grease bearing (7) and push onto support (33). Closed side of retainer should be toward dust cap (6) end of support. Screw axle (16) into support (33) until axle protrudes approximately 1-1/8 inches (Fig. B30). Install dust cap (6-Fig. B29) and brake anchor (4) and tighten lock nut (3). Grease brake discs (34 and 35) while assembling. Five of the internally splined steel discs (34) are thinner than one (thick) disc. Install one thin internal splined disc (34), followed by one brass external splined disc (35). Alternate the thin internal splined discs and the brass external splined discs until all five thin internally splined steel discs and five externally splined brass discs are installed. Install one thick internally splined steel disc, pressure plate (36) and retaining ring (37). Refer to Fig. B31. Hook coupling (38-Fig. B29) over ends of retarder spring of pressure plate (36). Lower window in coupling should be over lower end of retarder spring. NOTE: Coupling (38) has short, flat projections and coupling (13) has longer projections with a lip to catch over edge of the low speed driving clutch (39). Hook coupling (13) over ends of retarder spring on high speed clutch (14). Lower window in coupling should be over lower end of retarder

spring. Hook the projections of coupling (13) over notches in low speed clutch (39). Coat the clutch subassembly (13, 14 & 39) with grease except for bore in end of high speed clutch (14) and install in hub. Insert the previously assembled axle, bearing, brake disc assembly and brake arm assembly into hub. Lugs on the brass external discs (35) must align with grooves in hub and projections on coupling (38) must enter notches in low speed clutch (39) over projections (13). NOTE: Special tool (part number AB-103) is available for aligning the brake friction discs. Turn the unit over and clamp brake arm end of axle in a soft jawed vise.

Position indexing spring (18) over sleeve on high speed driving screw. NOTE: Install indexing spring carefully, with the short lugs (L-Fig. B32) toward bearing race of the drive screw. Internal springing pieces will engage cutouts in sleeve of high speed driving screw. Grease bearing race in the high speed driving screw, locate the eleven loose bearing balls (20-Fig. B29) in race, then install low speed driving screw as shown. Grease bearing (17) and install in hub race. NOTE: Closed side of bearing retainer should be out with bearing balls down, against race in hub. Hold driving screws (40 and 41) together and carefully insert into hub while turning clockwise until seated.

Fig. B31—Disc brake parts should be thoroughly lubricated when assembling. The one thick internal splined disc is shown at (T). Be sure that both windows in coupling (38) are correctly positioned over ends of retarder spring that is installed on pressure plate (36).

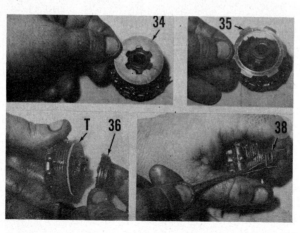

Fig. B32—The three short protruding lugs (L) should be toward bearing race of drive screw (40) as shown.

CAUTION: Be careful when installing to prevent damaging indexing spring (18) or losing bearing balls (20). Grease bearing (24) and insert in race with closed side of retainer out. Screw adjusting cone and sun gear (25) onto axle until sun gear just contacts the planet gears, then continue turning sun gear while turning sprocket counter-clockwise. Tighten adjusting cone and sun gear (25) down until seated, then loosen approximately 1/8-turn. Wheel should turn freely with only a slight amount of play at wheel rim.

TROUBLE SHOOTING. Following is a list of some troubles and possible remedies. Refer to MAINTENANCE or REPAIR section for additional adjustment and disassembly procedures.

1. Unit will not shift. Disassemble hub and inspect indexing spring (18-Fig. B29) and bore of clutch (14).
   a. Make certain that perpendicular lugs on indexing spring are not bent or broken. Renew spring (18) if damaged.
   b. Check for wear on external prongs of indexing spring (18) which drag on notches in bore of clutch (14). Prongs should have turned up ends. Renew spring (18) and/or clutch (14) if damaged.
   c. Assemble clutch (14) and indexing spring (18) on driving screw (40). Rotate clutch back and forth and notice that indexing spring (18) is shifting. Renew damaged parts as necessary.

2. Slips when pedaling forward.
   a. Insufficient retarder pressure. Disassemble and check retarder springs. Install new retarder springs if weak.

   b. Engaging clutches worn out. Disassemble and check condition of clutches (14 and 39). Renew clutches and retarder springs if condition is questionable.

3. Pedals rotate backward excessively when brake is applied (indicating slippage).
   a. Insufficient retarder pressure. Renew retarder spring on pressure plate (36).

4. Poor braking or failure to stop as quickly as desired.
   a. Disassemble and check condition of brake discs (34 and 35).

5. Cracking or grinding noises.
   a. Chain dirty, broken or adjusted too tight. Inspect chain and clean, renew or adjust as required.
   b. New sprocket used with old chain or old sprocket used with new chain. It is best to renew chain when it is necessary to install new sprocket because old sprocket is worn out. Check condition of old sprockets when installing a new chain.

   c. Dust caps rubbing on hub. Check dust caps and renew if bent. Be sure that dust caps are correctly assembled.
   d. Hub bearing is damaged. Disassemble and check condition.

7. Excessive lost motion between forward and backward (braking) position of pedals.
   a. Incorrect bearing cone adjustment. Refer to MAINTENANCE paragraphs and adjust bearings.
   b. Brake discs worn out. Refer to REPAIRS paragraphs, disassemble and renew brake discs.

8. Squealing noises when brake is applied.
   a. Lack of lubrication or incorrect type of lubricant. Disassemble and lubricate.

9. Unit binds, detent noise.
   a. Check frame plates to be sure they are parallel. Straighten plates (frame) if necessary. Axle attaching plates on frame are bent if noise disappears when axle attaching nuts are loosened.
   b. Bent axle. Install new axle if bent. Do not attempt to straighten.

Sachs Torpedo Duomatic

The model 101 hub is not equipped with brake and model 102 has a back-pedal type brake. Both models are shifted by pack pedaling a small amount. Gears automatically change from low to high and from high to low.

MAINTENANCE. Hub should be lubricated with oil through fitting (11-Fig. S5) at approximately monthly intervals. Hub should be disassembled, cleaned and thoroughly lubricated with grease at least once each year. Hub should be disassembled and thoroughly lubricated more often on 102 models if brake is used extensively. Refer to the REPAIR paragraphs for disassembly instructions.

Hub bearings should be adjusted to permit wheel to rotate freely without excessive play. Adjust bearings, by loosening axle nut (1) and lock nut (3A), then turning bearing adjusting nut (3B). A special spanner wrench (Sachs part number 0324 100 100) is available for turning nuts (3A, 3B & 38). Tighten lock nut (3A) after turning adjusting nut (3B). Be sure to recheck bearing adjustment after tightening lock nut (3A).

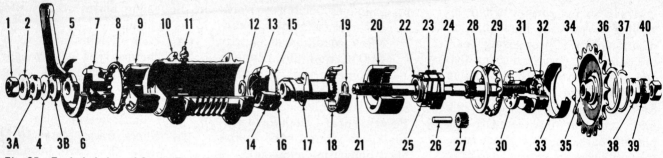

1 2 5 7 8 9 10 11 12 13 15 19 20 22 23 24 28 29 31 32 34 36 37 40

3A 4 3B 6 14 16 17 18 21 25 26 27 30 33 35 38 39

Fig. S5—Exploded view of Sachs Torpedo Duomatic two speed hub. Model 102 with brake pedal is shown but model 101 hubs are similar except for brake parts.

1. Axle nut	8. Ball bearing	15. Retaining ring	22. Friction spring	27. Planet gear (3 used)	32. Dust cap
2. Washer	(S2049)	16. Pawl for brake cone	23. Pawl for pawl	28. Washer for planet	33. Dust cap
3A. Lock nut	9. Brake shell	(2 used)	carrier (4 used)	gear carrier	34. Sprocket
3B. Adjusting nut	10. Hub	17. Drive bushing	24. Retaining rings (2	29. Ball bearing	35. Fixed cone
4. Lock washer	11. Lubrication fitting	18. Drive ring	used)	(S2049)	36. Washer
5. Brake arm	12. Snap ring	19. Thrust washer	25. Pawl carrier	30. Planet gear carrier	37. Retaining ring
6. Dust cap	13. Friction spring	20. Internal gear	26. Pivot for planet	31. Ball bearing	38. Lock nut
7. Lever cone	14. Brake cone	21. Axle	gear (3 used)	(S2048)	39. Washer
					40. Axle nut

REPAIR. Remove wheel and hub from bicycle, then proceed as follows: Grip the sprocket end of axle (21-Fig. S5) in a soft jawed vise. Remove nut (1), washer (2), lock nut (3A), washer (4) and adjusting nut (3B). Lever (5), dust cap (6), lever cone (7), bearing (8) and brake shell (9) can be lifted out of hub. Lift hub (10) off of the remaining parts. Turn brake cone (14) counter-clockwise to remove from drive bushing (17). Lift drive ring (18) and internal gear (20) off. Remove lock washer (12), then pull drive bushing (17) off of axle. NOTE: Be careful not to lose thrust washer (19). Remove nut (40), washer (39), nut (38) and fixed cone (35), then remove the remaining parts from axle.

Clean and inspect all parts especially bearings and bearing races (7, 8, 10, 29, 30, 31 & 35). Special petroleum jelly and oil mixture is available from Sachs (Part No. 0369 111 000) for lubricating the disassembled axle. Lubricate all parts before and during assembly. Approximately 2 cc of grease is required for lubricating the brake shell (9) and 1 cc is required for planet gear assembly (26, 27, 30, 31 and 32). Be sure to grease the groove for friction ring (13).

Use the following procedure

when assembling: Grease bearing (31) and locate in bearing race of planet carrier (30) with closed side of bearing carrier toward outside. Press dust cap (32) into bore of planet carrier. Assemble planet gears (27) and pivot shafts (26) in carrier (30). Slide planet carrier assembly (26, 27, 30, 31 & 32) onto axle (21) with internal teeth of planet carrier toward long side of axle. NOTE: Long side of axle is determined by lengths at sides of axle gear. Install fixed cone (35) and tighten nut (38) against fixed cone. Clamp axle (21) in a soft jawed vise, next to the fixed bearing cone (35). Grease bearing (29) and position on planet carrier (30) with closed side of bearing carrier toward sprocket (34). Position washer (28) over carrier and thrust washer (19) over axle. note; Thrust washer (19) should be inside the internal teeth of planet carrier. Install internal gear (20) over planet gears. Insert pawl carrier assembly (22, 23, 24 & 25) over axle and into gear (20). NOTE: Friction spring (22) should be toward side shown. It may be necessary to compress pawls (23) when inserting into gear (20). Install drive bushing (17) over axle, with gear inside pawl carrier (25). NOTE: Rotate drive bushing (17) so that gear will engage teeth of planet wheel

carrier (30). Groove in axle should be accessible for easy installation of snap ring (12). Install drive ring (18) with ridge on outside diameter against the internal gear (20). Turn brake friction cone assembly (13, 14, 15 & 16) onto drive bushing (17). NOTE: Friction spring (13) must be on side shown and hole in underside of brake cone (14) must engage end of friction spring (22). Position hub (10) over the assembled parts on axle. NOTE: Two of the teeth inside hub (10) are shorter than the others. The two short teeth are opposite each other and should engage the two projections on drive ring (18). Insert brake shell (9) with retaining lugs up toward lever cone (7). Slots in other end of brake shell (9) should engage ends of friction spring (13). Position bearing (8) in hub race with closed side of bearing carrier toward outside. Install lever cone (7) with the two slots engaging the lugs on brake shell (9). Turn adjusting nut (3B) onto axle threads to remove excessive bearing play. NOTE: Do not tighten nut (3B) enough to cause bearings to bind. Install lock washer (4) and lock nut (3A). Recheck bearing adjustment after tightening lock nut (3A). Change setting of nut (3B) if bearing adjustment is incorrect with lock nut (3A) tightened.

Three Speed Rear Hubs

Brampton

Refer to the following service section for Sturmey Archer AW hub while repairing Brampton three speed unit. Design and even some parts are identical.

Hercules

Refer to the following service section for Sturmey Archer AW hub while repairing Hercules three speed unit. Design and even some parts are identical.

Sachs Torpedo

The model 415 hub is not equipped with a brake and bicycles using the 415 hub are usually equipped with a rim acting caliper rear brake. Model 515 hub is equipped with a back-pedal type brake. Both models are manually shifted by a handle bar mounted gear shift control. A neutral position is located between the III (high) gear position and II (Middle) gear position. The II (middle) gear position drives the rear wheel at the same speed as the sprocket. Low gear (I position) drives the rear wheel at a 26.6 per cent speed reduction. High gear (III position) drives the rear wheel at an increased (approximately 36 per cent faster than the sprocket) speed.

Sachs Model 415

MAINTENANCE. Hub should be lubricated with oil through fitting (9-Fig. S11) at approximately monthly intervals. Lubricate hub more often if used on long tours. Hub should be disassembled, cleaned and thoroughly lubricated with grease at least once each year. Refer to the REPAIR paragraphs for disassembly instructions. Remove control wire from housing and lubricate the wire and control mechanism occasionally to insure smooth movement.

Hub bearings should be adjusted to permit the wheel to rotate freely without excessive play. Adjust bearings after loosening axle nut (1-Fig. S12) and lock nut (3) on left side. Turn bearing adjusting nut (5) as required to adjust the bearings. A special spanner wrench (Sachs part number 0524 001 200) is available for turning nuts (3, 5 & 45). Tighten lock nut (3) after adjusting nut (5). Recheck bearing adjustment after tightening lock nut (3).

CONTROL ADJUSTMENT. Correct adjustment is important to prevent damage to the hub and

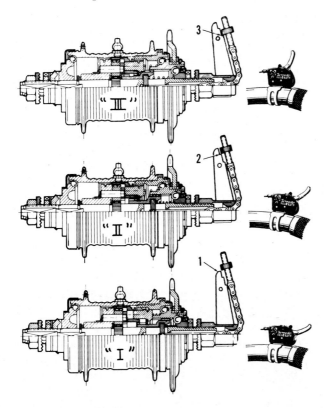

Fig. S10—Cross sectional drawings of 415 hub in I [low] position, II [medium] position and III [high speed] position. Gear reduction in low gear [I] position and overdrive in high gear [III] position are accomplished by the planetary gear set in the hub. Medium [II] position provides a normal 1 to 1 relation between the sprocket and the hub.

Fig. S11—View of 415 hub (TOP) and 515 hub (BOTTOM). Lubrication fitting is shown at (9) and adjusting gage at (48). Bearing adjustment is accomplished by loosening nut (3) and turning the adjusting nut (5).

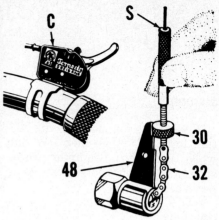

Fig. S13—View of shift control (C) and control chain (32). Sleeve (S) on end of control cable is threaded onto end of control chain and locked with nut (30).

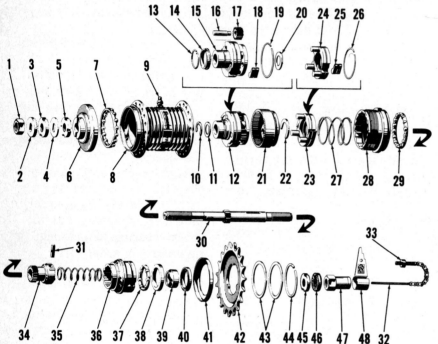

Fig. S12—Exploded views of the 415 hub.

1. Left axle nut	14. Locating sleeve	25. Pawl (same as 18)	39. Fixed cone
2. Plate	15. Planet carrier	26. Pawl spring ring	40. Cone dust cap
3. Lock nut	16. Journal pin (3 used)	27. Spring	41. Dust cover
4. Lock washer	17. Planet gear (3 used)	28. Ratchet bushing	42. Sprocket (17 to 22 teeth)
5. Adjusting nut	18. Ratchet pawl (4 used)	29. Bearing (S1020)	43. Spacer washers (2 used)
6. Bearing cone	19. Pawl spring ring	30. Axle	44. Retaining ring
7. Bearing (S2049)	20. Thrust washer	31. Sliding block	45. Lock nut (same as 3)
8. Hub	21. Gear ring	32. Pull rod & chain	46. Plate (same as 2)
9. Lubrication fitting	22. Gear change plate	33. Lock nut	47. Chain guide axle nut
10. Snap ring	23. Pawl carrier assembly	34. Clutch gear	48. Adjusting gage
11. Thrust washer	24. Pawl carrier	35. Spring	
12. Planet carrier assembly		36. Driver	
13. Retaining ring		37. Bearing (S2048)	
		38. Driver dust cap	

and again check location of lock nut (1). Adjust shift cable if edge of the lock nut does not align as shown at (1, 2 & 3) or if shift control will not stay in I position. Shift cable can be adjusted in two ways. Normally the threaded adjusting sleeve (S-Fig. S13) can be turned onto threaded part of chain. Be sure to lock the adjustment with nut (30) after correctly set. Control cable pulleys (P-Fig. S14) can be relocated if turning the sleeve (S-Fig. S13) will not provide correct adjustment.

Adjustment can be accomplished without using the special gage, by adjusting controls to provide free turning of pedals in NEUTRAL position. Adjustment in this way is usually more difficult and more care should be exercised. Be sure to check operation in gears I, II and III and recheck NEUTRAL position.

REPAIR. Remove wheel and hub from bicycle, refer to Fig. S12 and proceed as follows: Remove axle nuts (1 & 47) and washers (2 & 46). Clamp sprocket end of axle (30) in a soft jawed vise and remove lock nut (3) and washer (4). NOTE: Special tool (part number 0524 001 200) is available from manufacturer for turning nuts (3, 5 & 45). Remove adjusting nut (5), bearing cone (6)

for rider safety. Shift the control to the high (III) position and move the pedals backward slightly to shift the hub. Attach special gage (48-Fig. S12 or Fig. S13) and locate gage parallel with the control chain. Turn lock nut down until edge is flush with lower step of gage as shown at (3-Fig. S10). Move shift control to II position and check location of lock nut (2). Move shift control to I position move snap ring (10) and thrust washer (11), then lift planet carrier assembly (12) and ring gear (21) off of axle. Refer to Fig. S15. Push one side of pawl carrier down (Fig. S16) and remove gear change plate (22). Lift pawl carrier (23-Fig. S12), large spring (27), ratchet bushing (28) and bearing (29) off. Unscrew control chain (32) from sliding block (31) and remove lock nut (45). Remaining parts can then be removed from axle and disassembled for inspection and lubrication. CAUTION: Do not damage spring rings (19 and 26) or retaining ring (13) when removing.

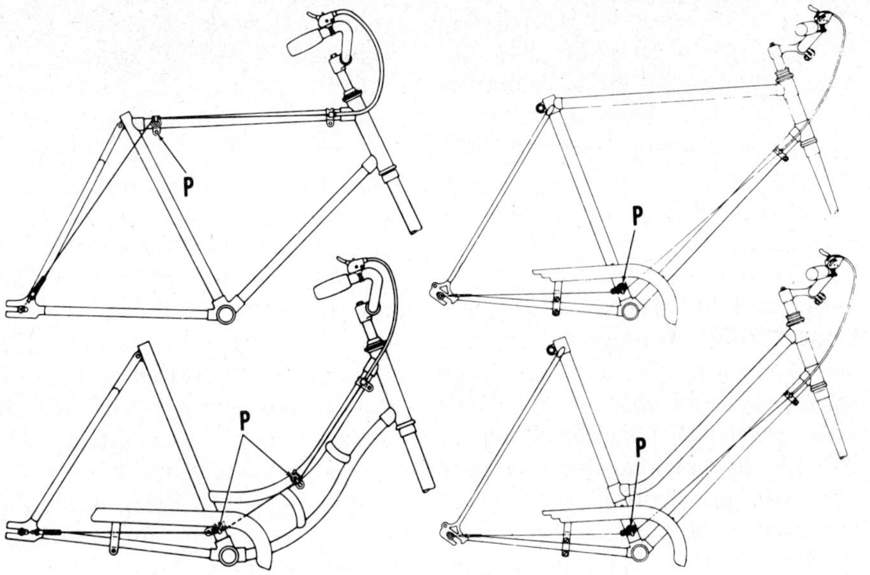

Assemble spring ring (19-Fig. S17) on carrier with locating slots (S) between ends of the spring ring. Slide pawls (18-Fig. S18) under spring ring (19). Coat both sides of thrust washer (20-Fig. S12) with Molykote Paste G (molybdenum disulphide) or graphite containing grease. Locate thrust washer (20-Fig. S19) in recess of planet carrier. Coat planet gears (17-Fig. S12) and journal pins (16) with 50:50 mixture of petroleum jelly and oil. Slide planet gears into position in carrier, then insert journal pins (16) with smaller end toward large end of planet carrier. Slide the locating sleeve (14-Fig. S20) onto planet carrier with large diameter against planet gear journal pins (16). Retaining ring (13)

Fig. S14—Location of the pulley (P) can be changed to adjust control cable. Be sure that pulley is straight so that cable will not fall off.

Fig. S15—View showing method of removing snap ring (10-Fig. S12).

and bearing (7). Grip the ratchet bushing (28) in a soft jawed vise or in special tool (number 0583 101 000) and unscrew unit from hub (8). The unit is equipped with standard (right hand) thread. Re-

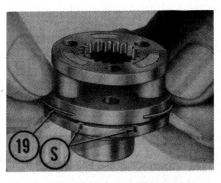

Fig. S17—Locate pawl retaining ring with ends between slots (S) of carrier.

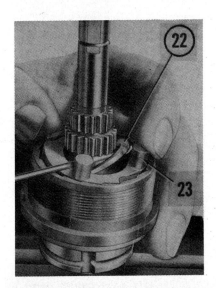

Fig. S16—View showing method of removing gear change plate (22-Fig. S12).

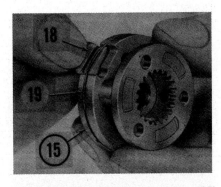

Fig. S18—View of planet carrier (15) showing installation of pawls (18) under retaining spring ring (19).

Fig. S19—Thrust washer (20) should be lubricated with molybdenum disulphide or graphite grease while assembling.

should fit into recess in carrier shoulder. Install spring ring (26-Fig. S21) in groove of pawl carrier (24), with locating slot (S) between ends of spring ring. NOTE: Ends of spring ring (19-Fig. S17) are further apart than ends of spring ring (26-Fig. S21) and the two spring rings can be identified by the width of the gap. Slide pawls (25-Fig. S22) under the installed spring ring.

Lubricate bearing (37-Fig. S12) with bearing grease and insert into bore of driver (36) with closed side of bearing carrier toward outside. Press dust cap (38) into bore of driver, with cupped (open) side toward outside of driver.

Grease axle (30) and slide clutch gear (34) into position on right end of axle. Align hole in clutch gear and hole in axle and insert the sliding block (31) through both pieces. NOTE: Rounded side of sliding block (31) should be toward gear on axle (30). Screw pull rod (32) into sliding block. Lubricate splines in

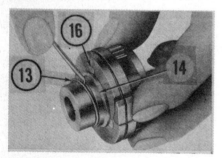

Fig. S20—Large diameter of retaining ring (14) should hold journal pins (16) in place. Retaining ring (13) should fit into groove in planet carrier.

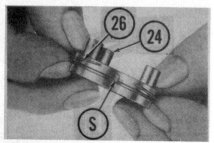

Fig. S21 — Ends of spring ring (26) should be at sides of slot (S) when seated in groove of pawl carrier (24).

driver (36) and position over splines of clutch gear (34). Oil small spring (35) lightly and install over axle, then install fixed cone (39). Tighten lock nut (45), to hold the fixed cone in position.

Clamp axle in a soft jawed vise with pull rod and chain (32) down. Grease bearing (29) and install over race of driver (36) with closed side of bearing carrier down (toward sprocket). Oil large spring (27) and position on driver (36). Position ratchet bushing (28), oil the pawl carrier assembly (23) and position pawl carrier assembly over axle on large spring (27). Push the pawl carrier down while guiding pawls into ratchet dogs, then install the horse shoe collar as shown in (Fig. S23). NOTE: Insert horse shoe collar between the two pins which are furthest apart. Grease bore of ring gear (21-Fig. S12) and position onto pins of pawl carrier (23). NOTE: The three drive pins are unequally spaced. Oil planet carrier assembly (12) lightly and locate over axle and into ring gear (21). Grease thrust washer (11) and slide down over axle. Press snap ring (10) into groove. Remove unit from vise and check for freedom of operation. Screw assembled unit, including ratchet bushing (28), into the hub (8).

Lubricate bearing (7) with grease and position in hub. Closed side of bearing carrier should be toward outside. Install the bearing cone (6).

Adjust hub bearings by turning nut (5) to permit wheel to rotate

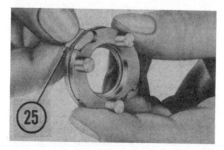

Fig. S22—Slide pawls (25) under the spring ring as shown.

freely without excessive play. Tighten lock nut (3) after setting nut (5) and be sure to recheck bearing adjustment after tightening lock nut (3). A special wrench (part number 0524 001 200) is available from the manufacturer for turning nuts (3, 5 & 45).

NOTE: Do not attempt to adjust bearings by loosening nut (45). This nut should be tight against fixed cone (39) and should only be loosened in correct sequence when disassembling the hub as previously outlined.

Refer to CONTROL ADJUSTMENT paragraphs for adjusting the control cable.

TROUBLE SHOOTING. The following lists some troubles and possible remedies. Refer to the appropriate MAINTENANCE, CONTROL ADJUSTMENT or REPAIR section for more detailed service procedures.

1. Hub slips when pedaling forward.
    a. Wrong gear adjustment. Adjust controls.
    b. Wrong grease causes the pawls to stick. Disassemble hub, clean and lubricate using correct lubricant.

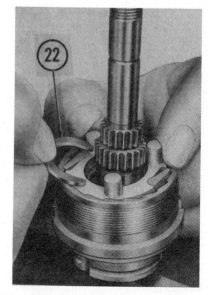

Fig. S23—Hold pawl carrier down as shown and install horse shoe collar (22) under teeth of clutch gear.

c. Wrong installation of pawl spring rings (19 & 26-Fig. S12) permitting pawls (18 & 25) to fall out of pockets. Ends of spring rings should be on sides of locating slots (S-Fig. S17 and S21). Disassemble and inspect for damage.

d. Wrong installation or damage to ball bearings (7, 29 & 37 - Fig. S12). Clean and inspect bearings and races. Renew parts as necessary, lubricate, assemble and adjust bearings.

e. Broken teeth on planetary gears. Inspect and renew parts as required.

f. Lugs on drive chain sprockets broken or worn off. Renew parts as necessary.

2. No shifting of gears.

a. Wrong gear adjustment. Adjust controls.

b. Sliding block (31-Fig. S12) broken, caused by incorrect assembly. Clutch teeth (34 & 36) not correctly engaged when fixed cone (39) was tightened. Renew parts as necessary.

c. Pull rod and chain (32) damaged. Renew and check threads in sliding block (31).

d. Shift cable and/or pulleys damaged. Renew parts as necessary.

e. Control lever damaged. Check very carefully. Lubricate or renew control lever as necessary.

3. Stiff changing of gears.

a. Chain links of pull rod (32) too stiff, caused by damage or rust, etc. Lubricate or renew as necessary.

b. Pull rod caught in guide nut (47). Renew nut and/or pull rod as necessary.

c. Bad positioning of cable. Check for misalignment, bends, etc. Relocate or renew as necessary.

d. Dry or rusted cable in housing or guide pulleys. Renew or lubricate.

e. Bent or squeezed cable housing. Renew cable and housing.

4. Wheel hard to turn.

a. Wheel bearings incorrectly adjusted. Bearings may be adjusted too loose or too tight. Readjust bearings. Disassemble and check for damage if condition is questionable.

5. Too much axial play in rear wheel.

a. Axle nuts (1 & 47) loose. Adjust chain and tighten nuts. Be sure that wheel is centered in frame.

b. Bearing adjustment too loose. Refer to MAINTENANCE section for adment procedure.

c. Worn-out or damaged bearings. Refer to REPAIR section for disassembly, lubrication and adjustment procedure.

6. Pedals move when free-wheeling.

a. Hub bearings adjusted too tight or lock nuts (3 and 45) loose. Recheck bearing adjustment.

b. Chain too tight. Adjust chain to have slight play.

7. Noises: Squealing noise when pedaling forward, knocking when pedaling forward at normal or high speed can all be caused by similar problems.

a. Wrong or not enough lubricant. Hub should be disassembled, cleaned, inspected, lubricated and reassembled.

b. Bearing noises are most often caused by dry or damaged bearings. Disassemble, clean, inspect and renew, if necessary.

Sachs Model 515

MAINTENANCE. Hub should be lubricated with oil through fitting (9-Fig. S25) at approximately monthly intervals. Lubricate hub more often if used on long tours. Hub should be disassembled, cleaned and thoroughly lubricated with grease at least once each year. Hub should be disassembled and lubricated more often if the brake is used extensively. Refer to the REPAIR paragraphs for disassembly instructions. Remove control wire from housing and lubricate wire and control mechanism occasionally to insure smooth movement.

Hub bearings should be adjusted to permit wheel to rotate freely without excessive play. Adjust bearings after loosening axle nut (1) and lock nut (3) on left side. Turn bearing adjusting nut (5) as required to adjust bearings. A special spanner wrench (Sachs part number 0524 001 200) is available for turning nuts (3, 5, & 45). Tighten lock nut (3) after adjusting nut (5). Recheck bearing adjustment after tightening lock nut (3).

CONTROL ADJUSTMENT. Correct adjustment is important to prevent damage to hub and for rider safety. Shift control to high (III) position and move pedals backward slightly to shift hub. Attach special gage (48-Fig. S25) and locate gage parallel with control chain. Turn lock nut down until edge is flush with lower step of gage as shown at (3-Fig. S10).

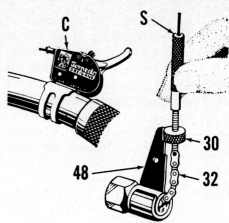

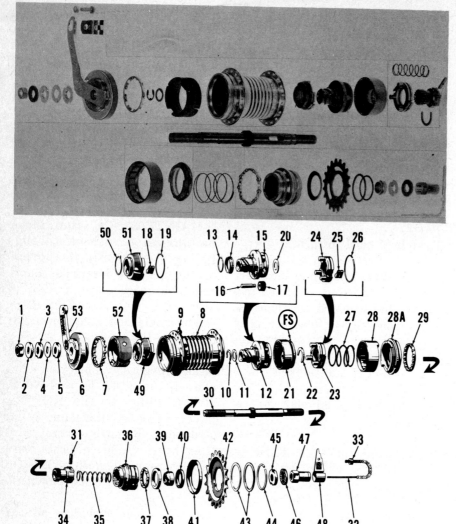

Fig. S26—View of shift control (C) and control chain (32). Sleeve (S) on end of control cable is threaded onto end of control chain and locked with nut (30).

Fig. S25—Exploded view of Sachs 515 hub. Friction spring (FS) is no longer used and should be removed from early units.

1. Left axle nut	16. Jounal pin (3 used)	29. Bearing (S1020)	43. Spacer washers (2 used)
2. Plate	17. Planet gear (3 used)	30. Axle	44. Retaining ring
3. Lock nut	18. Ratchet pawl (4 used)	31. Sliding block	45. Lock nut (same as 3)
4. Lock washer	19. Pawl spring ring	32. Pull rod & chain	46. Plate (same as 2)
5. Adjusting nut	20. Thrust washer	33. Lock nut	47. Chain guide axle nut
6. Bearing cone	21. Gear ring	34. Clutch gear	48. Adjusting gage
7. Bearing (S2049)	22. Gear change plate	35. Spring	49. Braking cone assembly
8. Hub	23. Pawl carrier assembly	36. Driver	50. Friction spring
9. Lubrication fitting	24. Pawl carrier	37. Bearing (S2048)	51. Braking cone
10. Snap ring	25. Pawl (same as 18)	38. Driver dust cap	52. Braking shell
11. Thrust washer	26. Pawl spring ring	39. Fixed cone	53. Brake lever
12. Planet carrier assembly	27. Spring	40. Cone dust cap	
13. Retaining ring	28. Ratchet bushing	41. Dust cover	
14. Locating sleeve	28A. Retainer	42. Sprocket (17 to 22 teeth)	
15. Planet carrier			

Move shift control to II position and check location of lock nut (2). Move shift control to I position and again check location of lock nut (1). Adjust shift cable if edge of lock nut does not align as shown at (1, 2 and 3) or if shift control will not stay in I position. Shift cable can be adjusted in two ways. Normally the threaded adjusting sleeve (S-Fig. S26) can be turned onto threaded part of chain. Be sure to lock the adjustment with nut (30) after correctly set. Control cable pulleys (P-Fig. S27) can be relocated if turning the sleeve (S-Fig. S26) will not provide correct adjustment.

Adjustment can be accomplished without using the special gage by adjusting controls to provide free turning of pedals in NEUTRAL position. Adjustment in this way is usually more difficult and more care should be exercised. Be sure to check operation in gears I, II and III and recheck NEUTRAL position.

REPAIR. Remove wheel and hub from bicycle, refer to Fig. S25, and proceed as follows: Remove axle nuts (1 and 47) and washers (2 and 46). Clamp sprocket end of axle (30) in a soft jawed vise and remove lock nut (3) and washer (4). NOTE: Special tool (part number 0524 001 200) is available from manufacturer for turning nuts (3, 5 and 45). Remove adjusting nut (5), bearing cone (6) and bearing (7). Turn the driver (36) to push brake shell (52) and brake cone assembly (49) out of hub (8). Grip retainer (28A) in a soft jawed vise or in special tool (number 0583 101 000) and unscrew unit from hub (8). Unit is equipped with standard (right hand) thread. Remove snap ring (10) and thrust washer (11). Then lift planet carrier assembly (12) and ring gear (21) from axle.

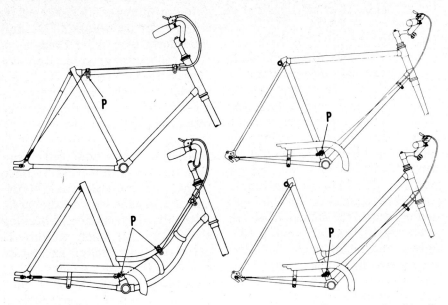

Fig. S31—View of brake cone showing method of installing pawls (18) under spring (19). Friction spring (50) must be installed in direction shown.

Fig. S27—Location of the pulley (P) can be changed to adjust control cable. Be sure that pulley is straight so that cable will not fall off.

Fig. S28—View showing method of removing snap ring (10-Fig. S25).

Refer to Fig. S28. Push one side of pawl carrier down (Fig. S29) and remove gear change plate (22). Lift pawl carrier (23-Fig. S25), large spring (27), ratchet bushing (28), retainer (28A) and bearing (29) off. Unscrew control chain (32) from sliding block (31) and remove lock nut (45). Remaining parts can then be removed from axle and disassembled for inspection and lubrication. CAUTION: Do not damage spring rings (19 and 26) or retaining ring (13) when removing.

Assemble spring ring (19-Fig. S30) on brake cone (51) with locating slots (S) between ends of

spring ring. Slide pawls (18-Fig. S31) under spring ring and install friction spring (50) in correct direction as shown. Coat both sides of thrust washer (20-Fig. S25) with Molykote Paste G (molybdenum disulphide) or graphite containing grease. Locate thrust washer (20-Fig. S32) in recess of planet carrier. Coat planet gears (17-Fig. S25) and journal pins (16) with 50:50 mixture of petroleum jelly and oil. Slide planet gears into position in carrier, then insert journal pins (16) with smaller end toward large end of planet carrier. Slide locating sleeve (14-Fig. S33) onto planet carrier with large diameter against planet gear journal pins (16). Retaining ring (13) should fit into recess in carrier shoulder. Install spring

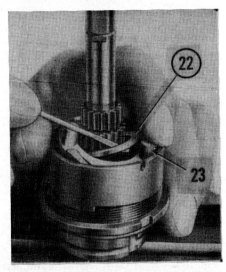

Fig. S29—View showing method of removing gear change plate (22-Fig. S25).

Fig. S30—Locate pawl retaining spring ring with ends between slots (S) of the brake cone. Refer to Fig. S31 for installation of friction spring.

Fig. S32—Thrust washer (20) should be lubricated with molybdenum disulphide or graphite grease while assembling. Planet carrier shown is for 415 models but assembly is similar for 515 models.

ring (26-Fig. S34) in groove of pawl carrier (24), with locating slot (S) between ends of spring ring. NOTE: Ends of spring ring (19-Fig. S30) are further apart than ends of spring ring (26-Fig. S34) and the two spring rings can be identified by the width of the gap. Slide pawls (25-Fig. S35) under the installed spring ring.

Some early 515 models may have a friction spring (FS-Fig. S25) installed in groove of ring gear (21). Later units are not equipped with the friction spring and latest models do not have a groove in the ring gear. It is suggested that friction spring (FS) be discarded from early models so equipped, when the unit is being serviced.

Lubricate bearing (37) with bearing grease and insert into bore of driver (36) with closed side of bearing carrier toward outside. Press dust cap (38) into bore of driver, with cupped

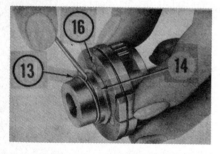

Fig. S33—Large diameter of retaining ring (14) should hold journal pins (16) in place. Retaining ring (13) should fit into groove in planet carrier. Model 415 unit is shown but 515 is similar.

(open) side toward outside of driver.

Grease axle (30) and slide clutch gear (34) into position on right end of axle. Align hole in clutch gear and hole in axle and insert sliding block (31) through both pieces. NOTE: Rounded side of sliding block (31) should be toward gear on axle (30). Screw pull rod (32) into sliding block. Lubricate splines in driver (36) and position over splines of clutch gear (34). Oil small spring (35) lightly and install over the axle, then install fixed cone (39). Tighten lock nut (45), to hold fixed cone in position.

Clamp axle in a soft jawed vise with the pull rod and chain (32) down. Grease bearing (29) and install over race of driver (36) with closed side of bearing carrier down (toward sprocket). Oil large spring (27) and position on driver (36). Position retainer (28A) and ratchet (28) on axle and driver, oil pawl carrier assembly (23) and position pawl carrier assembly over axle on large spring (27). Push pawl carrier down while guiding pawls into ratchet dogs, then install horse shoe collar as shown in Fig. S36. NOTE: Insert horse shoe collar between the two pins which are furthest apart. Grease bore of ring gear (21-Fig. S25) and position onto pins of pawl carrier (23). NOTE: The three drive pins are unequally spaced. Oil planet carrier assembly (12) lightly and locate over

axle and into ring gear (21). Grease thrust washer (11) and slide down over axle. Press snap ring (10) into groove. Remove unit from the vise and check for freedom of operation. Screw the assembled unit, including ratchet retainer (28A), into hub (8).

Oil the brake cone assembly (49) lightly and screw it onto planet carrier (12). CAUTION: Do not grease the brake cone assembly. Coat outside of braking shell (52) with 50:50 mixture of petroleum jelly and oil and locate in hub so that slot engages end of friction spring (50). Pack about 3 cc of petroleum jelly and oil mixture into the braking shell.

Lubricate bearing (7) with grease and position in hub. Closed side of bearing carrier should be toward outside. Install bearing cone (6). NOTE: Be sure that notches in cone (6) correctly engage projections on braking shell (52).

Adjust hub bearings by turning nut (5) to permit wheel to rotate freely without excessive play. Tighten lock nut (3) after setting

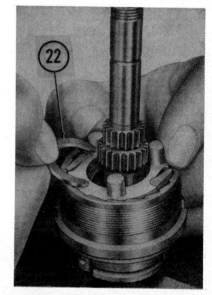

Fig. S36—Hold pawl carrier down as shown and install horse shoe collar (22) under teeth of clutch gear.

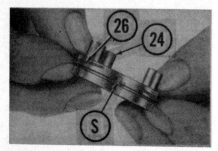

Fig. S34—Ends of spring ring (26) should be at sides of slot (S) when seated in groove of pawl carrier (24).

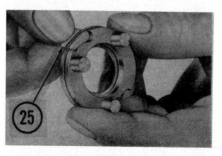

Fig. S35—Slide pawls (25) under the spring ring as shown.

nut (5) and be sure to recheck bearing adjustment after tightening lock nut (3). A special wrench (part number 0524 001 200) is available from the manufacturer for turning nuts (3, 5 & 45).

NOTE: Do not attempt to adjust bearings by loosening nut (45). This nut should be tight against fixed cone (39) and should only be loosened in correct sequence when disassembling the hub as previously outlined.

Refer to CONTROL ADJUSTMENT paragraphs for adjusting the control cable.

TROUBLE SHOOTING. The following lists some troubles and possible remedies. Refer to the appropriate MAINTENANCE, CONTROL ADJUSTMENT or REPAIR section for more detailed service procedures.

1. Hub slips when pedaling forward.
   a. Wrong gear adjustment. Adjust Controls.
   b. Wrong grease causes pawls to stick. Disassemble hub, clean and lubricate using correct lubricant.
   c. Wrong installation of pawl spring rings (19 & 26-Fig. S25), permitting pawls (18 and 25) to fall out of pockets. Ends of spring rings should be on sides of locating slots (S-Fig. S30 and S34). Disassemble and inspect for damage.
   d. Wrong installation or damage to ball bearings (7, 29 and 37-Fig. S25). Clean and inspect bearings and races. Renew parts as necessary, lubricate, assemble and adjust bearings.
   e. Broken teeth on planetary gears. Inspect and renew parts as required.

   f. Lugs on drive chain sprockets broken or worn off. Renew parts as necessary.

2. No shifting of gears.
   a. Wrong gear adjustment. Adjust controls.
   b. Sliding block (31-Fig. S25) broken, caused by incorrect assembly. Clutch teeth (34 & 36) not correctly engaged when fixed cone (39) was tightened. Renew parts as necessary.
   c. Pull rod and chain (32) damaged. Renew and check threads in sliding block (31).
   d. Shift cable and/or pulleys damaged. Renew parts as necessary.
   e. Control lever damaged. Check very carefully. Lubricate or renew control lever as necessary.

3. Stiff changing of gears.
   a. Chain links of pull rod (32) too stiff, caused by damage or rust, etc. Lubricate or renew as necessary.
   b. Pull rod caught in guide nut (47). Renew nut and/ or pull rod as necessary.
   c. Bad positioning of cable. Check for misalignment, bends, etc. Relocate or renew as necessary.
   d. Dry or rusted cable in housing or guide pulleys. Renew or lubricate.
   e. Bent or squeezed cable housing. Renew cable and housing.

4. Wheel hard to turn.
   a. Wheel bearings incorrectly adjusted. Bearings may be adjusted too loose or too tight. Readjust bearings. Disassemble and check for damage if condition is questionable.

   b. Brake arm may have twisted causing bearings to be twisted. Clip should be used to hold brake arm (53) to bicycle frame.

5. Too much axial play in rear wheel.
   a. Axle nuts (1 and 47) loose. Adjust chain and tighten nuts. Be sure that wheel is centered in frame.
   b. Bearing adjustment too loose. Refer to MAINTENANCE section for adjustment procedure.
   c. Worn-out or damaged bearings. Refer to REPAIR section for disassembly, lubrication and adjustment procedure.

6. Pedals move when freewheeling.
   a. Hub bearings adjusted too tight or lock nuts (3 and 45) loose. Recheck bearing adjustment.
   b. Chain too tight. Adjust chain to have slight play.

7. Hub slips when braking.
   a. Wrong gear adjustment. Adjust controls.
   b. Wrong grease, brake cylinder slips. Disassemble hub, clean and lubricate using correct lubricant.
   c. Insufficient or no friction at brake cylinder. Renew friction spring (50). Be sure to lubricate groove and install in correct direction.

8. Abrupt braking or locking of the hub.
   a. Braking parts dry, rusted, galled or not lubricated. Disassemble, inspect, lubricate and install new parts if damaged.
   b. Clip holding brake lever (53) to frame too large. Install clip that fits.

9. Brake sticks after application.
   a. The large square thread inside brake cone (49) and on end of planet carrier (15) is rusted and/or dry. Disassemble, clean and lubricate.
   b. Braking surface of cone (6) rusted and/or dry. Disassemble, clean and lubricate.
   c. Gear on axle (30) dry. Disassemble, clean and lubricate.

10. Noises: Squealing noise when pedaling forward, knocking when pedaling forward at normal or high speed and brake noises can all be caused by similar problems.
   a. Wrong or not enough lubricant. Hub should be disassembled, cleaned, inspected, lubricated and reassembled.

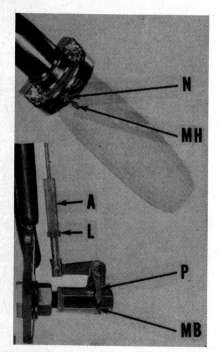

Fig. SH11—Control adjustment can usually be accomplished by turning adjuster (A).

A. Adjuster	MH. Handgrip mark
L. Lock nut	N. Normal mark
MB. Belcrank mark	P. Pointer

b. Bearing noises are most often caused by dry or damaged bearings. Disassemble, clean, inspect and renew, if necessary.

Schwinn Approved Styre

Refer to the following service section for Sturmey Archer AW hub while repairing Schwinn Approved Styre three speed unit. Design and even some parts are identical.

Shimano 3.3.3. Without Back Pedaling Brake

This three speed rear hub is shifted by a handlebar mounted remote control. Unit may be shifted while pedalling lightly, but it is recommended that the unit be shifted while coasting whenever possible.

MAINTENANCE. Hub should be lubricated with about 2 cc of oil at approximately one month intervals. Use a very light sewing machine or spindle oil and squirt oil into hub through lubrication fitting in center of hub. Lubricate hub more often on long tours. Hub should be disassembled, cleaned, inspected and thoroughly lubricated at one year intervals.

CONTROL ADJUSTMENT. Correct adjustment is important to prevent damage to the hub and for the safety of the rider. Shift the control to Normal ("N" or "2") position and move pedals backward slightly to shift hub. Pointer (P-Fig. SH11) of belcrank should be exactly aligned with mark (MB). Adjust shift cable if mark is not aligned. Shift cable can be adjusted in two ways. Normally the threaded adjusting sleeve (A) can be turned onto threaded part of belcrank shaft to provide the correct setting. Be sure to lock adjustment with lock nut (L)

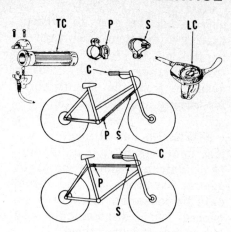

Fig. SH12—Views showing normal routing of control cables for three speed rear hub. Shimano twist control is shown at (TC) and lever control at (LC). Pulleys are identified by (P) and cable housing stop by (S). Controls (C) are usually located on handlebar.

after it is correctly set. Control cable pulleys (P-Fig. SH12) and cable stoppers (S) can be relocated if turning adjustment sleeve (A-Fig. SH11) will not provide correct adjustment. Be sure that cable operates smoothly and is not binding in control, pulleys or cable housing.

REPAIR. Remove wheel and hub from bicycle, refer to Fig. SH13 and proceed as follows: Remove belcrank (31) and withdraw push rod (12) from right end of axle. Remove nuts (1, 3, 28 & 30) and washers (2, 4 & 29) from ends of axles. Unscrew bearing cones (5 & 5R) from ends of axle, remove dust caps (7 & 7R), bearings (8 & 8R) and spring (6). Driver assembly (24) and bearing (23) can be withdrawn. All of the bearings (8, 8R & 23) may be inspected and serviced at this time without further disassembly. Unscrew ball cup (22) from hub, then the axle and planetary gear assembly may be withdrawn from hub. Remove sliding keys (13 & 14), then slide axle out of planet assembly. Remove snap ring (17), to separate ring gear (16), ratchet (18) and ratchet (20). Remove snap ring (32) to remove pins

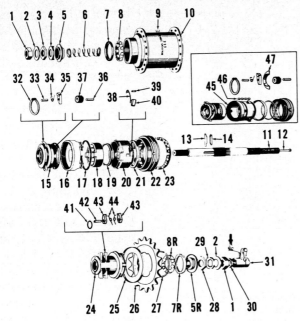

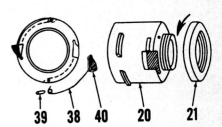

Fig. SH14—Drawing showing correct assembly of pawls (43), springs (44) and driver (24). Spring should enter small holes (H).

Fig. SH13—Exploded view of typical Shimano three speed rear hub without back pedaling brake. Planetary assembly shown in inset uses pins (46) to hold planet carrier to ratchet and ring gear unit (45). Other differences may also be noticed on some units.

1. Axle nuts	15. Planet cage	32. Snap ring
2. Washers	16. Ring gear	33. Pin
3. Lock nut	17. Snap ring	34. Spring
4. Lock washer	18. Ratchet	35. Pawl
5. Left bearing cone	19. Pawl guide	36. Pin
5R. Right bearing cone	20. Ratchet	37. Planet gear
6. Spring	21. Pawl retaining nut	38. Spring
7. Dust cap	22. Ball cup	39. Pin
7R. Right hand dust cap	23. Bearing with retainer	40. Ratchet pawl
8. Bearing with retainer	24. Driver	41. Snap ring
8R. Right bearing	25. Dust cap	42. Pin
9. Lubrication fitting	26. Sprocket	43. Pawls
10. Hub	27. Retaining ring	44. Springs
11. Axle with sun gear	28. Lock nut	45. Ratchet and ring gear
12. Control push rod	29. Lock washer	assembly
13. Long sliding key	30. Lock nut	46. Pins
14. Short sliding key	31. Control belcrank	47. Pawl plate

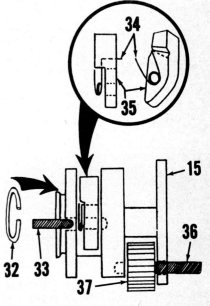

Fig. SH15—Ratchet assembly must be assembled as shown. Nut (21) has left hand thread.

(33), ratchet pawls (35) and ratchet spring (34). Remove pawl retaining nut (21) to remove ratchet pawls (40), pins (39) and springs (38). NOTE: Retaining nut (21) is equipped with a left hand thread and must be removed by turning clockwise. Remove snap ring (41) to remove pin (42), pawls (43) and springs (44). Sprocket (26) and dust cap (25) can be removed after removing retaining ring (27).

Clean and inspect all parts carefully. Check gear teeth and renew any that are broken, chipped or excessively worn. Renew any ratchet or pawl that is broken or if engaging ends are worn off round. Renew any spring which is broken, bent or is in any other way different than a new spring. Renew bearings if retainer is bent or worn or if balls are missing, broken, nicked or worn. Check bearing races carefully, especially if bearing balls are damaged. Renew bearing races (cups and cones) if nicked, worn or cracked. Check sliding keys and renew if worn or broken.

Reassemble driver (24), ratchet (20) and planet cage (15) as subassemblies before beginning to assemble hub. Locate pawls and springs as shown in Fig. SH14. Beveled, projection on pawls should be together and edge of springs should be behind pawls. Other end of spring should engage small holes (H) in driver (24). Pawl guide (19-Fig. SH13) is fixed in position inside ratchet (20). There is no reason to remove the pawl guide; however,

Fig. SH16—Pawl (35) and spring (34) must be installed as shown.

if loose, drive guide back into its original location. Install pawl springs (38) and retaining pins (39). Hold spring down and position pawls (40) over the springs as shown in Fig. SH15. Install retaining nut (21) to hold pawls in position. **NOTE:** Nut (21) has left **hand thread. Tighten by turning counter-clockwise.** Assemble planet cage assembly as shown in Fig. SH16. Be sure that springs (34) and pawls (35) are installed as indicated. Snap ring (32) holds pins (33) in place.

Assemble planet gear set as follows: Hold ratchet pawls (35-Fig. SH17) down and slide ring gear (16) over pawls and planet gears. Slide ratchet (18) into ring gear so that the two lugs engage the two slots in planet cage (15). Locate ratchet (20) around lugs of ring gear (16) and install snap ring (17). Snap ring (17) engages ring gear (16) and ratchet (20) holding the assembly (A) together.

Fig. SH17—Assemble planet and ratchet subassembly to form the assembly shown at (A).

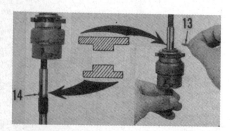

Fig. SH18—Short sliding key (14) and long sliding key (13) must be assembled correctly for the unit to operate properly.

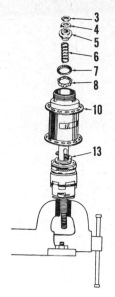

Fig. SH19—Hold axle in soft jawed vise while assembling parts shown. Be sure that sliding key (13) remains in place while assembling.

Position shorter sliding key (14-Fig. SH18) in axle slot as shown, then slide planet gear set over axle and key. Install longer sliding key (13) in slot above planet gear set. Slide hub (10-Fig. SH19) over axle and planet gear set, then install bearing (8), seal (7), spring (6) and bearing cone (5). Tighten cone against shoulder of axle, then loosen cone only enough to install lock washer (4). Tighten lock nut (3) against washer. Invert unit and install ball cup (22-Fig. SH20). Hold ratchet pawls (40) in, using a small rod (R) or screwdriver. Install bearing (23) into bearing cup, with closed side of retainer out. Re-

tainer will rub on ball cup race if bearing is installed wrong. Press pawls (43) in while turning driver (24) and sprocket (26) counterclockwise. When driver is fully seated, install right side bearing (8R-Fig. SH13), dust cap (7R) and adjustable cone (5R). Slide push rod (12) into end of axle.

Adjust hub bearings by turning cone (5R) until wheel rotates freely without excessive play. Tighten lock nut (28) after bearing cone (5R) is set. Recheck bearing adjustment after lock nut is tight. Install wheel in bicycle frame, and correctly tighten chain. Turn lock nut (30) onto axle, then turn belcrank (31) onto axle until the small screw contacts the axle. The joint of belcrank which attaches to cable should be aligned with cable, then tighten lock nut (30) against belcrank. Refer to control adjustment paragraph for final adjusting of the control cable.

TROUBLE SHOOTING. The following lists some troubles and possible remedies. Refer to the appropriate MAINTENANCE, CONTROL ADJUSTMENT or REPAIR section for more detailed service procedures.

Check action of push rod (12-Fig. SH13) within the axle when control belcrank assembly (31) is removed. Push the rod (12) in, then release and measure the working distance. The correct

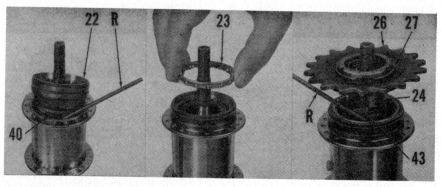

Fig. SH20—A small rod (R) may be used to hold the pawls in while installing ball cup (22) and driver (24).

stroke is 10 MM (13/32-inch) and rod should move in smoothly and should return (out) easily under spring pressure. If difficulty is noticed, check the following: Be sure push rod is not bent. Be sure that left bearing cone (5), lock washer (4) and lock nut (3) are all installed and tight. Be sure that the two sliding keys (13 & 14) are correctly installed as shown in Fig. SH18. Check installation of all ratchet pawls.

If unit slips in high "H" or "3", check condition of pawls (43-Fig. SH13) and springs (44). These pawls may be traded around to equalize wear on both edges, but the offset portions must be installed together as shown in Fig. SH14. Check also condition of pawls (40-Fig. SH13) and springs (38).

If the unit slips in normal and low "N" and "L" or "1" and "2" positions, check pawls (35) and springs (34).

If the unit does not rotate smoothly or at all, disassemble the unit and inspect for broken parts and rust.

A cracking noise from the rear hub is usually caused by a damaged bearing (8, 8R or 23). Be sure to check accompanying races (5, 10, 22, 24 and 5R) if bearings are damaged. Grinding or cracking noise may also be caused by dirt or broken parts within the unit.

Shimano 3.3.3. Tri-Matic With Back Pedaling Brake

This three speed rear hub is shifted by handlebar mounted remote control. Unit may be shifted while pedalling lightly, but it is recommended that unit be shifted while coasting whenever possible.

MAINTENANCE. Hub should be lubricated with about 2 cc of oil at approximately one month intervals. Use a light oil such as sewing machine or spindle oil and

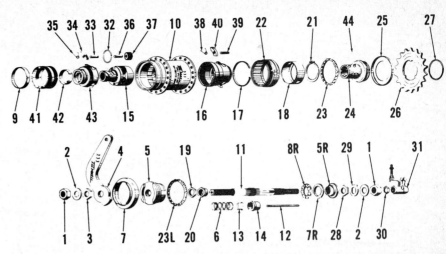

Fig. SH25—Exploded view of Shimano Tri-Matic three speed rear hub with back pedaling brake.

1. Axle nuts	14. Sliding clutch	30. Lock nut
2. Washers	15. Pinion cage	31. Belcrank
3. Lock nuts	16. Ring gear	32. Retaining ring
4. Brake arm	17. Pawl cage spring	33. Pin
5. Brake cone	18. Pawl cage	34. Ratchet pawl
5R. Right bearing cone	19. Lock nut	35. Spring
6. Clutch spring	20. Nut	36. Pin
7. Dust cap	21. Snap ring	37. Planet pinion
7R. Right dust cap	22. Ball cap	38. Spring
8R. Ball and retainer	23. Bearing with retainer	39. Pin
9. Spring band	24. Driver	40. Ratchet pawl
10. Hub	25. Dust cap	41. Brake shoe
11. Axle	26. Sprocket	42. Retarder spring
12. Push rod	27. Snap ring	43. Clutch sleeve
13. Sliding key	28. Lock nut	44. Engagement balls
	29. Lock washer	

squirt oil into hub through lubrication fitting in center of hub. Lubricate hub more often on long tours. The hub should be disassembled, cleaned, inspected and thoroughly lubricated at one year intervals.

CONTROL ADJUSTMENT. Correct adjustment is important to prevent damage to hub and for rider safety. Shift control to Normal ("N" or "2") position and move pedals backward slightly to shift hub. Pointer (P-Fig. SH26) of belcrank should be exactly aligned with mark (MB). Adjust shift cable if mark is not aligned. Shift cable can be adjusted in two ways. Normally the threaded adjusting sleeve (A) can be turned onto threaded part of belcrank shaft to provide the correct setting. Tighten lock nut (L) after adjustment is correctly set. Con-

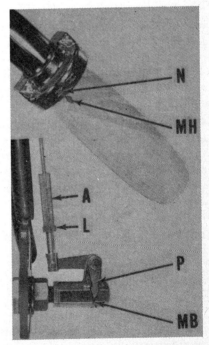

Fig. SH26—The control adjustment can usually be accomplished by turning adjuster (A).

A. Adjuster
L. Lock nut
MB. Belcrank mark

MH. Handgrip mark
N. Normal mark
P. Pointer

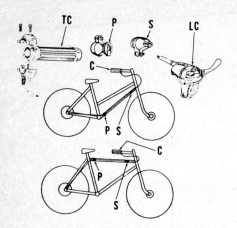

Fig. SH27—Views showing normal routing of control cables for three speed rear hub. Shimano twist control is shown at (TC) and lever control at (LC). Pulleys are identified by (P) and cable housing stop by (S). Controls (C) are usually located on handlebar.

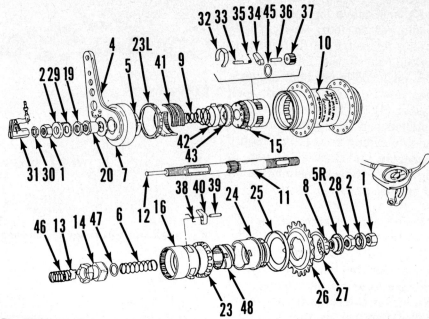

Fig. SH28—Exploded view of Shimano 3 CC three speed, coaster brake, cartridge type rear hub.

1. Axle nuts			36. Pin
2. Washers	11. Axle	24. Driver	37. Planet pinion
4. Brake arm	12. Push rod	25. Dust cap	38. Spring
5. Brake cone	13. Sliding key	26. Sprocket	39. Pin (same as 36)
5R. Right bearing	14. Sliding clutch	27. Snap ring	40. Ratchet pawl
cone	15. Carrier assy.	28. Locknut	41. Brake shoe
6. Clutch spring	16. Ring gear	29. Lockwasher	42. Retarder spring
(long)	19. Locknut	30. Locknut	43. Spring guide
7. Dust cap	20. Stop nut	31. Shift bellcrank	45. Thrust washer
8. Ball bearing &	23. Ball bearing	32. Stop spring	46. Clutch spring
retainer	(right)	33. Pin	(short)
9. Release spring	23L. Ball bearing	34. Ratchet pawl	47. Clutch washer
10. Hub	(left)	35. Spring	48. Lead piece

trol cable pulleys (P-Fig. SH27) and cable stoppers (S) can be relocated if turning adjustment sleeve (A-Fig. SH26) will not provide correct adjustment. Be sure that cable operates smoothly and is not binding in control, pulleys or cable housing.

REPAIR. Refer to information regarding similar hub in preceding section and to Fig. SH25. Inspect engagement balls (44) carefully. Bearings (23 & 23L) are different and should not be interchanged. Closed side of retainer for bearings (8R, 23 & 23L) should be toward outside when assembling. Be sure to install retarder spring (42) on clutch sleeve (43) in direction shown. Tang on end of retarder spring should engage brake shoe (41).

Shimano 3 CC (3 Speed, Coaster Brake, Cartridge Type)

This three speed rear hub is shifted by a remote control usually mounted on the handlebar. Unit may be shifted while pedalling lightly, but it is recommended that shifting occur whenever possible.

MAINTENANCE AND ADJUSTMENT. Refer to information regarding lubrication and cable adjustment in the preceding paragraphs regarding similar Shimano 3.3.3. Trimatic hub with Back Pedalling Brake.

REPAIR. Remove wheel and hub from bicycle, refer to Fig. SH28 and proceed as follows: Remove bellcrank (31) and withdraw push rod (12) from left end of axle. Remove nuts (1, 19, 20, 28 and 30) and washers (2 and 29) from ends of axles. Unscrew bearing cones (5 and 5R) from ends of axle, remove bearing (8) and spring (6). Driver assembly (24) and bearing (23) can be withdrawn. All of the bearings (8, 23 and 23L) may be inspected and serviced at this time without further disassembly. The axle and planetary gear assembly may be withdrawn from left side of hub. Remove sliding clutch (14), key (13) and spring (46), then slide axle out of planet assembly.

TROUBLESHOOTING. The following lists some troubles and possible remedies. Refer to the appropriate MAINTENANCE, CONTROL ADJUSTMENT or REPAIR section for more detailed service procedures.

Check action of push rod (12—Fig. SH28) within the axle when control bellcrank assembly (31) is removed. Push the rod (12) in, then release and measure the working distance. The correct stroke is 10 mm (13/32-inch) and rod should move in smoothly and should return (out) easily under spring pressure. If difficulty is noticed, check the following: Be sure push rod is not bent. Be sure that brake cone (5), nut (20) and locknut (19) are all installed and tight. Be sure that sliding key (13) is correctly installed as shown. Check installation of all ratchet pawls and condition of ratchet springs.

If the unit does not rotate smoothly or at all, disassemble the unit and inspect for broken parts and rust.

A cracking noise from the rear hub is usually caused by a damaged bearing. Be sure to check accompanying races if bearings are damaged. Grinding or cracking noise may also be caused by dirt or broken parts within the unit.

Clean and inspect all parts carefully. Check gear teeth and renew any that are broken, chipped or excessively worn. Renew any ratchet or pawl that is broken or if engaging ends are worn off round. Renew any spring which is broken, bent or is in any other way different than a new spring. Renew bearings if retainer is bent or worn or if balls are missing, broken, nicked or worn. Check bearing races carefully, especially if bearing balls are damaged. Renew bearing races (cups and cones) if nicked, worn or cracked. Check sliding key and renew if worn or broken.

Install bearing (23) into bearing cup, with closed side of retainer out. Retainer will rub on ball cup race if bearing is installed wrong.

Adjust hub bearings by turning cone (5R) until wheel rotates freely without excessive play. Tighten locknut (28) after bearing adjustment is set. Recheck bearing adjustment after locknut is tight. Install wheel in bicycle frame, and correctly tighten chain. Turn locknut (30) onto axle, then turn bellcrank (31) onto axle. The joint of bellcrank which attaches to cable should be aligned with cable, then tighten locknut (30) against bellcrank. Refer to control adjustment paragraph for final adjusting of the control cable.

Sturmey Archer "AW"

Unit is identified by model stamped on hub below name. Model AW is not equipped with a brake and is usually equipped with a rim acting caliper rear brake. Unit is usually shifted by a handlebar mounted remote con-

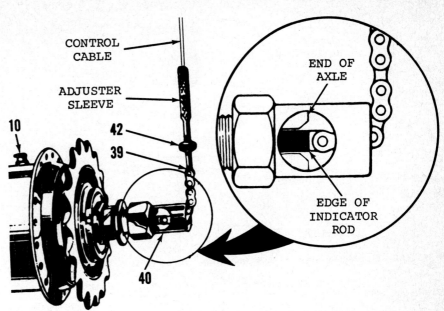

Fig. SA1—Edge of rod (39) is used as an indicator for adjusting control cable. Fitting (10) permits lubrication of assembled hub.

trol. Low speed position on control unit is marked "1", "L", or "I" and rear hub is driven at a slower speed than rear sprocket. The normal drive, locks hub and rear sprocket together and drives the unit similar to a single speed hub. Normal position if marked "2", "N" or "II" on remote control. The high speed drives rear wheel hub at an increased (faster than sprocket) speed and remote control position is marked "3", "H" or "III".

Although hub may be shifted while light pressure is exerted on pedals, this procedure is not recommended. A freewheel pause in pedalling helps to engage the unit for smoother shifts. Hub mechanism will also last longer with this technique.

MAINTENANCE. Hub should be lubricated with light machine oil or special Sturmey Archer oil through lubrication opening in hub. Interval of lubrication should be about every two weeks. Control cable and housing should be lubricated with oil frequently as should remote control assembly and any pulleys used. Adjust hub bearings to permit wheel to rotate freely without excessive play. Adjust bearings by turning

bearing cone (5L-Fig. SA2) on left side only. CAUTION: Do not change the setting of bearing cone on right side or internal damage may result. Tighten lock nut (3) after adjustment is complete. Recheck bearing adjustment and control cable adjustment after axle nuts are tight. Refer to REPAIR section if setting of right bearing cone was disturbed.

CONTROL ADJUSTMENT. Correct adjustment is important to prevent damage to hub and for rider safety. Shift remote control to normal position and check location of indicator rod (Fig. SA1). Edge of indicator must be aligned with end of axle as shown ("2", "N" or "II"). Usually adjustment can be accomplished by loosening lock nut (42) and turning adjuster sleeve. Control cable pulleys can be relocated if necessary to provide additional adjustment.

REPAIR. Remove wheel and hub from bicycle, refer to Fig. SA2 and proceed as follows: Remove nuts (1 & 40) and axle lock washers (2) from both ends of axle. Remove lock nut (3), washer (4) and bearing cone (5L) from left end of axle. Use a hammer

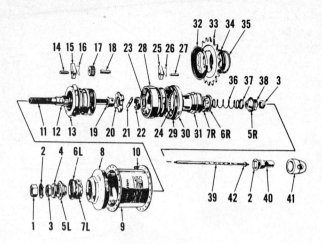

Fig. SA2—Exploded view of AW rear hub. Refer to text when assembling.

1. Axle nut	10. Lubrication fitting	23. Thrust washer
2. Axle positioning washers	11. Axle	24. Bearing balls (3/16-inch diameter)
3. Lock nuts	12. Sun gear	25. Ring gear pawl
4. Spacer washers	13. Planet cage	26. Spring
5L & 5R. Bearing cones	14. Pin	27. Pin
6L & 6R. Dust caps	15. Low gear pawl	28. Ring gear
7L & 7R. Bearings with retainers	16. Spring	29. Right hand ball ring
8. Left ball cup	17. Planet pinion	30. Dust cap
9. Hub shell	18. Pinion pin	31. Driver
	19. Clutch sleeve	32. Dust cap
	20. Clutch	
	21. Axle key	
	22. Thrust ring	

33. Sprocket
34. Spacer washers
35. Retaining ring
36. Clutch spring
37. Spring cap
38. Special lock washer
39. Indicator rod
40. Right hand axle nut
41. Plastic protector cap
42. Lock nut

and punch or appropriate special wrench and unscrew ball ring (29) from right end of hub (9).

NOTE: Mark hub (9) and ball ring (29) before loosening the ball ring. Ball ring has two different start threads but original position should be maintained upon reassembly.

Lift axle and planet assembly out of hub. Remove pins (14), low gear pawls (15) and springs (16). Clamp left end of axle in a soft jawed vise and remove lock nut (3), lock washer (38) and right bearing cone (5R). Lift parts off in the following order: Clutch spring (36), driver (31), ball ring (29) and ring gear (28). Remove pins (27), ring gear pawls (25) and springs (26). Remove thrust ring (22) and washer (23). Unscrew indicator rod (39), push axle key (21) out and remove sliding clutch (20) and sleeve (19). Lift planet cage (13) off and remove pins (18) and pinions (17).

Ball cup on left end of hub is threaded into hub shell with left hand thread and may be removed by turning clockwise.

Check clutch (20) for freedom of movement in slots of clutch driver (31). Check to be sure that axle is straight and not bent. Check all gear teeth for wear or chips. Check all six bearing races for wear or pitting. Check pinion pins (18), sliding clutch (20) and ring gear (28) splines for rounding off at the engagement points. Check pawls (15 & 25) and pawl ratchets for wear.

To assemble, install left side ball cup in hub shell. Place ring gear (28) with gear teeth down against a flat surface. Place pawl spring (26) along side of a pawl (25) so that loop is over pin hole and bent end is under long nose of pawl. Grip nose of pawl and foot of spring and slide the pawl, tail first, between flanges of ring gear, then push pin (27) through the flange, pawl and spring. Coat channels of dust caps of left hand ball cup (8), driver (31) and in

recess of right hand ball ring (29). CAUTION: Do not use grease anywhere else. Clamp left end of axle in a soft jawed vise and install planet cage (13). Install planet gears (17) and pins (18) in planet cage. Small ends of pins (18) should protrude. Install sleeve (19) with flange down and clutch (20) with recess engaging flange of sleeve. Install axle key (21) with flat of key facing upward, then screw indicator rod (39) into key to hold parts (19, 20 & 21) in position. Install thrust ring (22) and washer (23). Make sure that slots in thrust ring engage flat ends of key (21). Install ring gear (28) over axle and planet carrier and position ball ring (29) over axle with threaded side toward ring gear. The twenty four 3/16-inch diameter bearing balls (24) and dust cap (30) must be installed on ball ring before locating ball ring over axle. Install bearing (7R) in driver with closed side of retainer toward outside, press dust cap (6R) into driver (31). Install driver assembly, spring (36), cap (37) and bearing cone (5R) over right end of axle. Tighten the right hand bearing cone finger tight, back it off 1/2 turn, install special lock washer (38) and tighten lock nut (3). NOTE: Never back the bearing cone off more than 1/2 turn. The preceding setting for the right bearing cone must not be changed or incorrect operation and damage may result.

Remove assembly from vise, invert and clamp right end of axle in soft jawed vise. Install pawls (15) in planet cage as follows: Locate pawl between flanges with flat driving edge pointing toward right. Insert pawl pin (14) through the outside flange and half way through the pawl. Grip the bent end of pawl spring (16) and slide spring between lower side of pawl and lower flange. Loop in spring should align with pawl pin hole and push pin through. Both ends of spring will be between right side of pawl and planet cage and right edge of pawl will be pushed out. Remove the unit from vise and pour about 2 teaspoons of oil into planet cage.

Insert gear unit vertically upward into hub and screw ball ring (29) into hub. NOTE: The previously installed marks should align when ball ring is tight. If marks don't align, unscrew ball ring and reinstall using the other thread. Install left side bearing cone (5L), washers (4) and lock nut (3). Tighten left bearing cone only enough to remove play from bearings without causing bearings to bind.

There must always be two 1/16-inch thick spacer washers (34) used. The location behind or in front of the sprocket and offset of the sprocket will be determined by alignment of front chainwheel. Install these three parts as they were removed and check alignment. If chainwheel and rear sprocket are not aligned, change the order of assembly.

TROUBLE SHOOTING. The major cause of trouble is faulty control adjustment. Sluggish gear change or stiffness may be caused by lack of lubrication or lubrication with stiff grease. Refer to Fig. SA2 and the following for other suggested faults.

1. No low gear.
   a. Low gear pawls (15) upside down. Disassemble and install correctly.
   b. Thrust collar (22) not seating over key (21). Disassemble and install correctly.
   c. Incorrect spring (36). Disassemble and install correct spring.

2. Slips in low gear.
   a. Sliding clutch (20) worn. Install new sliding clutch.

   b. Indicator rod (39) not completely screwed into key (21). Disconnect control cable, turn indicator rod to tighten and readjust control cable.
   c. Right hand bearing cone (5R) incorrectly adjusted. Refer to REPAIR section and reset.
   d. Control cable binding. Check and renew if necessary.
   e. Bent or damaged chain on indicator rod (39). Renew if damaged.

3. Fluctuates between 1st (L) and 2nd (N) gear.
   a. Worn ring gear pawls (25). Renew damaged parts.

4. Slips in 2nd (N) gear.
   a. Ring gear dogs and/or clutch (20) worn. Renew damaged parts.
   b. Indicator rod (39) not completely screwed into key (21). Disconnect control cable, turn indicator rod to tighten and readjust control cable.

5. Slips in top (3rd, H) gear.
   a. Pinion pins (18) and/or clutch (20) worn. Disassemble, inspect and renew worn parts.
   b. Very weak or distorted spring (36). Disassemble and renew spring.

   c. Incorrect setting of right hand bearing cone (5R). Refer to REPAIR section and reset.
   d. Grit between clutch sleeve (19) and axle. Disassemble and clean.

6. Hub is hard to turn. Difficult to pedal.
   a. Too many balls (24) in ball ring. Install only 24.
   b. Bearing cones (5L & 5 R) incorrectly set. Refer to REPAIR Section and readjust.
   c. Frame ends not parallel. Straighten and align ends of frame.
   d. Corrosion inside hub. Disassemble, clean and reassemble using a non-corrosive lubricant.
   e. Bent dust caps. Install new caps.

7. Sluggish gear change.
   a. Distorted spring (36). Install new spring.
   b. Bent axle (11). Install new axle.
   c. Worn chain on indicator rod (39). Install new indicator rod.
   d. Control cable guide pulley out of alignment. Align pulley and readjust cable.
   e. Cable needs lubrication, is bent or has frayed wire. Lubricate or renew as necessary.

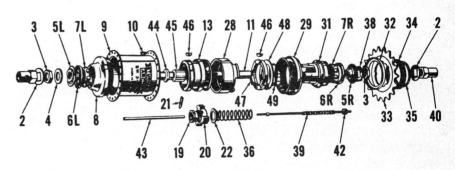

Fig. SA3—Exploded view of SW rear hub. Unit is not equipped with brake. Refer to Fig. SA2 for legend except the following.

43. Push rod	45. Clutch	47. Ratchet ring
44. Lock nut	46. Pawls	48. Washer
		49. Spring

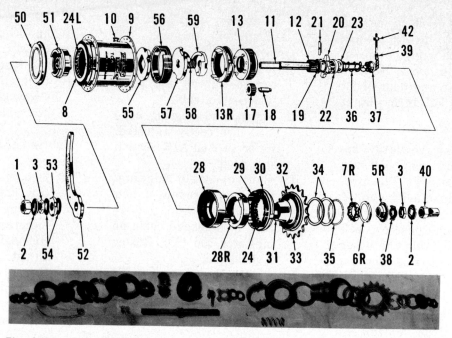

Fig. SA5—Exploded views of old style TCW rear hub. The unit includes a back pedaling coaster brake. Brake arm (52) must be firmly attached below left side chain stay.

1. Axle nut
2. Axle positioning washers
3. Lock nut
5R. Right bearing cone
6R. Dust cap
7R. Right bearing with retainer
8. Left ball cup
9. Hub shell
10. Lubrication fitting
11. Axle
12. Sun gear

13. Planet cage
13 R. Ratchet assembly
17. Planet pinion
18. Pinion pin
19. Clutch sleeve
20. Clutch
21. Axle key
22. Thrust ring
23. Thrust washer
24 & 24L. Bearing balls (3/16-inch diameter)
28. Ring gear

28R. Ring gear ratchet
29. Right hand ball ring
30. Dust cap
31. Driver
32. Dust cap
33. Sprocket
34. Spacer washers
35. Retaining ring
36. Clutch spring
37. Spring cap
38. Special lock washer
39. Indicator rod and chain

40. Right hand axle nut
42. Lock nut
50. Dust cap
51. Left hand cone
52. Brake arm
53. Lock nut
54. Washers
55. Brake plate
56. Brake band
57. Brake thrust plate
58. Spring
59. Brake cam

f. Control handle needs lubrication or is damaged. Lubricate or renew as necessary.

Other Sturmey Archer 3 Speed Hubs

The various hubs can be identified by model stamped on hub below name. Refer to the accompanying illustrations (Figs. SA3 through SA7) and to the service procedures outlined for the AW hub. On models with back pedaling brake, noisy or shuddering brake may be caused by loose brake arm clip. Be sure that brake arm is securely clamped below left chain stay. Scratching noise or extreme brake operation may be caused by lack of lubrication. Lubricate unit through fitting in hub with light machine oil or special Sturmey Archer oil.

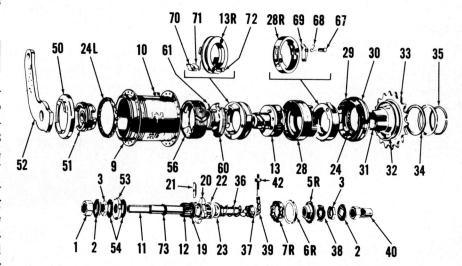

Fig. SA6—Exploded view of TCW Mark 3 rear hub. Hub is marked "TCW III". Brake actuating parts (51, 56, 60 & 61) and planet carrier (13) with large screw are most obvious changes from earlier unit. Refer to SA5 for legend except the following.

13R. Pawl ring
28R. Pawl ring
60. Brake thrust plate

61. Brake actuating spring
67. Pawl pin

68. Spring
69. Pawl

70. Pawl
71. Spring
72. Pawl pin

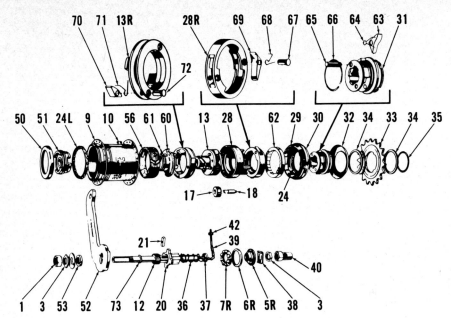

Fig. SA7—Exploded view of S3C rear hub. Hub is similar to TCW Mark 3 except for differences in driver (31) and ratchet (62 through 66). Refer to Fig. SA5 for legend except the following.

13R. Pawl ring
28R. Pawl ring
 60. Brake thrust plate
 61. Brake actuating spring

62. Ratchet ring
63. Pawl
64. Spring
65. Pin

66. Snap ring
67. Pawl pin
68. Spring

69. Pawl
70. Pawl
71. Spring
72. Pawl pin

Fig. SA9—View showing correct method of installing pawl springs (68) on models equipped with pawl retainer (28R). Pins (67) are riveted in place and hold pawls (69) and end is filed flush with retainer. Turn pawl back as far as it will go, insert spring (68) between retainer and pawl, with bent end of spring under short end of pawl. Turn pawl back to correct position.

Four And Five Speed Rear Hubs

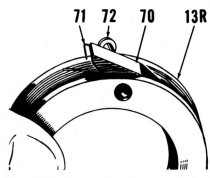

Fig. SA8—View showing method of assembling pawls (70), springs (71) and pins (72) in pawl ring (13R).

Styre 3 Speed Hub

Refer to the preceding service section for Sturmey Archer AW hub while repairing Styre three speed unit. Design and even some parts are identical.

Sturmey Archer

The four speed hub is identified by FW stamped on hub below name. Five speed hubs have S5 stamped below name. Four speed hub is similar to the five speed unit except for compensating spring (S-Fig. SA41) and collar (P). The following procedures describe the five speed S5 hub, but can be used for most service on four speed FW hub also.

The S5 hub provides five different drive ratios. Top (5th) gear drives the wheel 50% faster than sprocket, 4th gear drives wheel 26.6% faster than sprocket, Normal (3rd) gear drives the wheel the same speed as sprocket, 2nd gear drives the wheel 21.1% slower than sprocket and Low (1st) gear drives the wheel 33.3% slower than sprocket.

Although the hub may be shifted while a light pressure is exerted on pedals, this procedure is not recommended. A freewheel pause in pedalling helps to engage the unit for smoother shifts.

Hub mechanism will also last longer with this technique.

MAINTENANCE. Hub should be lubricated frequently with light machine oil or special Sturmey Archer oil through lubrica-

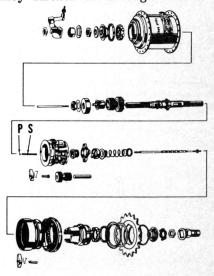

Fig. SA41—Exploded view of FW four speed rear hub. Unit is similar to five speed unit shown in Fig. SA53 except for minor differences including compensating spring (S) and collar (P). Refer to Fig. SA53.

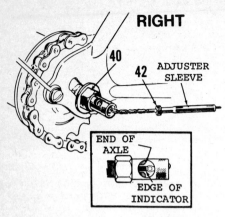

Fig. SA51—Control cable adjustment on right side should cause edge of indicator to align with end of axle when control lever is in center position.

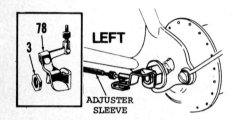

Fig. SA52—Control cable at left side operates a belcrank which pushes a rod in to change speeds. Belcrank must be firmly attached and cable must be correct length to permit both full in and full out movement of the rod.

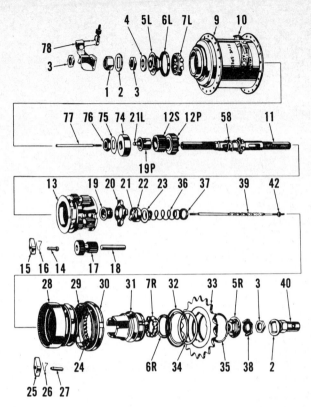

Fig. SA53—Exploded view of the Sturmey Archer "S5" five speed rear hub.

1. Axle nut	17. Planet gear	31. Driver
2. Axle positioning washer	18. Planet pin	32. Dust cap
3. Lock nut	19. Clutch sleeve	33. Sprocket (16 to 20 teeth)
4. Spacer washer	19P. Pinion sleeve	34. Spacer washer (2 used)
5L & 5R. Left and right	20. Clutch	35. Retaining ring
bearing cones	21. Axle key	36. Clutch spring
6L & 6R. Dust caps	21L. Low gear axle key	37. Spring cap
7L & 7R. Bearings with	22. Thrust ring	38. Special lock washer
retainers	23. Thrust washer	39. Indicator rod
9. Hub shell	24. Bearing balls (3/16-inch)	40. Right hand axle nut
10. Lubrication fitting	25. Ring gear pawl	42. Lock nut
11. Axle	26. Spring	58. Low gear spring
12P. Primary sun gear	27. Pin	74. Dog ring
12S. Secondary sun gear	28. Ring gear	75. Lock washer
13. Planetary cage	29. Ball ring	76. Lock nut for dog ring
14. Pin	30. Dust cap	77. Gear push rod
15. Low gear pawl		78. Belcrank, left side
16. Spring		

tion fitting (10-Fig. SA53) in hub. Interval of lubrication should usually be at least every two weeks. Shift controls, cables, cable housings pulleys and indicator rod chain should be lubricated often with oil. Adjust hub bearings to permit wheel to rotate freely without excessive play. Adjust bearings by turning bearing cone (5L) on left side only. CAUTION: Do not change setting of bearing cone on right side or internal damage may result. Tighten lock nut (3) after adjustment is complete. Recheck bearing adjustment after axle nuts are tight. Refer to REPAIR Section if setting of the right bearing cone was disturbed.

CONTROL ADJUSTMENT. Correct adjustment is important to prevent damage to the hub and for rider safety.

Move right hand control to the center position and check the position of indicator rod in relation to end of axle. These parts can be viewed through the round opening of the right hand axle nut (40-Fig. SA51). End of indicator rod should be flush with end of axle as shown. If incorrect, loosen lock nut (42) and turn the cable adjuster sleeve. Usually the adjustment can be accomplished by turning sleeve, but additional adjustment can be made by relocating cable pulleys.

The left hand control pushes control rod in. Be sure that belcrank (78-Fig. SA52) is tight against left axle nut and that lock nut (3) is tight against belcrank.

Arm on belcrank must align with cable. Push left hand lever forward and loosen cable slightly by turning adjuster sleeve. Pull hand control lever back and screw the adjuster sleeve until all slack is just removed from cable. Check adjustment by engaging all of the gears. After determining that control cable is adjusted correctly, tighten lock nuts against cable adjuster sleeves on both sides.

REPAIR. Remove wheel and hub from bicycle. Refer to Fig. SA53 and proceed as follows: Remove control belcrank (78), axle nut (1), lock nut (3), washers (2 & 4) and bearing cone (5L) from left

Fig. SA54—View showing installation of pawls (15), springs (16) and pins (14) in planet carrier (13). Pins are riveted in place. It is important that both ends of pin are flush with planet carrier after installation.

end of axle. Use a hammer and punch or appropriate special wrench and unscrew ball ring (29) from right end of hub (9).

NOTE: Mark hub (9) and ball ring (29) before loosening the ball ring. Ball ring has two different start threads but the original position should be maintained upon reassembly.

Lift axle and planet assembly out of hub. Clamp left end of axle in a soft jawed vise and remove lock nut (3), lock washer (38) and right bearing cone (5R). Lift parts off in the following order: Cap (37), clutch spring (36), driver (31), ball ring (29) and ring gear (28). Remove thrust ring (22) and washer (23). Unscrew indicator rod (39), push axle key (21) out and remove sliding clutch (20) and sleeve (19). Remove pins (18) and pinions (17), then lift planet cage (13) off. Low gear pawl pins (14) are riveted in position. Refer to Fig. SA54 if necessary to remove these pins.

Unscrew and remove push rod (77-Fig. SA53), then clamp right end of axle in a soft jawed vise. Straighten edge of tab lock washer (75) and remove nut (76), tab

washer (75) and dog ring (74). Push the two sun gears (12P & 12S) along axle so that larger one (12P) engages axle dogs. Move sleeve (19P) in opposite direction to expose axle key (21L) and push the key out. Slide sleeve (19P), sun gears (12P & 12S) and spring (58) from axle.

Check clutch (20) for freedom of movement in slots of clutch driver (31). Check to be sure that axle is straight and not bent. Check all gear teeth for wear or chips. Check all six bearing races for wear or pitting. Check all engagement dogs and splines for rounding off at engagement points. Check pawls (15 & 25) and pawl ratchets for wear.

Assemble the subassemblies to prepare for assembling the axle. Grease bearing (7L) lightly and position in bearing race in left side of hub. Closed side of bearing retainer should be toward outside. Install dust cap (6L) with recess toward outside. Assemble similar bearing (7R) and dust cap (6R) in driver (31) with closed side of retainer and recess in dust cap toward outside. Install dust cap (32), washers (34), sprocket (33) and retainer ring (35), if sprocket was removed from driver (31).

Position the twenty four 3/16-inch diameter bearing balls (24) in groove of ball race (29) and install dust cap (30). Be sure that balls are free to turn with dust cap in place.

Place ring gear (28) with gear teeth down against a flat surface. Place pawl spring (26) along side of a pawl (25) so that loop is over pin hole and bent end is under long nose of pawl. Grip nose of pawl and foot of spring and slide the pawl, tail first, between flanges of ring gear, then push pin (27) through the flange, pawl and spring. Refer to Fig. SA54 if

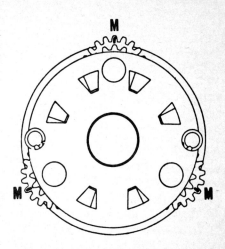

Fig. SA55—The planet gears must be timed when installed. Be sure that all three timing marks (M) are exactly as shown when planet gears are installed and meshed with sun gears.

pawl pins (14) are removed. If pins (14) come loose or project above flush with surface, serious damage will result.

Complete assembly of hub as follows: Slide spring (58), large sun gear (12P), small sun gear (12S) and sleeve (19P) on end of axle with short slot. Push these parts over against spring until large gear engages lugs on axle, then withdraw sleeve (19P) enough to insert key (21L). Be sure that threaded hole in key is aligned for installation of push rod (77), then release gears. Insert push rod (77) through end of axle and thread into key (21L). Install dog ring (74) so that it engages the axle squarely, then install tab washer (75) and nut (76). Tighten nut securely, then bend edges of tab washer (75) over sides of nut (76). Clamp left end of axle in a soft jawed vise, hold planet cage (13) in position, then install planet gears (17) and pins (18). CAUTION: Install each of the planet pinions carefully being sure that marked tooth (M-Fig. SA55) on each of the three gears is straight out as shown. To check timing, install ring gear (28-Fig. SA53) and rotate several revolutions. Ring gear should rotate very easily. Remove ring gear after testing. Install clutch sleeve (19) with flange down and clutch (20) with recess engaging flange of sleeve. Install axle key (21) with flat of key facing upward, then screw indicator rod (39) into key to hold parts (19, 20 & 21) in position. Install thrust ring (22) and washer (23). Make sure that slots in thrust ring engage flat ends of key (21). Install ring gear (28) over axle and planet carrier and position ball ring (29) over axle with threaded side toward ring gear. Install driver assembly, spring (36), cap (37) and bearing cone (5R) over right end of axle. Tighten right hand bearing cone finger tight, back it off ½ turn, install special lock washer (38) and tighten lock nut (3). NOTE: Never back the bearing cone off more than ½-turn. The preceding setting for right bearing cone must not be changed or incorrect operation and damage may result.

Pour about two teaspoons of oil into planet cage, then insert gear unit vertically upward into hub. Screw ball ring (29) into hub and check the previously installed marks. If marks do not align when ball ring is tight, unscrew and reinstall ball ring using the other thread. Install left side bearing cone (5L), washers (4) and lock nut (3). Tighten left bearing cone only enough to remove play from bearings without causing bearings to bind.

TROUBLE SHOOTING. The major cause of trouble is faulty control adjustment. Sluggish gear change or stiffness may be caused by lack of lubrication or lubrication with stiff grease. Refer to Fig. SA53 and the following for other suggested faults.

1. No super low (1st) gear·
   a. Control cable on left side too loose. Adjust cable.

   b. Low gear pawls (15) upside down or reversed. Disassemble and install correctly.

2. Difficulty engaging lower two gears (1st & 2nd). NOTE: This must not be confused with the fact that a stronger pull on control cable is necessary than for high and middle gears.
   a. Cable needs lubrication. Lubricate or renew control cable.
   b. Distorted or damaged low gear spring (58). Disassemble and renew spring.
   c. Axle key (21L) bent. Install new key.

3. Slips in super low (1st) gear.
   a. Bent or kinked cable. Install new control cable.
   b. Distorted or damaged low gear spring (58). Disassemble and renew spring.
   c. Incorrectly installed pawl springs. Disassemble and check installation of pawl springs.

4. Alternates between super low gear (1st) or second (2nd) and normal gear (3rd).
   a. Faulty ring gear pawls (25). Disassemble and renew.

5. Slips in super low (1st) gear and second (2nd) gear.
   a. Lock nut (76) loose. Disassemble, check for damage, retighten lock nut reset tab washer (75).
   b. Weak low gear spring (58). Install new spring.
   c. Teeth in dog ring (74) worn. Install new dog ring.

6. Slips in second (2nd) gear and fourth (4th) gear.
   a. Control cable on left side too tight. Adjust cable.

7. Slips in normal (3rd) gear.
   a. Ring gear (28) and sliding clutch (20) worn. Damage probably caused by incorrect cable adjustment. Install new ring gear and sliding clutch and make sure controls are maintained in proper adjustment.

8. Slips in fourth (4th) and super high (5th) gears.
   a. Planet cage dogs and clutch (20) worn. Probably caused by incorrect control adjustment or very weak spring (36). Install new parts as necessary and adjust controls.
   b. Incorrect adjustment of right hand cone (5R). Readjust cone as described in REPAIR Section.
   c. Tight spring (36) or dirt restricting spring action. Clean or renew as necessary.

9. Hub turns stiffly. Drag on pedals when freewheeling.
   a. Planet pinions not correctly timed (Fig. SA55). Disassemble and assemble correctly.
   b. Too many balls (24-Fig. SA53) installed in ball race (29). Install only 24.
   c. Left cone (5L) adjusted incorrectly. Adjust and check operation.
   d. Frame ends not parallel. Straighten and align ends of frame.
   e. Corrosion inside hub. Disassemble, clean and reassemble using a non-corrosive lubricant.
   f. Bent dust caps. Install new caps.

10. No gears at all.
    a. Pawls stuck by incorrect oil, grease, dirt or rust. Disassemble, clean and lubricate with light ma-

chine oil or special Sturmey Archer oil.

11. Sluggish gear change.
    a. Distorted spring (36). Install new spring.
    b. Bent axle (11). Install new axle.

c. Worn chain on indicator rod (39). Install new indicator rod.

d. Control cable guide pulley out of alignment. Align pulley and readjust cable.

e. Cable needs lubrication, is bent or has frayed wire. Lubricate or renew as necessary.

f. Control handle needs lubrication or is damaged. Lubricate or renew as necessary.

Derailleur Systems

Derailleurs manufactured by various companies vary in design and the procedures for servicing and adjusting will be different. Most operate in a similar way and principles suggested for a unit that appears to be similar may be applicable for repairing models not specifically included in this section. Refer also to the following general suggestions regarding all derailleurs:

Do not strain the cables unnecessarily by moving control levers when machine is at rest. Don't move levers except with a definite purpose even when pedalling.

Do not attempt to change gears while pedalling backwards. Damage is sure to result. See Fig. D2.

Do not expect control cable to last indefinitely without proper treatment. All of the cables should be kept well oiled.

Do not leave your machine in top gear when stopping. Change to a lower gear well in advance of reaching a difficult situation whenever possible.

Do not expect bearings and bushings of derailleur to lubricate themselves. Keep parts cleaned and lubricated at all times.

GENERAL ADJUSTMENTS

Most derailleurs can be adjusted to correct alignment, to set cable and control position and to limit high and low speed positions.

ALIGNMENT. Special care is taken when designing derailleurs to be sure that chain is moved in and out in a straight line. Incorrect installation can cause derailleur to operate on an angle and result in poor shifting.

Front derailleur is usually clamped onto seat tube. Install front derailleur so that outside section of guide clears the largest

DIRECTION OF CHAIN TRAVEL

Fig. D2—View of typical rear derailleur showing path of the chain. Attempting to shift either derailleur while chain is stopped or while pedalling backwards will probably bend or break some parts.

REAR DERAILLEUR FRONT DERAILLEUR CONTROL LEVERS

Fig. D1—Views showing installation of typical derailleur parts. Friction on control levers is adjustable and must be set high enough to prevent unwanted gear changes.

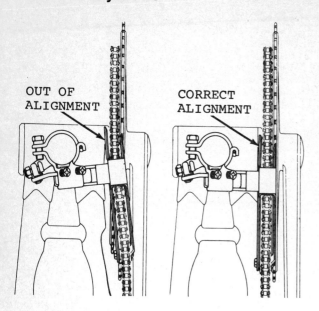

OUT OF ALIGNMENT

CORRECT ALIGNMENT

Fig. D3—Misalignment will cause incorrect shifting and unnecessary wear. Front derailleur is shown but rear derailleur can also be out of alignment.

chainwheel by about 1/8-inch and chain guide is parallel with chainwheel. Refer to Fig. D3. Tighten clamp and be sure that unit is tight on seat tube. Front lip of inside rail is usually bent out slightly as shown to assist shifting chain to the large outside sprocket.

Rear derailleur must also move straight in and out to change gears while maintaining alignment with sprockets. Rear derailleur usually also includes the tensioner rollers which establish a path for chain before going over rear sprockets. If rear derailleur is not properly aligned, chain will have a tendency to creep toward a side and eventually change gears. Misalignment is most often caused by an accident which results in a bent fork end or bent derailleur mounting lug. Misalignment should be corrected by straightening or renewing the bent part. Remove derailleur and rear wheel before attempting to straighten any bent parts. Sprockets, chain and guide (tension) holders will all be in a straight line (Fig. D4) if parts are aligned.

CABLE ADJUSTMENT. Cable should be routed so it will not bind and will be free to operate smoothly inside cable housing.

Move control lever forward, loosen cable attachment and retighten after slack is removed from cable. Check operation of control throughout range of travel to be sure that control permits complete movement. Reposition cable in clamp if necessary to permit adequate movement.

LIMIT STOPS. Limit stops are provided to keep derailleur from overshifting the chain past sprockets or chainwheels. The exact location of these stops varies with the make. Refer to individual illustrations for locations. The low speed adjustment stop is

indicated by "L" and high speed stop by "H" in all of the drawings of specific derailleurs.

The high speed limit stop on rear derailleur controls shifting onto the small high speed sprocket. Chain will be permitted to come out past the small sprocket and lodge between sprocket and frame if high speed stop (H) doesn't stop the derailleur soon enough. The chain won't shift onto small high speed sprocket if high speed stop (H) is screwed in too far. Similarly, low speed stop (L) should prevent chain from shifting past large sprocket and lodging between hub flange and low speed sprocket. Derailleur cage may also shift into the wheel and catch spokes if incorrect. The chain may not move onto large sprocket if low speed stop screw (L) is screwed in too far. Since the chain is usually slightly out of line, stops for rear derailleur should be adjusted so they operate correctly regardless of the position of the front derailleur.

Limit stops for front derailleur operate like those on the rear. Check operation carefully with the bicycle on a stand to be sure that all gears can be easily engaged.

MAINTENANCE. All derailleur parts and controls should be

Fig. D4—Idler wheels must always remain parallel with sprockets. Incorrect alignment is usually a result of an accident which has bent frame (fork ends) and/or rear derailleur assembly.

lubricated frequently. Aluminum derailleur parts can corrode and prevent free, easy movement. Steel will, of course, rust if not properly protected and lubricated. Control cables and housings are susceptible to rust which can prevent smooth shifts. Cable wear may make it necessary to adjust the cable before all gears can be engaged. Many parts of the derailleurs may be obtained and installed individually; however, it may be more desirable and sometimes less expensive to install a complete new derailleur assembly.

Belri

REAR DERAILLEUR. To adjust, move control lever forward, then loosen clamp screw (8-Fig. BE1). Turn top adjuster screw (H) until rollers and derailleur cage are aligned with small (outside) sprocket. Tighten clamp screw (8) and shift unit to low gear by moving control lever. NOTE: Turn chainwheels in normal direction while shifting derailleurs if chain is installed. Hold

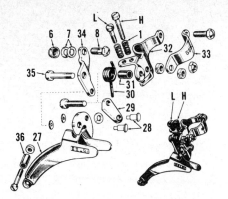

Fig. BE2—Exploded view of Belri front derailleur.

shift mechanism in line with large sprocket and turn low speed stop screw (L) to prevent overshifting past large sprocket. All moving parts should be lubricated with oil.

Chain tension is maintained by spring (14). Tension should be maintained at a minimum to reduce friction. Adjustment is possible by attaching end of spring (14) in a different slot of tension cup (23).

FRONT DERAILLEUR. Install the unit on seat tube so that

derailleur cage (27-Fig. BE2) is parallel with chainwheels and clears the teeth of largest chainwheel. Install chain through derailleur cage and around smallest chainwheel. Turn stop screw (L) until the cage (27) is centered directly over small chainwheel. Install control cable through clamp screw (8), be sure that control lever is forward, then tighten clamp nut (6). Pull control lever back, which should move derailleur cage out toward large sprocket. NOTE: Be sure to turn chainwheels while shifting. Turn stop screw (H) as required to center the cage over large chainwheel when control lever is fully toward rear.

Campagnolo Valentino

REAR DERAILLEUR. To adjust, move control lever forward, then loosen cable clamp screw (8-Fig. CA1). Turn high speed adjuster screw (H) until rollers and derailleur cage are aligned with small (outside) sprocket. Tighten cable clamp screw (8), and shift unit to low gear by moving control lever. NOTE: Turn chainwheels in normal direction while shifting derailleurs if

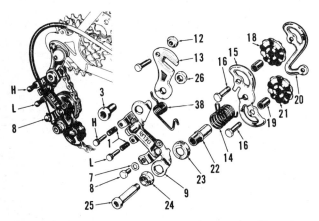

Fig. BE1—Exploded view of Belri rear derailleur assembly.

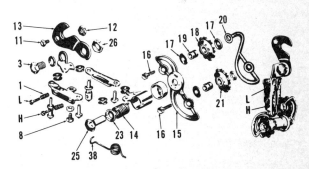

Fig. CA1—Exploded view of Campagnolo Valentino Extra rear derailleur.

1. Adjustment lock spring	8. Cable attaching bolt	15. Outer cage plate	20. Inner (wheel side) cage plate
2. Cover	9. Main body	16. Bolt	21. Lower idler (jockey) wheel
3. Arm pivot or pivot snap ring	10. Tension spring	17. Cap or bearing cone	22. Tension adjusting sleeve
4. Lock spring	11. Attaching screw	18. Upper idler (jockey) wheel	23. Tension spring cup
5. Cable adjuster	12. Adapter nut	19. Bushing or bearing balls	24. Lock nut
6. Nut	13. Adapter		
7. Cable holder	14. Chain tension spring		

25. Pivot bolt	32. Housing
26. Lock nut	33. Cap
27. Front derailleur cage	34. Belcrank
28. Pivots	35. Pivot screw
29. Lever	36. Roller
30. Shift spring	37. Spindle
31. Spring sleeve	38. Shift spring
	39. Spring cup

chain is installed. Hold shift mechanism in line with large sprocket and turn low speed stop screw (L) to prevent over-shifting past large sprocket. All moving parts of derailleur should be lubricated frequently with oil.

Chain tension is controlled by spring (14). Tension should be maintained at a minimum to reduce friction. To adjust, reposition end of spring in different hole of cage (15).

FRONT DERAILLEUR. Install on seat tube so that derailleur cage (27-Fig. CA2) is parallel with chainwheels and clears teeth of largest chainwheel. Install chain through derailleur cage and around smallest chainwheel. Loosen set screw (L) and center cage (27) directly over small chainwheel, then retighten set screw (L). Install control cable up through bracket and clamp in lever (34). Be sure that control lever is forward, then tighten clamp screw (8). Pull control lever back which should move derailleur cage out toward large chainwheel. NOTE: Be sure to turn chainwheels while shifting. Turn

stop screw (H) as necessary to center cage over large chainwheel when control lever is fully toward rear.

Campagnolo Nuovo Record

REAR DERAILLEUR. To adjust, move control lever forward, then loosen cable clamp screw (8-Fig. CA3). Turn lower adjusting screw (H) until rollers and derailleur cage are aligned with small (outside) sprocket. Tighten cable clamp screw (8) and shift unit to low gear by moving control lever. NOTE: Turn chainwheels in normal direction while shifting derailleurs if chain is installed. Hold shift mechanism in line with large sprocket and turn

low speed stop screw (L) to prevent overshifting past large sprocket. All moving parts of derailleur and chain should be lubricated frequently with oil.

Chain tension is controlled by spring (14). Tension should be maintained at a minimum to reduce friction. To adjust, reposition end of spring in different hole of cage (15).

FRONT DERAILLEUR. Install on seat tube so that derailleur cage (27-Fig. CA4) is parallel with chainwheels and clears teeth of largest chainwheel. Install chain through derailleur cage and around smallest chainwheel. Turn stop screw (L), to center cage (27) directly over small chainwheel. Install control

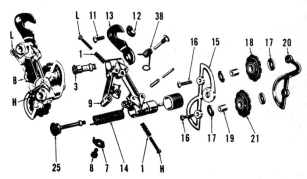

Fig. CA3—Exploded view of Campagnolo Nuovo Record rear derailleur.

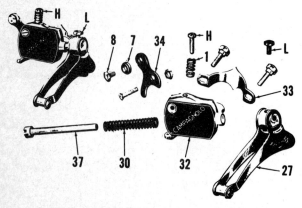

Fig. CA2—Exploded view of Campagnolo Valentino front derailleur.

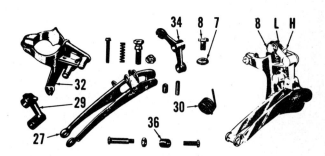

Fig. CA4—Exploded view of Campagnolo Record front derailleur.

1. Adjustment lock spring	8. Cable attaching bolt	15. Outer cage plate	20. Inner (wheel side) cage plate
2. Cover	9. Main body	16. Bolt	21. Lower idler (jockey) wheel
3. Arm pivot or pivot snap ring	10. Tension spring	17. Cap or bearing cone	22. Tension adjusting sleeve
4. Lock spring	11. Attaching screw	18. Upper idler (jockey) wheel	23. Tension spring cup
5. Cable adjuster	12. Adapter nut	19. Bushing or bearing balls	24. Lock nut
6. Nut	13. Adapter		
7. Cable holder	14. Chain tension spring		

25. Pivot bolt	32. Housing
26. Lock nut	33. Cap
27. Front derailleur cage	34. Belcrank
28. Pivots	35. Pivot screw
29. Lever	36. Roller
30. Shift spring	37. Spindle
31. Spring sleeve	38. Shift spring
	39. Spring

cable up through lever (34), be sure that control lever is forward, then tighten clamp screw (8). Pull control lever back which should move derailleur cage out toward large chainwheel. NOTE: Be sure to turn chainwheels while shifting. Turn stop screw (H) as necessary to center cage over large chainwheel when control lever is fully toward rear.

Campagnolo Sport Extra

REAR DERAILLEUR. To adjust, move control lever forward, then loosen cable clamp screw (8-Fig.CA5). Turn adjuster screw (H) until rollers and derailleur cage are aligned with small (outside) sprocket. Tighten cable clamp screw (8) and shift unit to low gear by moving control lever. NOTE: Turn chainwheels in normal direction while shifting derailleurs if chain is installed. Hold shift mechanism in line with large sprocket and turn low speed stop screw (L) to prevent overshifting past large sprocket. All moving parts of derailleur and chain should be lubricated with oil.

Chain tension is controlled by spring (10).

Cyclo Benelux

These units are available for use with multi-speed rear hubs or with standard free wheeling unit. Although several differences in application and changes in design may be noted, adjustment procedure will be similar for all models.

REAR DERAILLEUR. To adjust, move control lever forward,

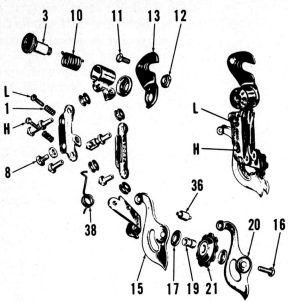

Fig. CA5—Exploded view of Campagnolo Sport Extra rear derailleur.

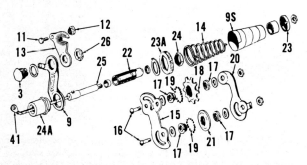

Fig. CY1—Exploded view of original Benelux rear derailleur.

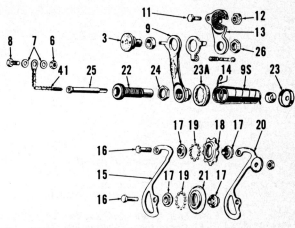

Fig. CY2—Exploded view of Benelux Mark 7 rear derailleur. Spring cup (23A) is used to adjust tension of spring (14). Toggle chain is shown at (41).

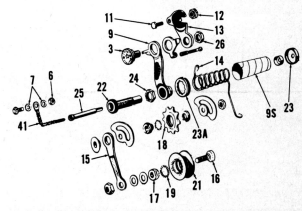

Fig. CY3—Exploded view of Benelux Mark 8 Tourist rear derailleur. Bearings in idler sprocket (18) and tension pulley (21) are adjustable.

1. Adjustment lock spring	8. Cable attaching bolt	15. Outer cage plate	20. Inner (wheel side) cage plate	25. Pivot bolt	32. Housing
2. Cover	9. Main body	16. Bolt	21. Lower idler (jockey) wheel	26. Lock nut	33. Cap
3. Arm pivot or pivot snap ring	10. Tension spring	17. Cap or bearing cone	22. Tension adjusting sleeve	27. Front derailleur cage	34. Belcrank
4. Lock spring	11. Attaching screw	18. Upper idler (jockey) wheel	23. Tension spring cup	28. Pivots	35. Pivot screw
5. Cable adjuster	12. Adapter nut	19. Bushing or bearing balls	24. Lock nut	29. Lever	36. Roller
6. Nut	13. Adapter			30. Shift spring	37. Spindle
7. Cable holder	14. Chain tension spring			31. Spring sleeve	38. Shift spring
					39. Spring

then loosen cable clamp (8-Fig. CY4). Loosen nut (24), then turn knurled adjusting sleeve (22) until idler wheel is aligned with low speed sprocket as shown at (L). Tighten lock nut (24) and cable

clamp screw (8) after low speed setting is correct. Stop screw (S) is provided on some models to adjust for chain length. Turn screw (S) so that three rivets (one complete link) of chain is

between large (low speed) sprocket and top idler wheel. Tension of spring (14-Fig. CY1, Fig. CY2 and Fig. CY3) moves derailleur in to engage lower speed sprockets and provides tension for chain. To adjust, push cup (23A) off locating stud, turn and reposition on cup. Tension of spring should be maintained at the minimum required for adequate operation.

FRONT DERAILLEUR. Two types have been used. The rod operated unit is shown in Fig. CY7 and the cable operated unit in Fig. CY6. On all models, install unit on seat tube so that derailleur cage (27) is parallel with chainwheels and clears teeth of largest chainwheel. On units controlled by control rod (34R-Fig. CY7), position upper bracket (33U) approximately 4¾ inches above lower clamp (33). On all models, loosen set screw (L-Fig. CY8) and center derailleur cage over small chainwheel. Shift front derailleur to large chainwheel and

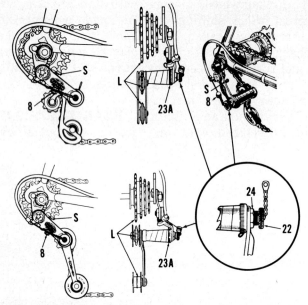

Fig. CY4—Views of installed Benelux rear derailleurs. Upper left drawings are of Mark 7; lower left are of Mark 8 Tourist: Drawing at upper right is of installation on multi-speed rear hub. Inset shows details of adjuster.

   L. Low speed sprocket and idler rollers
   S. Chain tension adjusting stop screw
   8. Cable clamp screw
 22. Adjusting sleeve
23A. Spring retaining cup
 24. Lock nut

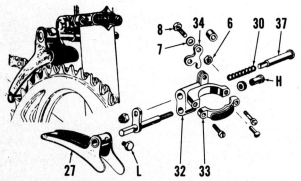

Fig. CY6—Exploded and installed drawings of cable operated Benelux front derailleur.

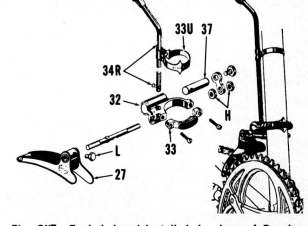

Fig. CY7—Exploded and installed drawings of Benelux front derailleur operated by a control rod. Upper support clamp (33U) should be located approximately 4-3/4 inches above lower clamp.

1. Adjustment lock spring	8. Cable attaching bolt	15. Outer cage plate	20. Inner (wheel side) cage plate	25. Pivot bolt	32. Housing
2. Cover	9. Main body	16. Bolt	21. Lower idler (jockey) wheel	26. Lock nut	33. Cap
3. Arm pivot or pivot snap ring	10. Tension spring	17. Cap or bearing cone	22. Tension adjusting sleeve	27. Front derailleur cage	34. Belcrank
4. Lock spring	11. Attaching screw	18. Upper idler (jockey) wheel	23. Tension spring cup	28. Pivots	35. Pivot screw
5. Cable adjuster	12. Adapter nut	19. Bushing or bearing balls	24. Lock nut	29. Lever	36. Roller
6. Nut	13. Adapter			30. Shift spring	37. Spindle
7. Cable holder	14. Chain tension spring			31. Spring sleeve	38. Shift spring
					39. Spring cup

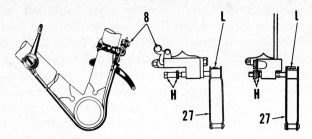

Fig. CY8—View showing adjustment locations for cable and rod operated Benelux front derailleurs.

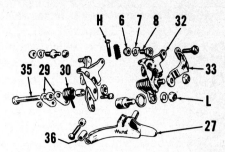

Fig. H3—Exploded view of Huret 1964 Allvit front derailleur.

check for correct alignment with large chainwheel. If alignment is incorrect, adjust by turning adjustment nuts (H). On models with rod control, recheck alignment with small chainwheel and readjust with set screw (L) if necessary.

Huret Allvit and Super Allvit

The length of the rear derailleur cage (15 & 20-Fig. H1 and Fig. H2) determines the range of sprockets that can be used. The standard unit (Fig. H1) has a range of 30 teeth to 13 teeth on rear sprockets and 36 to 53 on chainwheels. Super Allvit unit (Fig. H2) has a range of 34 teeth to 13 teeth on rear sprockets and 26 to 53 on chainwheels.

The Avant front derailleur is often used with the Allvit rear unit. Refer to the following section for service of Avant front derailleur.

REAR DERAILLEUR. To adjust, move control lever forward, then loosen cable clamp screw (8-Fig. H1 or Fig. H2). Turn top adjuster screw (H) until rollers and derailleur cage are aligned with small (outside) sprocket. Tighten cable clamp nut (6) and shift unit to low gear by moving control lever. NOTE: Turn chainwheels in normal direction while shifting derailleurs if chain is installed. Hold shift mechanism in line with large sprocket and turn low speed stop screw (L) to prevent overshifting past large sprocket. All moving parts of de-

railleur and chain should be lubricated frequently with oil.

Chain tension is controlled by spring (14). Tension should be maintained at a minimum to reduce friction. To adjust spring tension, hook end of spring over one of the two tabs (T1 or T2) on derailleur cage (15).

FRONT DERAILLEUR. On the model 1964 Allvit models, install on seat tube so that derailleur cage (27-Fig. H3) is parallel with chainwheels and clears teeth of largest chainwheel. Install chain through derailleur cage and around smallest chainwheel. Loosen nut (L), center cage (27) directly over small chainwheel, then retighten nut (L). Install control cable up behind washer (7), be

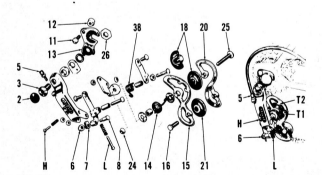

Fig. H1—Exploded view of Huret Allvit rear derailleur. Chain tension is increased by hooking spring (14) on tang (T2).

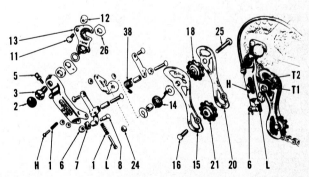

Fig. H2—Exploded view of Huret Super Allvit rear derailleur. A longer derailleur cage (15 or 20) is used, permitting more capacity of sprockets and chain wheels.

1. Adjustment lock spring	8. Cable attaching bolt	15. Outer cage plate	20. Inner (wheel side) cage plate	25. Pivot bolt
2. Cover	9. Main body	16. Bolt	21. Lower idler (jockey) wheel	26. Lock nut
3. Arm pivot or pivot snap ring	10. Tension spring	17. Cap or bearing cone	22. Tension adjusting sleeve	27. Front derailleur cage
4. Lock spring	11. Attaching screw	18. Upper idler (jockey) wheel	23. Tension spring cup	28. Pivots
5. Cable adjuster	12. Adapter nut	19. Bushing or bearing balls	24. Lock nut	29. Lever
6. Nut	13. Adapter			30. Shift spring
7. Cable holder	14. Chain tension spring			31. Spring sleeve

32. Housing
33. Cap
34. Belcrank
35. Pivot screw
36. Roller
37. Spindle
38. Shift spring
39. Spring cup

sure that control lever is forward, then tighten clamp nut (6). Pull control lever back which should move derailleur cage out toward large chainwheel. NOTE: Be sure to turn chainwheels while shifting. Turn stop screw (H) as necessary to center cage over large chainwheel when control lever is fully toward rear.

Huret Avant "700"

This front derailleur is often used in combination with Huret Allvit or Svelto rear derailleur.

FRONT DERAILLEUR. Install on seat tube so that derailleur cage (27-Fig. H4) is parallel with chainwheels and clears teeth of largest chainwheel. Install chain through derailleur cage and around smallest chainwheel. Turn stop screw (L) to center cage (27) directly over small chainwheel. Install control cable up behind washer (7), be sure that control lever is forward, then tighten clamp nut (6). Pull control lever back which should move derailleur cage out toward large chain-

wheel. NOTE: Be sure to turn chainwheels while shifting. Turn stop screw (H) as necessary to center cage over large chainwheel when control lever is fully toward rear.

Huret Jubilee

The Huret Jubilee derailleur is a light alloy unit. The length of the rear derailleur cage (15 & 20-Fig. H5) determines the range of sprockets that can be used. Short unit has a range of 24 teeth to 13 teeth on rear sprockets and longer derailleur cage will accept rear sprockets of 13 teeth through 28 teeth. On all models, chainwheels should have from 36 to 53 teeth.

REAR DERAILLEUR. To adjust, move control lever forward, then loosen cable clamp screw (8-Fig. H5). Turn adjuster screw (H) until rollers and derailleur cage are aligned with small (outside) sprocket. Tighten cable clamp screw (8) and shift unit to low gear by moving control lever. NOTE: Turn chainwheels in nor-

mal direction while shifting derailleurs if chain is installed. Hold shift mechanism in line with large sprocket and turn low speed stop screw (L) to prevent overshifting past large sprocket. All moving parts of derailleur and chain should be lubricated with oil.

Chain tension is controlled by spring (14). Tension should be maintained at a minimum to reduce friction. To adjust, disassemble and hook end of spring (14) in other hole in derailleur body (9).

FRONT DERAILLEUR. Install on seat tube so that derailleur cage (27-Fig. H6) is parallel with chainwheels and clears teeth of largest chainwheel. Install chain through derailleur cage and around smallest chainwheel. Turn stop screw (L) to center cage (27) directly over small chainwheel. Install control cable up behind washer (7), be sure that control

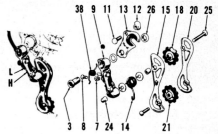

Fig. H5—Exploded view of Huret Jubilee rear derailleur.

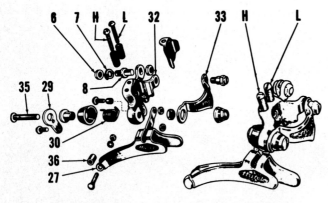

Fig. H4—Exploded view of Huret Avant front derailleur. This unit is often used in conjunction with Allvit rear unit.

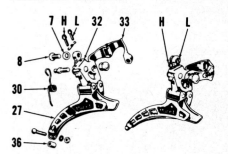

Fig. H6—Exploded view of Huret Jubilee front derailleur.

1. Adjustment lock spring	8. Cable attaching bolt
2. Cover	9. Main body
3. Arm pivot or pivot snap ring	10. Tension spring
4. Lock spring	11. Attaching screw
5. Cable adjuster	12. Adapter nut
6. Nut	13. Adapter
7. Cable holder	14. Chain tension spring

15. Outer cage plate	20. Inner (wheel side) cage plate
16. Bolt	21. Lower idler (jockey) wheel
17. Cap or bearing cone	22. Tension adjusting sleeve
18. Upper idler (jockey) wheel	23. Tension spring cup
19. Bushing or bearing balls	24. Lock nut

25. Pivot bolt	32. Housing
26. Lock nut	33. Cap
27. Front derailleur cage	34. Belcrank
28. Pivots	35. Pivot screw
29. Lever	36. Roller
30. Shift spring	37. Spindle
31. Spring sleeve	38. Shift spring
	39. Spring cup

lever is forward, then tighten clamp screw (8). Pull control lever back which should move derailleur cage out toward large chainwheel. NOTE: Be sure to turn chainwheels while shifting. Turn stop screw (H) as necessary to center cage over large chainwheel when control lever is fully toward rear.

Huret Luxe

REAR DERAILLEUR. To adjust, move control lever forward, then loosen cable clamp nut (6-Fig. H7). Turn top adjuster screw (H) until rollers and derailleur cage are aligned with small (outside) sprocket. Tighten cable

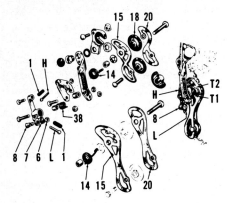

Fig. H7—Exploded view of Huret Luxe rear derailleur. Two different lengths of derailleur cage (15 & 20) are available to accomodate different sprocket ranges.

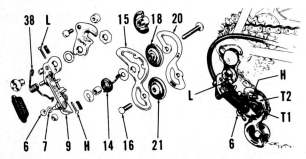

Fig. H8—Exploded of Huret Svelto rear derailleur. Chain tension can be increased by hooking end of spring (14) over tang (T2).

clamp nut (6) and shift unit to low gear by moving control lever. NOTE: Turn chainwheels in normal direction while shifting derailleurs if chain is installed. Hold shift mechanism in line with large sprocket and turn low speed stop screw (L) to prevent overshifting past large sprocket. All moving parts of derailleur and chain should be lubricated with oil.

Chain tension is controlled by spring (14). Tension should be maintained at a minimum to reduce friction. To adjust spring tension, hook end of spring over one of the two tabs (T1 or T2) on derailleur cage (15).

Huret Svelto

The capacity of the Svelto derailleur is within the range of 13 to 24 teeth on the rear sprocket. Unit is often used in combination with a Huret Avant front derailleur.

REAR DERAILLEUR. To adjust, move control lever forward, then loosen cable clamp nut (6-Fig. H8). Turn adjuster screw (H)

until rollers and derailleur cage are aligned with small (outside) sprocket. Tighten cable clamp nut (6) and shift unit to low gear by moving control lever. NOTE: Turn chainwheels in normal direction while shifting derailleurs if chain is installed. Hold shift mechanism in line with large sprocket and turn low speed stop screw (L) to prevent overshifting past large sprocket. All moving parts of derailleur and chain should be lubricated with oil.

Chain tension is controlled by spring (14). Tension should be maintained at a minimum to reduce friction. To adjust spring tension, hook end of spring over one of the two tabs (T1 or T2) on derailleur cage (15).

Schwinn

The length of the rear derailleur cage (15 & 20-Fig. SC1 and Fig. SC2) determines the range of sprockets that can be used.

REAR DERAILLEUR. To adjust, move control lever forward, then loosen cable clamp screw (8-

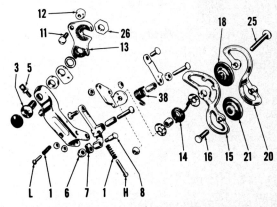

Fig. SC1—Exploded view of rear derailleur typical of some Schwinn units.

1. Adjustment lock spring	8. Cable attaching bolt	15. Outer cage plate	20. Inner (wheel side) cage plate	25. Pivot bolt	32. Housing
2. Cover	9. Main body	16. Bolt	21. Lower idler (jockey) wheel	26. Lock nut	33. Cap
3. Arm pivot or pivot snap ring	10. Tension spring	17. Cap or bearing cone	22. Tension adjusting sleeve	27. Front derailleur cage	34. Belcrank
4. Lock spring	11. Attaching screw	18. Upper idler (jockey) wheel	23. Tension spring cup	28. Pivots	35. Pivot screw
5. Cable adjuster	12. Adapter nut	19. Bushing or bearing balls	24. Lock nut	29. Lever	36. Roller
6. Nut	13. Adapter			30. Shift spring	37. Spindle
7. Cable holder	14. Chain tension spring			31. Spring sleeve	38. Shift spring
					39. Spring cup

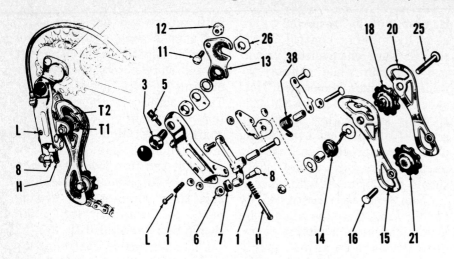

Fig. SC2—Exploded view of rear derailleur typical of some Schwinn units. Chain tension can be adjusted by hooking end of spring (14) over tang (T2).

wheel. Turn stop screw (L) to center cage (27) directly over small chainwheel. Install control cable up behind washer (7), to be sure that control lever is forward, then tighten clamp nut (6). Pull control lever back which should move derailleur cage out toward large chainwheel. NOTE: Be sure to turn chainwheels while shifting. Turn stop screw (H) as necessary to center cage over large chainwheel when control lever is fully toward rear.

Shimano Crane, Dura Ace, Eagle, Thunder Bird, Titlist, Tourney

These derailleurs are similar but not exactly alike. Several variations of these units are available and only a few are illustrated. Crane rear derailleurs are manufactured of light alloy material. Titlist rear derailleur is manufactured with light alloy body and a steel cage. Tourney model rear derailleurs are similar to Titlist models except that some body parts are also steel. Eagle rear derailleurs are all steel con-

Fig. SC1 or Fig. SC2). Turn top adjuster screw (H) until rollers and derailleur cage are aligned with small (outside) sprocket. Tighten cable clamp nut (6) and shift unit to low gear by moving control lever. NOTE: Turn chainwheels in normal direction while shifting derailleurs if chain is installed. Hold shift mechanism in line with large sprocket and turn low speed stop screw (L) to prevent overshifting past large sprocket. All moving parts of derailleur and chain should be lubricated frequently with oil.

Chain tension is controlled by spring (14). Tension should be maintained at a minimum to re-

duce friction. To adjust spring tension, hook end of spring over one of the two tabs (T1 or T2) on derailleur cage (15).

FRONT DERAILLEUR. Install front derailleur on seat tube so that derailleur cage (27-Fig. SC3) is parallel with chainwheels and clears teeth of largest chainwheel. Install chain through derailleur cage and around smallest chain-

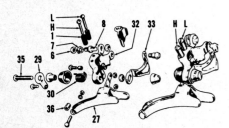

Fig. SC3—Exploded view of front derailleur typical of some Schwinn units.

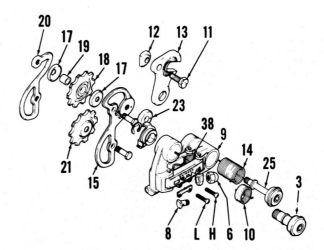

Fig. SH1—Exploded view of Shimano Crane rear derailleur.

1. Adjustment lock spring	8. Cable attaching bolt	15. Outer cage plate	20. Inner (wheel side) cage plate	25. Pivot bolt	32. Housing
2. Cover	9. Main body	16. Bolt	21. Lower idler (jockey) wheel	26. Lock nut	33. Cap
3. Arm pivot or pivot snap ring	10. Tension spring	17. Cap or bearing cone	22. Tension adjusting sleeve	27. Front derailleur cage	34. Belcrank
4. Lock spring	11. Attaching screw	18. Upper idler (jockey) wheel	23. Tension spring cup	28. Pivots	35. Pivot screw
5. Cable adjuser	12. Adapter nut	19. Bushing or bearing balls	24. Lock nut	29. Lever	36. Roller
6. Nut	13. Adapter			30. Shift spring	37. Spindle
7. Cable holder	14. Chain tension spring			31. Spring sleeve	38. Shift spring
					39. Spring

struction with a built in guard to protect the unit from falls. Lark rear derailleur is made of steel like Eagle models except it is not equipped with a guard. Standard Crane, Titlist, Tourney, Eagle, Lark SS and Lark GTO models are equipped with standard length rear cage. A longer derailleur cage is used on Crane GS, Titlist GS, Tourney GS, Eagle GS and Eagle GTO models. Lark W is designed for use as 5 speed (no front derailleur) with a special twist grip control.

Dura-Ace front derailleur is made of light alloy metal. The Titlist front derailleur is equipped with a light alloy metal body and steel guide plate. Thunder Bird and Thunder Bird GTO front derailleurs are similar in design to Titlist and Dura-Ace models, but are made of steel. The 3.3.3. front derailleur is designed differently than the other models. The 3.3.3. unit is made of steel.

REAR DERAILLEUR. To adjust, move control lever forward, then loosen cable clamp nut (6- Fig. SH1, Fig. SH2, Fig. SH3 or Fig. SH4). Turn adjuster screw (H) until rollers and derailleur cage are aligned with small (outside) sprocket. Tighten cable clamp nut (6) and shift unit to low gear by moving control lever. NOTE: Turn chainwheels in normal direction while shifting derailleurs if chain is installed. Hold shift mechanism in line with large sprocket and turn low speed stop screw (L) to prevent overshifting past large sprocket. All moving parts of derailleur and chain should be lubricated with oil.

Chain tension is controlled by springs (10 and 14). Tension should be maintained at a minimum to reduce friction.

FRONT DERAILLEUR. On Dura-Ace, Titlist, Thunder Bird and Thunder Bird GTO models,

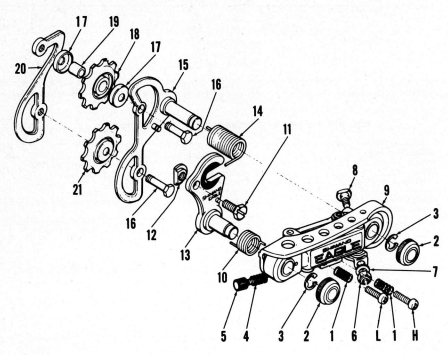

Fig. SH2—Exploded view of Shimano Eagle rear derailleur with standard capacity.

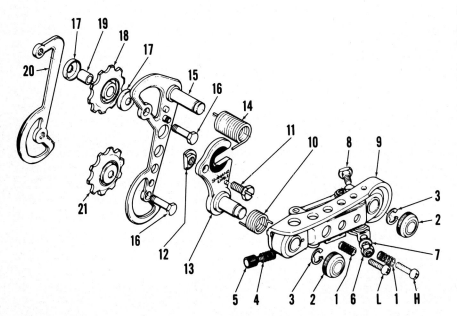

Fig. SH3—Exploded view of Shimano Eagle rear derailleur with increased capacity because of the long derailleur cage (15 & 20).

1. Adjustment lock spring	8. Cable attaching bolt	15. Outer cage plate	20. Inner (wheel side) cage plate	25. Pivot bolt	32. Housing
2. Cover	9. Main body	16. Bolt	21. Lower idler (jockey) wheel	26. Lock nut	33. Cap
3. Arm pivot or pivot snap ring	10. Tension spring	17. Cap or bearing cone	22. Tension adjusting sleeve	27. Front derailleur cage	34. Belcrank
4. Lock spring	11. Attaching screw	18. Upper idler (jockey) wheel	23. Tension spring cup	28. Pivots	35. Pivot screw
5. Cable adjuster	12. Adapter nut	19. Bushing or bearing balls	24. Lock nut	29. Lever	36. Roller
6. Nut	13. Adapter			30. Shift spring	37. Spindle
7. Cable holder	14. Chain tension spring			31. Spring sleeve	38. Shift spring
					39. Spring cup

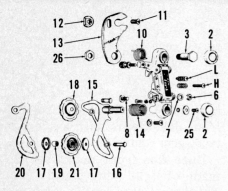

Fig. SH4—Exploded view of Shimano Lark rear derailleur.

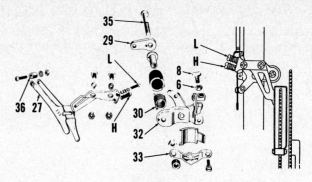

Fig. SH6—Views of Shimano 3.3.3. front derailleur.

1. Adjustment lock spring	8. Cable attaching bolt
2. Cover	9. Main body
3. Arm pivot or pivot snap ring	10. Tension spring
4. Lock spring	11. Attaching screw
5. Cable adjuster	12. Adapter nut
6. Nut	13. Adapter
7. Cable holder	14. Chain tension spring
	15. Outer cage plate
	16. Bolt
	17. Cap or bearing cone
	18. Upper idler (jockey) wheel
	19. Bushing or bearing balls

install on seat tube so that derailleur cage (27-Fig. SH5) is parallel with chainwheels and clears teeth of largest chainwheel. Install chain through derailleur cage and around smallest chainwheel. Turn stop screw (L) to center cage (27) directly over small chainwheel. Install control cable up through screw (8), be sure that control lever is forward, then tighten clamp nut (6). Pull control lever back which should move derailleur cage out toward large chainwheel. NOTE: Be sure to turn chainwheels while shifting. Turn stop screw (H) as necessary to center cage over large chainwheel when control lever is fully toward rear.

Installation procedure for 3.3.3. model (Fig. SH6) is similar. Position derailleur cage (27) over small chainwheel by turning stop screw (L), connect cable in clamp, then adjust high speed stop (H). Stop screws (L & H) are toward left side of bicycle.

Shimano Positron

This derailleur system is equipped with a detent assembly which assures positive location of the rear derailleur cage and permits movement of control lever while chain is stopped. The front derailleur may be any of several types, but is often the Shimano Thunderbird type described and adjusted in the previous paragraphs.

To adjust the Positron unit, shift rear derailleur until the detent ball is positioned in the middle notch as shown in inset (A – Fig. SH7). Loosen the cable clamp screw, then turn the derailleur screw (Fig. SH8) as necessary to locate the derailleur

pulleys directly below the middle sprocket. It will be necessary to turn pedals in normal direction if chain is not on center sprocket when beginning adjustment. Correct adjustment may not be possible if derailleur is bent or otherwise seriously damaged.

Move the control lever to the "3" or center position, then remove slack from cable, but be careful not to move the rear derailleur. Tighten the cable clamp (Fig. SH7) to retain cable position, then check operation by pedalling and changing gears, both up and down.

Refer to Fig. SH9 for exploded view of Positron 400 rear derailleur and to Fig. SH10 for Positron II positive pre-select system (PPS). The push and pull action of the cable should not require adjustment, but cable must be maintained in good condition and properly lubricated.

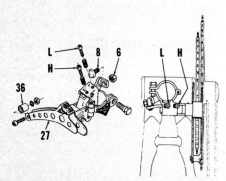

Fig. SH5—Views of Shimano Thunder Bird front derailleur.

Fig. SH7—Refer to text for adjusting Shimano PPS rear derailleur. Inset "A" shows the detent ball in middle notch.

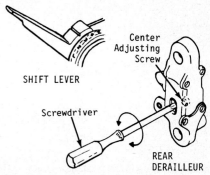

Fig. SH8—Turn center adjusting screw as necessary to align pulleys directly below the middle sprocket.

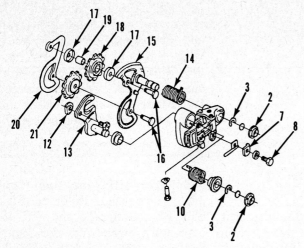

Fig. SH9—Exploded view of Shimano Positron 400 positive pre-select rear derailleur.

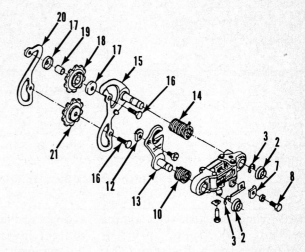

Fig. SH10—Exploded view of Shimano Positron II positive pre-select rear derailleur.

Simplex

Total capacity is 37 teeth for standard Prestige and Criterium models. Largest rear sprockets should not exceed 28 teeth for Prestige; 30 for Criterium. Small sprocket on both Prestige and Criterium models should have a minimum of 13 teeth. Mini Prestige model is designed for five speeds (rear sprockets) only.

REAR DERAILLEUR. To adjust, move control lever forward, then loosen cable clamp screw (8-Fig. SM1, Fig. SM2, Fig. SM3, Fig. SM5 or Fig. SM7). Turn top adjuster screw (H) until rollers and derailleur cage are aligned with small (outside) sprocket. Tighten cable clamp screw (8) and shift unit to low gear by moving control lever. NOTE: Turn chainwheels in normal direction while shifting derailleurs if chain is installed. Hold shift mechanism in line with large sprocket and turn low speed stop screw (L) to prevent overshifting past large sprocket. All moving parts of derailleur and chain should be lubricated with oil.

Chain tension is controlled by springs (10 and 14). Tension should be maintained at a minimum to reduce friction. To adjust, loosen lock nut (24) and use Allen wrench to turn spring bolt (25). Turn bolt clockwise to in-

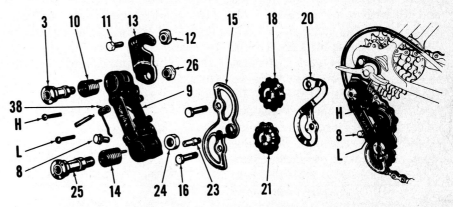

Fig. SM1—Exploded view of Simplex Prestige rear derailleur.

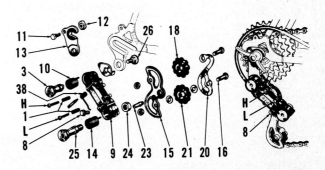

Fig. SM2—Exploded view of Simplex Prestige N1 rear derailleur.

20. Inner (wheel side) cage plate	25. Pivot bolt	32. Housing
21. Lower idler (jockey) wheel	26. Lock nut	33. Cap
	27. Front derailleur cage	34. Belcrank
22. Tension adjusting sleeve	28. Pivots	35. Pivot screw
23. Tension spring cup	29. Lever	36. Roller
24. Lock nut	30. Shift spring	37. Spindle
	31. Spring sleeve	38. Shift spring
		39. Spring cup

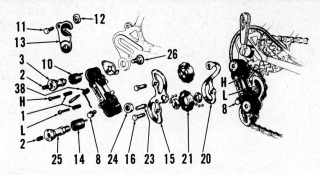

Fig. SM3—Exploded view of Simplex Criterium rear derailleur.

crease chain tension, then tighten lock nut (24). Upper spring is similarly adjusted with bolt (3) after loosening nut or screw (26). Initial setting (without chain) should provide both springs (10 and 14) with ½-turn preload.

FRONT DERAILLEUR. On standard Prestige and Criterium models, install on seat tube so that derailleur cage (27-Fig. SM4) is parallel with chainwheels and clears teeth of largest chainwheel. Install chain through derailleur cage and around smallest chainwheel. Loosen set screw (L), center cage (27) directly over small chainwheel, then retighten set screw (L). Install control cable up through lever (34), housing (32)

and clamp block (6). Be sure that control lever is forward, then tighten clamp screw (8). Pull control lever back which should have derailleur cage out toward large chainwheel. NOTE: Be sure to turn chainwheels while shifting. Turn stop screw (H) as necessary to center cage over large chainwheel when control lever is fully toward rear.

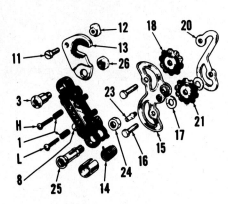

Fig. SM5—Exploded view of Simplex Mini Prestige rear derailleur. Unit is used as five speed only.

Installation procedure for Super Competition model (Fig. SM6) and Prestige Super L. J. model (Fig. SM7) is similar. Position derailleur cage (27) over small chainwheel by turning stop screw (L), connect cable in clamp (8), then adjust high speed stop (H).

Sun Tour

Several different Sun Tour models are used. Refer to Figs. ST1, ST2, ST3, ST4 and ST5 for exploded views of rear derailleurs and Figs. ST7 and ST8 for front derailleurs. The V-GT and V models of rear derailleurs and Compe-V front derailleur are made of light alloy metal while others are made of steel.

REAR DERAILLEUR. To adjust, move control lever forward, then loosen cable clamp screw (8-Fig. ST6). Turn top adjuster screw (H) until rollers and derailleur cage are aligned with small (outside) sprocket. Tighten cable clamp screw (8) and shift unit to low gear by moving control lever. NOTE: Turn chainwheels in normal direction while shifting derailleurs if chain is installed. Hold shift mechanism in line with large sprocket and turn low speed stop screw (L) to prevent overshifting

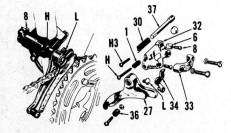

Fig. SM4—Exploded view of Simplex front derailleur typical of Prestige and Criterium models. A shorter stop screw (H3) is used when used with three chain wheels.

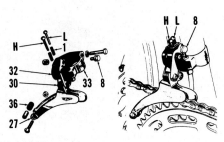

Fig. SM6—Exploded view of Simplex Super Competition front derailleur.

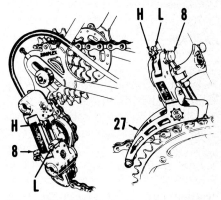

Fig. SM7—Installed drawings of Simplex Prestige Super L. J. derailleurs.

1. Adjustment lock spring	8. Cable attaching bolt
2. Cover	9. Main body
3. Arm pivot or pivot snap ring	10. Tension spring
4. Lock spring	11. Attaching screw
5. Cable adjuster	12. Adapter nut
6. Nut	13. Adapter
7. Cable holder	14. Chain tension spring

15. Outer cage plate	20. Inner (wheel side) cage plate
16. Bolt	21. Lower idler (jockey) wheel
17. Cap or bearing cone	22. Tension adjusting sleeve
18. Upper idler (jockey) wheel	23. Tension spring cup
19. Bushing or bearing balls	24. Lock nut

25. Pivot bolt	32. Housing
26. Lock nut	33. Cap
27. Front derailleur cage	34. Belcrank
28. Pivots	35. Pivot screw
29. Lever	36. Roller
30. Shift spring	37. Spindle
31. Spring sleeve	38. Shift spring
	39. Spring

past large sprocket. All moving parts of derailleur and chain should be lubricated with oil.

Chain tension is controlled by spring (10-Figs. ST1, ST2, ST3, ST4 and ST5). Tension should be maintained at a minimum to reduce friction.

FRONT DERAILLEUR. Install derailleur on seat tube so that derailleur cage (27-Fig. ST7 and ST8) is parallel with chainwheels and clears teeth of largest chainwheel. Install chain through derailleur cage and around smallest chainwheel. Turn stop screw (L) to center cage (27) directly over small chainwheel. Install control

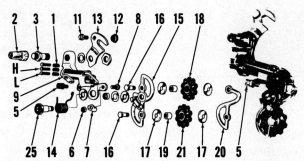

Fig. ST1—Exploded view of Sun Tour Skitter rear derailleur. Capacity is 28 teeth.

cable, be sure that control lever is forward, then tighten clamp screw (8). Pull control lever back which should move derailleur cage out toward large chainwheel.

NOTE: Be sure to turn chainwheels while shifting. Turn stop screw (H) as necessary to center cage over large chainwheel when control lever is fully toward rear.

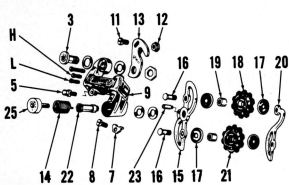

Fig. ST2—Exploded view of Sun Tour V rear derailleur. Capacity is 24 teeth.

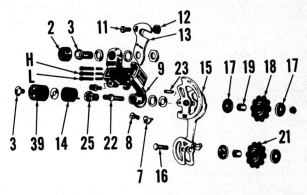

Fig. ST4—Exploded view of Sun Tour GT rear derailleur. Capacity is 36 teeth.

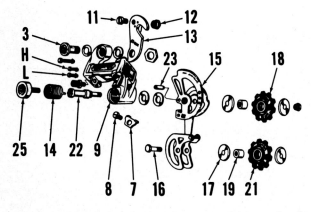

Fig. ST3—Exploded view of Suntour V-GT rear derailleur. Capacity is 36 teeth.

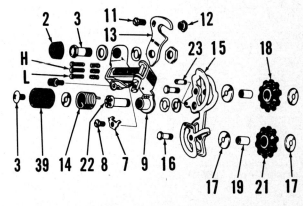

Fig. ST5—Exploded view of Sun Tour Honor rear derailleur. Capacity is 28 teeth.

1. Adjustment lock spring	8. Cable attaching bolt	15. Outer cage plate	20. Inner (wheel side) cage plate
2. Cover	9. Main body	16. Bolt	21. Lower idler (jockey) wheel
3. Arm pivot or pivot snap ring	10. Tension spring	17. Cap or bearing cone	22. Tension adjusting sleeve
4. Lock spring	11. Attaching screw	18. Upper idler (jockey) wheel	23. Tension spring cup
5. Cable adjuster	12. Adapter nut	19. Bushing or bearing balls	24. Lock nut
6. Nut	13. Adapter		
7. Cable holder	14. Chain tension spring		

25. Pivot bolt	32. Housing
26. Lock nut	33. Cap
27. Front derailleur cage	34. Belcrank
28. Pivots	35. Pivot screw
29. Lever	36. Roller
30. Shift spring	37. Spindle
31. Spring sleeve	38. Shift spring
	39. Spring cup

Fig. ST6—*View of Sun Tour Honor rear derailleur showing location of adjustment parts. Other Sun Tour models are similar.*

Triplex

REAR DERAILLEUR. To adjust, move control lever forward, then loosen cable clamp screw (8-Fig. T1). Turn top adjuster screw (H) until rollers and derailleur cage are aligned with small (outside) sprocket. Tighten cable clamp screw (8) and shift unit to low gear by moving control lever. NOTE: Turn chainwheels in normal direction while shifting derailleurs if chain is installed. Hold shift mechanism in line with large sprocket and turn low speed stop screw (L) to prevent overshifting past large sprocket. All moving parts of derailleur and chain should be lubricated with oil.

Chain tension is controlled by spring (14). Tension should be maintained at a minimum to reduce friction. To adjust, locate end of spring (14) in different hole in derailleur cage (15).

FRONT DERAILLEUR. Install derailleur on seat tube so that derailleur cage (27-Fig. T2) is parallel with chainwheels and clears teeth of largest chainwheel. Install chain through derailleur

cage and around smallest chainwheel. Turn stop screw (L) to center cage (27) directly over small chain wheel. Install control cable, be sure that control lever is forward, then tighten clamp screw (8). Pull control lever back which should move derailleur cage out toward large chainwheel. NOTE: Be sure to turn chainwheels while shifting. Turn stop screw (H) as necessary to center cage over large chainwheel when control lever is fully toward rear.

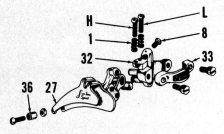

Fig. ST7—*Exploded view of Sun Tour Spirit front derailleur.*

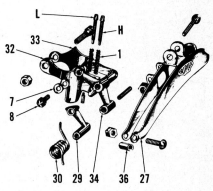

Fig. T2—*Exploded view of Triplex front derailleur.*

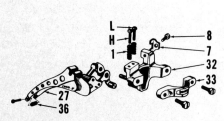

Fig. ST8—*Exploded view of Sun Tour Compe-V front derailleur.*

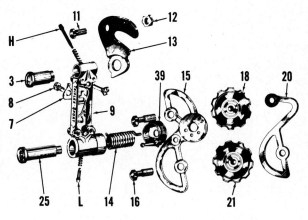

Fig. T1—*Exploded view of Triplex rear derailleur.*

1. Adjustment lock spring	8. Cable attaching bolt	15. Outer cage plate	20. Inner (wheel side) cage plate	25. Pivot bolt	32. Housing

1. Adjustment lock spring
2. Cover
3. Arm pivot or pivot snap ring
4. Lock spring
5. Cable adjuster
6. Nut
7. Cable holder

8. Cable attaching bolt
9. Main body
10. Tension spring
11. Attaching screw
12. Adapter nut
13. Adapter
14. Chain tension spring

15. Outer cage plate
16. Bolt
17. Cap or bearing cone
18. Upper idler (jockey) wheel
19. Bushing or bearing balls

20. Inner (wheel side) cage plate
21. Lower idler (jockey) wheel
22. Tension adjusting sleeve
23. Tension spring cup
24. Lock nut

25. Pivot bolt
26. Lock nut
27. Front derailleur cage
28. Pivots
29. Lever
30. Shift spring
31. Spring sleeve

32. Housing
33. Cap
34. Belcrank
35. Pivot screw
36. Roller
37. Spindle
38. Shift spring
39. Spring cup

METRIC CONVERSION

MM.	INCHES			MM.	INCHES			MM.	INCHES			MM.	INCHES			MM.	INCHES			MM.	INCHES		
1	0.0394	1/32	+	51	2.0079	2.0	+	101	3.9764	3 31/32	+	151	5.9449	5 15/16	+	201	7.9134	7 29/32	+	251	9.8819	9 7/8	+
2	0.0787	3/32	−	52	2.0472	2 1/16	−	102	4.0157	4 1/32	−	152	5.9842	5 31/32	+	202	7.9527	7 15/16	+	252	9.9212	9 29/32	+
3	0.1181	1/8	−	53	2.0866	2 3/32	−	103	4.0551	4 1/16	−	153	6.0236	6 1/32	−	203	7.9921	8.0	−	253	9.9606	9 31/32	−
4	0.1575	5/32	+	54	2.1260	2 1/8	+	104	4.0945	4 3/32	+	154	6.0630	6 1/16	+	204	8.0315	8 1/32	+	254	10.0000	10.0	
5	0.1969	3/16	+	55	2.1654	2 5/32	+	105	4.1339	4 1/8	+	155	6.1024	6 3/32	+	205	8.0709	8 1/16	+	255	10.0393	10 1/32	+
6	0.2362	1/4	−	56	2.2047	2 7/32	−	106	4.1732	4 3/16	−	156	6.1417	6 5/32	−	206	8.1102	8 1/8	−	256	10.0787	10 3/32	−
7	0.2756	9/32	−	57	2.2441	2 1/4	−	107	4.2126	4 7/32	−	157	6.1811	6 3/16	−	207	8.1496	8 5/32	−	257	10.1181	10 1/8	−
8	0.3150	5/16	+	58	2.2835	2 9/32	+	108	4.2520	4 1/4	+	158	6.2205	6 7/32	+	208	8.1890	8 3/16	+	258	10.1575	10 5/32	+
9	0.3543	11/32	+	59	2.3228	2 5/16	+	109	4.2913	4 9/32	+	159	6.2598	6 1/4	+	209	8.2283	8 7/32	+	259	10.1968	10 3/16	+
10	0.3937	13/32	−	60	2.3622	2 3/8	−	110	4.3307	4 11/32	−	160	6.2992	6 5/16	−	210	8.2677	8 9/32	−	260	10.2362	10 1/4	−
11	0.4331	7/16	−	61	2.4016	2 13/32	−	111	4.3701	4 3/8	−	161	6.3386	6 11/32	−	211	8.3071	8 5/16	−	261	10.2756	10 9/32	−
12	0.4724	15/32	+	62	2.4409	2 7/16	+	112	4.4094	4 13/32	+	162	6.3779	6 3/8	+	212	8.3464	8 11/32	+	262	10.3149	10 5/16	+
13	0.5118	1/2	+	63	2.4803	2 15/32	+	113	4.4488	4 7/16	+	163	6.4173	6 13/32	+	213	8.3858	8 3/8	+	263	10.3543	10 11/32	+
14	0.5512	9/16	−	64	2.5197	2 17/32	−	114	4.4882	4 1/2	−	164	6.4567	6 15/32	−	214	8.4252	8 7/16	−	264	10.3937	10 13/32	−
15	0.5906	19/32	−	65	2.5591	2 9/16	−	115	4.5276	4 17/32	−	165	6.4961	6 1/2	−	215	8.4646	8 15/32	−	265	10.4330	10 7/16	−
16	0.6299	5/8	+	66	2.5984	2 19/32	+	116	4.5669	4 9/16	+	166	6.5354	6 17/32	+	216	8.5039	8 1/2	+	266	10.4724	10 15/32	+
17	0.6693	21/32	+	67	2.6378	2 5/8	+	117	4.6063	4 19/32	+	167	6.5748	6 9/16	+	217	8.5433	8 17/32	+	267	10.5118	10 1/2	+
18	0.7087	23/32	−	68	2.6772	2 11/16	−	118	4.6457	4 21/32	−	168	6.6142	6 5/8	−	218	8.5827	8 9/16	−	268	10.5512	10 9/16	−
19	0.7480	3/4	−	69	2.7165	2 23/32	−	119	4.6850	4 11/16	−	169	6.6535	6 21/32	−	219	8.6220	8 5/8	−	269	10.5905	10 19/32	−
20	0.7874	25/32	+	70	2.7559	2 3/4	+	120	4.7244	4 23/32	+	170	6.6929	6 11/16	+	220	8.6614	8 21/32	+	270	10.6299	10 5/8	+
21	0.8268	13/16	+	71	2.7953	2 25/32	+	121	4.7638	4 3/4	+	171	6.7323	6 23/32	+	221	8.7008	8 11/16	+	271	10.6693	10 21/32	+
22	0.8661	7/8	−	72	2.8346	2 27/32	−	122	4.8031	4 13/16	−	172	6.7716	6 25/32	−	222	8.7401	8 3/4	−	272	10.7086	10 23/32	−
23	0.9055	29/32	−	73	2.8740	2 7/8	−	123	4.8425	4 27/32	−	173	6.8110	6 13/16	−	223	8.7795	8 25/32	−	273	10.7480	10 3/4	−
24	0.9449	15/16	+	74	2.9134	2 29/32	+	124	4.8819	4 7/8	+	174	6.8504	6 27/32	+	224	8.8189	8 13/16	+	274	10.7874	10 25/32	+
25	0.9843	31/32	+	75	2.9528	2 15/16	+	125	4.9213	4 29/32	+	175	6.8898	6 7/8	+	225	8.8583	8 27/32	+	275	10.8268	10 13/16	+
26	1.0236	1 1/32	−	76	2.9921	3.0	−	126	4.9606	4 31/32	−	176	6.9291	6 15/16	−	226	8.8976	8 29/32	−	276	10.8661	10 7/8	−
27	1.0630	1 1/16	+	77	3.0315	3 1/32	+	127	5.0000	5.0		177	6.9685	6 31/32	−	227	8.9370	8 15/16	−	277	10.9055	10 29/32	−
28	1.1024	1 3/32	+	78	3.0709	3 1/16	+	128	5.0394	5 1/32	+	178	7.0079	7.0	+	228	8.9764	8 31/32	+	278	10.9449	10 15/16	+
29	1.1417	1 5/32	−	79	3.1102	3 1/8	−	129	5.0787	5 3/32	−	179	7.0472	7 1/16	−	229	9.0157	9 1/32	−	279	10.9842	10 31/32	+
30	1.1811	1 3/16	−	80	3.1496	3 5/32	−	130	5.1181	5 1/8	−	180	7.0866	7 3/32	−	230	9.0551	9 1/16	−	280	11.0236	11 1/32	−
31	1.2205	1 7/32	+	81	3.1890	3 3/16	+	131	5.1575	5 5/32	+	181	7.1260	7 1/8	+	231	9.0945	9 3/32	+	281	11.0630	11 1/16	+
32	1.2598	1 1/4	+	82	3.2283	3 7/32	+	132	5.1968	5 3/16	+	182	7.1653	7 5/32	+	232	9.1338	9 1/8	+	282	11.1023	11 3/32	+
33	1.2992	1 5/16	−	83	3.2677	3 9/32	−	133	5.2362	5 1/4	−	183	7.2047	7 7/32	−	233	9.1732	9 3/16	−	283	11.1417	11 5/32	−
34	1.3386	1 11/32	−	84	3.3071	3 5/16	−	134	5.2756	5 9/32	−	184	7.2441	7 1/4	−	234	9.2126	9 7/32	−	284	11.1811	11 3/16	−
35	1.3780	1 3/8	−	85	3.3465	3 11/32	+	135	5.3150	5 5/16	+	185	7.2835	7 9/32	+	235	9.2520	9 1/4	+	285	11.2204	11 7/32	+
36	1.4173	1 13/32	+	86	3.3858	3 3/8	+	136	5.3543	5 11/32	+	186	7.3228	7 5/16	+	236	9.2913	9 9/32	+	286	11.2598	11 1/4	+
37	1.4567	1 15/32	−	87	3.4252	3 7/16	−	137	5.3937	5 13/32	−	187	7.3622	7 3/8	−	237	9.3307	9 11/32	−	287	11.2992	11 5/16	−
38	1.4961	1 1/2	−	88	3.4646	3 15/32	−	138	5.4331	5 7/16	−	188	7.4016	7 13/32	−	238	9.3701	9 3/8	−	288	11.3386	11 11/32	−
39	1.5354	1 17/32	+	89	3.5039	3 1/2	+	139	5.4724	5 15/32	+	189	7.4409	7 7/16	+	239	9.4094	9 13/32	+	289	11.3779	11 3/8	+
40	1.5748	1 9/16	+	90	3.5433	3 17/32	+	140	5.5118	5 1/2	+	190	7.4803	7 15/32	+	240	9.4488	9 7/16	+	290	11.4173	11 13/32	+
41	1.6142	1 5/8	−	91	3.5827	3 9/16	−	141	5.5512	5 9/16	−	191	7.5197	7 17/32	−	241	9.4882	9 1/2	−	291	11.4567	11 15/32	−
42	1.6535	1 21/32	−	92	3.6220	3 5/8	−	142	5.5905	5 19/32	−	192	7.5590	7 9/16	−	242	9.5275	9 17/32	−	292	11.4960	11 1/2	−
43	1.6929	1 11/16	+	93	3.6614	3 21/32	+	143	5.6299	5 5/8	+	193	7.5984	7 19/32	+	243	9.5669	9 9/16	+	293	11.5354	11 17/32	+
44	1.7323	1 23/32	+	94	3.7008	3 11/16	+	144	5.6693	5 21/32	+	194	7.6378	7 5/8	+	244	9.6063	9 19/32	+	294	11.5748	11 9/16	+
45	1.7717	1 25/32	−	95	3.7402	3 3/4	−	145	5.7087	5 23/32	−	195	7.6772	7 11/16	−	245	9.6457	9 21/32	−	295	11.6142	11 5/8	−
46	1.8110	1 13/16	−	96	3.7795	3 25/32	−	146	5.7480	5 3/4	−	196	7.7165	7 23/32	−	246	9.6850	9 11/16	−	296	11.6535	11 21/32	−
47	1.8504	1 27/32	+	97	3.8189	3 13/16	+	147	5.7874	5 25/32	+	197	7.7559	7 3/4	+	247	9.7244	9 23/32	+	297	11.6929	11 11/16	+
48	1.8898	1 7/8	+	98	3.8583	3 27/32	+	148	5.8268	5 13/16	+	198	7.7953	7 25/32	+	248	9.7638	9 3/4	+	298	11.7323	11 23/32	+
49	1.9291	1 15/16	−	99	3.8976	3 29/32	−	149	5.8661	5 7/8	−	199	7.8346	7 27/32	−	249	9.8031	9 25/32	−	299	11.7716	11 25/32	−
50	1.9685	1 31/32	−	100	3.9370	3 15/16	−	150	5.9055	5 29/32	−	200	7.8740	7 7/8	−	250	9.8425	9 27/32	−	300	11.8110	11 13/16	−

NOTE. The + or − sign indicates that the decimal equivalent is larger or smaller than the fractional equivalent.

METRIC TAP AND DRILL SIZES
WITH INCH EQUIVALENTS
AND CLOSEST INCH DRILL SIZE

Metric Tap Size	Metric Drill Size	Inch Equivalent of Metric Drill Size	Closest Inch Drill Size	Decimal Equivalent of Inch Drill Size
M3x0.5*	2.50	0.0984	#40	0.0980
M3.5x0.6*	2.90	0.1142	#33	0.1130
M4x0.7*	3.30	0.1299	#30	0.1285
M4.5x0.75*	3.70	0.1457	#26	0.1470
M5x0.8*	4.20	0.1654	#19	0.1660
M6x1*	5.00	0.1968	#9	0.1960
M7x1*	6.00	0.2362	15/64	0.2344
M8x1.25*	6.70	0.2638	17/64	0.2656
M8x1	7.00	0.2756	J	0.2770
M10x1.5*	8.50	0.3346	Q	0.3320
M10x1.25	8.70	0.3425	11/32	0.3438
M12x1.75*	10.20	0.4016	Y	0.4040
M12x1.25	10.80	0.4252	27/64	0.4219
M14x2*	12.00	0.4724	15/32	0.4688
M16x2*	14.00	0.5512	35/64	0.5469
M18x2.5*	15.50	0.6102	39/64	0.6094
M20x2.5*	17.50	0.6890	11/16	0.6875

*International Organization for Standardization metric sizes (ISO metrics).

The above guide may be used to determine the proper hole size for metric taps.

Metric taps are disignated by an "M" followed by the nominal tap size in MM and the width between threads (pitch) also in MM. For example a 10 MM tap with 1.5 MM pitch threads will have a designation of M10x1.5.

When no designation is given for thread pitch, such as a tap marked "M14", it is understood to have the standard ISO course pitch of 2 MM. In most instances, the entire designation M14x2, will be given; however, either designation is correct.

Additional numbers and letters following a dash (—) refer to tolerance limits and locations. Numbers in the tolerance designation refer to the amount of tolerance allowed. Numbers used in tolerance designations range from 3 to 9. General purpose hardware has a standard tolerance of 6. Tighter tolerances will be designated with a smaller number and looser tolerances will be designated with a larger number.

Letters are used in the tolerance designation to denote the location of the tolerance such as, the maximum diameter at the thread tips or the minimum diameter between threads. Capitals and lower case letters are used to denote if the tolerance applies to external threads (lower case) or internal threads (capitals).

Below are examples of ISO metric tap designations.

M7x1
M14
M18x2.5-7H
M16-6g

IDENTIFICATION INFORMATION

    Use this page to list information, which can help identify each bicycle in case of loss, then remove this page from book and store it in a safe place.

    Encourage each rider to **always** properly secure the bicycle. Proper storage, including locking, will reduce theft.

Owner	Brand	Color	Model Number	Serial Number

other manuals available from (TECHNICAL PUBLICATIONS)

NAME (optional)

_____

_____

_____

_____

PLACE POSTAGE HERE

(**TECHNICAL PUBLICATIONS**)

Intertec Publishing Corp.
P.O. 12901
Overland Park, KS 66212

Attn: Editorial Director

other manuals available from TECHNICAL PUBLICATIONS

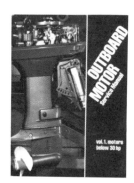

Questionnaire

1. Manual Purchased _____

2. I am a
   ☐ do-it-yourselfer
   ☐ professional mechanic specializing in the area of this manual
   ☐ teacher
   ☐ librarian

3. Strong features of this manual: _____

4. I would like to see this manual improved or expanded in the following way: _____

5. I would like to see the following manufacturers, models or materials included

in the next edition: _____
_____

6. I would like to see the following manuals or materials published: _____
_____

7. Other comments or suggestions: _____
_____

8. Purchased this manual through:
   ☐ Mail
   ☐ Telephone
   ☐ Equipment or Parts Store
   ☐ Bookstore
   ☐ Magazine (title) _____